The
Gospels
as Stories

The Gospels as Stories

A Narrative Approach
to Matthew, Mark,
Luke, and John

Jeannine K. Brown

Baker Academic
a division of Baker Publishing Group
Grand Rapids, Michigan

© 2020 by Jeannine K. Brown

Published by Baker Academic
a division of Baker Publishing Group
PO Box 6287, Grand Rapids, MI 49516-6287
www.bakeracademic.com

Printed in the United States of America

Library of Congress Cataloging-in-Publication Data
Names: Brown, Jeannine K., 1961– author.
Title: The gospels as stories : a narrative approach to Matthew, Mark, Luke, and John / Jeannine K. Brown.
Description: Grand Rapids : Baker Academic, a division of Baker Publishing Group, 2020. | Includes bibliographical references and index.
Identifiers: LCCN 2019050085 | ISBN 9780801049842 (paperback)
Subjects: LCSH: Bible. Gospels—Criticism, Narrative. | Narrative theology.
Classification: LCC BS2555.52 .B756 2020 | DDC 226/.066—dc23
LC record available at https://lccn.loc.gov/2019050085

ISBN 978-1-5409-6312-3 (casebound)

21   22   23   24   25   26   7   6   5   4   3   2

To Kate and Libby:
You are indispensable to my narrative

Contents

Figures

Preface

The Gospels as Stories has been a long time in the making. Although I did my doctoral work on a narrative-critical reading of the disciples in the Gospel of Matthew,[1] it took a while for the narrative method I had learned and was honing in my own work to filter into the courses I regularly taught on the Gospels. For example, I continued to follow the traditional route of assigning students a single passage (eight to ten verses) to test their abilities to interpret a Gospel. But each year I taught the Gospels, it seemed less and less helpful to focus students' attention on such a small bit of the text when whole vistas of a Gospel remained potentially unexplored. Coupled with my own desire to grasp the whole of a Gospel—to hear its "narrative logic"—I began assigning students and myself bigger and bigger projects.

Early on I developed a Gospel "plot/theme diagram" as an attempt to visualize a wider segment of the text. My first attempt at this kind of narrative diagramming focused on John 1–12, as I tried to get a sense of the flow of the first half of that Gospel through John's use of settings, discourses, controversies, the seven "signs," and Jesus' seven "I am" statements. From there I moved to Matthew, Mark, and Luke (for an example, see fig. 3.3: Diagram of Plot and Themes for Luke 4:14–9:50). And I began to press my students in similar ways to grapple with the Gospels as whole stories. A favorite assignment (at least for me, if not for them) is a plot/theme

---

1. Jeannine K. Brown, *The Disciples in Narrative Perspective: The Portrayal and Function of the Matthean Disciples*, SBLAB 9 (Atlanta: Society of Biblical Literature, 2002).

diagram of the Lukan travel narrative (9:51–19:27). Given that this section
of Luke is notoriously difficult to outline, I thought a different approach
for grasping the whole might be helpful. Students have tended to find it
so, and they certainly have a better grasp of Luke when they are done.

By teaching the Gospels differently, I learned to apply narrative criticism
more consistently (in a form that made particular sense to me) to my own
interpretation of the Gospels. Early work in my dissertation on characterization has been augmented by work on plotting (attending to the shaping
of each Gospel) and on intertextuality, with the conviction that the Gospel
writers use the Old Testament in careful and storied ways for narrating
their own stories of Jesus.[2] I've also become increasingly interested in the
theology of the Gospels, so much so that narrative theology has become
a keen interest of mine.[3] *The Gospels as Stories* is the result of these
various engagements with plotting (chaps. 2–3), characterization (chaps.
4–5), intertextuality (chaps. 6–7), and narrative theology (chaps. 8–9).

I am grateful for two very capable research assistants, Jenelle Lemons
and Ali Tonnesen, who read and interacted with the book in its various
stages. They helped me stay focused on real and thoughtful readers
throughout the process of writing. I'd also like to thank Jim Kinney at
Baker, who gave me my first opportunity to have a book published (beyond
my dissertation) and continues to be a valued conversation partner about
the direction of my scholarship and writing.

I dedicate this book to my daughters, Kate and Libby. They are lovers
of story. Kate, when she was a preschooler, would command during car
rides, "Tell me another story about Jesus." When I finally ran out of discrete stories, I began sharing with her how Matthew, for example, told a
whole string of stories about Jesus healing people (Matt. 8–9). Her love
of story pressed me to communicate more holistically about the Gospels.
Libby, as a language arts teacher to seventh and eighth graders, shares
her own love of story with her students. Her passion for literature—for
story—is contagious.

2. E.g., Jeannine K. Brown, "Genesis in Matthew's Gospel," in *Genesis in the New Testament*, ed. Maarten J. J. Menken and Steve Moyise (New York: T&T Clark, 2012), 42–59.
3. E.g., Jeannine K. Brown and Kyle Roberts, *Matthew*, THNTC (Grand Rapids: Eerdmans, 2018).

Abbreviations

AB	Anchor Bible
AsTJ	*Asbury Theological Journal*
AT	author's translation
BDAG	Danker, Frederick W., Walter Bauer, William F. Arndt, and F. Wilbur Gingrich. *A Greek-English Lexicon of the New Testament and Other Early Christian Literature*. 3rd ed. Chicago: University of Chicago Press, 2000.
BibInt	*Biblical Interpretation*
BLS	Bible and Literature Series
BNTC	Black's New Testament Commentaries
CBQ	*Catholic Biblical Quarterly*
CEB	Common English Bible (translation)
CH	*Church History*
CSB	Christian Standard Bible
DJG	*Dictionary of Jesus and the Gospels*. Edited by Joel B. Green, Jeannine K. Brown, and Nicholas Perrin. 2nd ed. Downers Grove, IL: InterVarsity, 2013.
GBS	Guides to Biblical Scholarship
GR	*Greece and Rome*
GW	God's Word (translation)
HBT	*Horizons in Biblical Theology*
Int	*Interpretation*
JBL	*Journal of Biblical Literature*
JETS	*Journal of the Evangelical Theological Society*
JSNT	*Journal for the Study of the New Testament*
JSNTSup	Journal for the Study of the New Testament Supplement Series
JSOT	*Journal for the Study of the Old Testament*
JTS	*Journal of Theological Studies*
LNTS	The Library of New Testament Studies
LXX	Septuagint
NC	narrative criticism

Neot	*Neotestamentica*
NETS	A New English Translation of the Septuagint
NICNT	New International Commentary on the New Testament
NIV	New International Version
NovTSup	Supplements to Novum Testamentum
NTE	New Testament for Everyone (translation)
NTS	*New Testament Studies*
RevExp	*Review and Expositor*
SBLAB	Society of Biblical Literature Academia Biblica
SBLSymS	Society of Biblical Literature Symposium Series
SNTSMS	Society for New Testament Studies Monograph Series
THNTC	Two Horizons New Testament Commentary
TN	travel narrative
ZECNT	Zondervan Exegetical Commentary on the New Testament
ZNW	*Zeitschrift für die neutestamentliche Wissenschaft und die Kunde der älteren Kirche*

Part One
Introduction

All narrative begins for me with listening. When I read, I listen. When I write, I listen—for silence, inflection, rhythm, rest.

Toni Morrison, *The Measure of Our Lives*

For me the Gospel of Mark is not a resource to be mined for historical nuggets or Christological jewels; it is the ground on which we walk.

Elizabeth Struthers Malbon, *Mark's Jesus*

1

The Turn to Gospels as Stories

Narrative Criticism in Gospel Studies

We "get" stories. We are drawn into their plotlines. We identify deeply with their characters. We are captivated by their settings. And we intuitively understand what a story is "doing"—what themes it communicates, what morals it highlights, what other stories it evokes or undermines. Neurobiologists suggest that story is hardwired into us; we make sense of our reality by interpreting it and retelling it as story.

So wouldn't coming to the Gospels in the New Testament be a relatively straightforward task? They are, after all, stories. They may be more than stories, but they certainly are not less.

Yet for all our comfort level with stories, we often do strange and odd things with the Gospels. In church contexts we chop them into very small pieces (single verses or individual episodes) and turn them into allegories for our own experiences. In the guild of biblical studies we have done things just as strange—at least if we consider that early church communities would have received and experienced a Gospel in its entirety, with large segments being read aloud in church gatherings.[1] We should

---

1. Justin Martyr, in about 156 CE, wrote that in church gatherings on Sunday, "the memoirs of the Apostles or the writings of the Prophets are read, as long as there is time." Saint Justin Martyr and Thomas B. Falls, *The First Apology, The Second Apology, Dialogue with Trypho, Exhortation to the Greeks, Discourse to the Greeks, The Monarchy or The Rule of God*, The

certainly recognize that the Gospel traditions predated the writing of the Gospels, and these traditions would have circulated as individual stories—a key tenet of **form criticism**.[2] Yet the Gospel writers brought together these traditions in thoughtful and distinctive ways, and the early church would have experienced Mark's Gospel, for example, as a unified work—as a story.

Such a holistic, storied reading is the focus of **narrative criticism**, a particular interpretive method used in Gospel studies. In this chapter, I describe narrative criticism as it has emerged over the last forty years or so, offering in the process a description of this method as well as its evolution into an eclectic and adaptable approach to reading the Gospels as stories.

Reading the Gospels: The Turn toward Narrative

To get a feel for how the Gospel narratives have been read by both church and academy, I'll illustrate with the fairy tale "The Princess and the Pea."

The Princess and the Pea

Once upon a time there was a prince who wanted to marry a princess; but she would have to be a real princess. He travelled all over the world to find one, but nowhere could he get what he wanted. There were princesses enough, but it was difficult to find out whether they were real ones. There was always something about them that was not as it should be. So he came home again and was sad, for he would have liked very much to have a real princess.

One evening a terrible storm came on; there was thunder and lightning, and the rain poured down in torrents. Suddenly a knocking was heard at the city gate, and the old king went to open it.

It was a princess standing out there in front of the gate. But, good gracious! What a sight the rain and the wind had made her look. The water

---

Fathers of the Church, vol. 6 (Washington, DC: The Catholic University of America Press, 2010), 67.

2. Bolded terms are defined in a glossary at the end of the book.

ran down from her hair and clothes; it ran down into the toes of her shoes and out again at the heels. And yet she said that she was a real princess.

Well, we'll soon find that out, thought the old queen. But she said nothing, went into the bedroom, took all the bedding off the bedstead, and laid a pea on the bottom; then she took twenty mattresses and laid them on the pea, and then twenty eider-down beds on top of the mattresses.

On this the princess had to lie all night. In the morning she was asked how she had slept.

"Oh, very badly!" said she. "I have scarcely closed my eyes all night. Heaven only knows what was in the bed, but I was lying on something hard, so that I am black and blue all over my body. It's horrible!"

Now they knew that she was a real princess because she had felt the pea right through the twenty mattresses and the twenty eider-down beds.

Nobody but a real princess could be as sensitive as that.

So the prince took her for his wife, for now he knew that he had a real princess; and the pea was put in the museum, where it may still be seen, if no one has stolen it.

There, that is a true story.

This is the original version of the story written by its author, Hans Christian Andersen, in 1835. Let's imagine, however, that we had this original telling of the story with two other versions on either side of it, without any notation about the date or origin of each.

Princess and the Pea (picture book)	"The Princess and the Pea" (as recorded above)	*Once upon a Mattress* (musical)

The first telling of the story is in storybook form with pictures, as well as a few more significant internal differences from the one recited above: (1) goose feathers instead of eiderdown, and (2) "if no one has stolen it" as the concluding line (i.e., missing the affirmation of its truth as a story).[3] The second telling is the one recorded above. The third version

3. "The Princess and the Pea," Reading A-Z, accessed July 27, 2019, https://www.readinga-z .com/book.php?id=1945.

is the musical *Once upon a Mattress*, which includes, among other additions, thirteen other supposed princesses who have been tested to see if they really are princesses before the main character appears—named in this version as Princess Winnifred the Woebegone.

Three versions, side by side, with no explicit indications of which came first. What might we do in response to this interesting mix of expressions of a single story?

Well, if we were like Gospels scholars of the nineteenth century, we might focus our attention on the historical question of which one came first and which others were derived from it. In this case, we might notice that the language of "eiderdown" is more obscure than the "goose feathers" of the storybook version and the "soft downy mattresses" of the musical. An eider is a large duck found in northern coastal regions, making this referent more (geographically) specific than "goose feathers" or "downy." We might then surmise that the middle of these versions was the original, with the others being derivative, since that very specific detail of "eiderdown" has been made more transferrable to other contexts in the first and third versions. In this historical work, we would be doing **source criticism**, a methodology used by Gospels scholars to determine which **Synoptic** Gospel—Matthew, Mark, or Luke—came first, with the conclusion usually drawn that Mark was written first and that Matthew and Luke used Mark as they wrote their stories of Jesus.[4]

Say we then decided to look at each of the differences between the story presumed to be written first (the middle example above) and the other two renderings. In this comparison of versions, we might note that pictures were added in the storybook, which could give us insight into the purposes and audience of that version: children in a stage of early reading ability. To gauge what was added in the musical, we could note the shift from an unnamed princess in the original to a named princess—Princess Winnifred the Woebegone. And this rather whimsical name could indicate the comedic purposes of the musical version. This kind of comparative study is what in Gospels scholarship has been called **redaction criticism**, an approach that saw its heyday in the latter part of the twentieth century. Redaction criticism has been used to highlight the specific audience and purposes of Matthew and

---

4. Given the distinctiveness of John's Gospel from Matthew, Mark, and Luke, it is not usually considered to have a direct literary (compositional) relationship with the Synoptic Gospels.

Luke when compared to their "redaction" or editing of their source, the Gospel of Mark.[5]

What do you notice about these various methods applied to "The Princess and the Pea"? What might become apparent is that these historical questions and methods have not yet addressed the stories themselves, although redaction criticism has begun to identify some of the more unique purposes of each telling (e.g., the comedic flavor of *Once upon a Mattress*). So, you might wonder, why not just study each story on its own terms? Doesn't this seem like an obvious place to start?

The answer outside of our analogy—in the history of Gospels research—is both yes and no. Yes, because in this research there was ongoing interest in the Gospels at the level of the whole book. Examples include the comparison of the Gospels to the genre of Greco-Roman biography as well as attention given to the Gospels as wholes in later forms of redaction criticism (sometimes called **composition criticism**).[6] And no, because attending to the Gospels as wholes had often been neglected in the history of the church and not only in New Testament scholarship of the past few hundred years. There has been a marked preference often given to the smaller parts of a Gospel rather than to their overarching stories.

Return with me for a moment to "The Princess and the Pea" analogy. I've suggested what historical approaches within scholarship, like source criticism and redaction criticism, might have looked like if this story, like the Gospels, would have shown up in multiple anonymous and undated renderings. How might this same analogy help to explain the ways the Gospels have been handled in the church, both ancient and contemporary? We can summarize some of these approaches under the rubrics of **amalgamating** (harmonizing), **atomizing** (dissecting), and **allegorizing**. Each of these ignored the narrative character of the Gospels in some significant way.

It is easy to imagine how the three renderings of "The Princess and the Pea" could be amalgamated. What better way to avoid losing any part of

---

5. I might also point out the importance of form criticism in the study of the Gospels, a method that has highlighted the individual Gospel units (pericopes), and specifically what they were (their genre) and how they functioned for Jesus' followers in the early oral period of Gospel transmission.

6. These biographies (Greek *bioi* or Latin *vitae*) were "a discrete but flexible genre that developed over the several centuries either side of the birth of Jesus of Nazareth." Richard Burridge, "Gospels: Genre," in *DJG*, 335–42, here 337.

these different rehearsals than to merge together all their various plot and formal details? The naming of the princess (Winnifred the Woebegone) only adds to the story, providing a richer, fuller telling, right? And certainly adding pictures helps the reader see what the original story was doing. Yet what to do with competing elements? Can you have a musical and a storybook at the same time? Would the goose feathers be added to the eiderdown for a doubly soft set of mattresses? Or would it create two sets of mattresses for two different princesses (one unnamed and one named) and so essentially change the plotline?

The amalgamation or harmonization of the four Gospels happened quite soon in the history of their interpretation. Tatian's *Diatessaron* ("harmony of the four"; ca. 170 CE) was an early example of such amalgamating—a tendency the church has continued to foster to the present. As with our analogous "harmonized" fairy tale, so too the Gospels present some difficulties for a coherent harmony. What do we do with differences in the ordering and details of, say, Peter's three denials of Jesus? Trying to account for these minor differences, there have been harmonies (amalgamations) produced that portray Peter denying Jesus six times, sometimes even nine times—in spite of the affirmation in each of the four Gospels that Peter denied Jesus just three times. At the risk of stating the obvious, the New Testament canon includes four portraits of Jesus and not a single amalgam, so we lose something by reconstructing a harmonized story we haven't been given.

A second approach that became commonplace in the church's use of the Gospels involves atomizing the text—taking its smaller pieces and treating them as stand-alone units. Whether individual sayings of Jesus (often at the verse level) or shorter passages (called **pericopes**), these now abstracted units were treated as fairly autonomous and free floating. They might then be combined easily with similar "pearls of wisdom" derived from another Gospel (potentially for amalgamation, as noted above) or from any other part of the Bible, for that matter. In this way, the narrative coherence of a single Gospel was often obscured. To illustrate via our analogy, what if a reader pulled out a single line of "The Princess and the Pea" in an attempt to let it speak on its own? For example,

"There was always something about them [other princesses] that was not as it should be."

Or,

"Nobody but a real princess could be as sensitive as that."

Finding the choicest parts of the story for quotation and possible application results in the quoted line being extracted from its original and storied purposes and potentially turned into something quite foreign to its contextual meaning. How different is this atomizing from what has been done with the Gospels, often with troubling exegetical consequences? For example, Jesus' words in Matthew, "I did not come to bring peace, but a sword" (10:34), could be used as license for Christian violence.[7] To take another example, "His blood is on us and on our children!" (Matt. 27:25) has sometimes been marshaled to indict all Jewish people for Jesus' death.[8] Wresting lines or brief stories from their narrative context (and, I should add, their historical setting) can mold these snippets into what we prefer them to say. They easily take on a life of their own.

A third way that the church appropriated the Gospels in their smaller parts was by allegorizing them. In allegorization, a reader mines an individual pericope for its storied details, heard to speak now within the reader's own context. Going back to our fairy tale, here's a whimsical example of allegorizing: *If you're a poor sleeper and female, then you might be a princess!* Allegorizing has been a long-standing practice within the history of biblical interpretation. For instance, church leaders as diverse as Origen, Venerable Bede, and Martin Luther saw within the picturesque details of Jesus' parables references to their own perspectives and concerns. One of the more colorful examples comes from Augustine, who interpreted the innkeeper in the parable of the good Samaritan as the apostle Paul.[9]

Yet it is not just Christians from the past who have tended toward allegorizing. It is easy enough to catch glimpses of allegories in contemporary sermons. Does Jesus' miraculous power in calming the storm (Luke 8:22–25) translate to Jesus calming the storms of our lives? If this sounds

---

7. In spite of its use in a context that indicates that loyalty to Jesus might result in *relational* divisions even within families.

8. For ways this second line from Matthew has been given a life of its own, to the detriment of Jewish people across history, see Jeannine K. Brown and Kyle Roberts, *Matthew*, THNTC (Grand Rapids: Eerdmans, 2018), 516–21.

9. For this example and many others, see Robert H. Stein, *An Introduction to the Parables of Jesus* (Philadelphia: Westminster, 1981), 42–47.

like an obvious meaning of Luke 8, then we've likely been privy to a kind
of allegorizing approach. Now, allegorizing does attend, at least in part,
to the narratival qualities of a Gospel, since a story from a Gospel is used
to address our own story in some way. Where it can stray off course is
by downplaying the wider context of the narrative being studied. Luke
puts Jesus' power on display in his Gospel (cf. 8:26–56; also 7:1–17), with
Christology as his primary focus in 8:22–25. Luke seems more interested
in answering the question, Who is Jesus? than the question, What can
Jesus do for me? Bending the narrative rather quickly toward the second
question may move us toward allegorizing.

I've drawn upon a simple fairy tale as an analogy to illustrate various
ways the Gospels have been studied and interpreted in the church and
in the academy that have not paid adequate attention to their storied
form—especially their overarching narrative structures. This leads us to
the role and contribution of narrative criticism in the interpretation of
the Gospels.

In the 1980s scholars began to place more concerted emphasis on the narrative shaping of the Gospels, a focus that developed into a methodology—
narrative criticism. This literary method was adapted from (though not
identical to) **narratology**, a method that had developed for the critical
analysis of literature in earlier decades. "Narrative criticism," nomen-
clature unique to biblical studies, was coined by David Rhoads, an early
practitioner of this method.[10] Central and early works that applied narrative criticism to the four Gospels are

- *Mark as Story* (1982) by David Rhoads and Donald Michie
- *Anatomy of the Fourth Gospel* (1983) by Alan Culpepper
- *Matthew as Story* (1986) by Jack Kingsbury
- *The Narrative Unity of Luke-Acts* (1986) by Robert Tannehill

This narrative turn in the study of the Gospels has been a welcomed
development for a number of reasons. Most centrally, it has highlighted
the Gospels as wholes—for example, all twenty-four chapters of Luke—
rather than dissecting them into their smallest parts. Attention to whole

10. David Rhoads, "Narrative Criticism and the Gospel of Mark," *Journal of the American
Academy of Religion* 50 (1982): 411–34, here 412.

books has allowed the storied shape of each Gospel to emerge more clearly. As Terence Donaldson notes, narrative methods tap into something organic in the Gospels themselves: "It needs to be recognized that the turn to narrative is not simply a scholarly fad. Rather, narrative criticism puts us in touch with something that is fundamental to the New Testament as a whole. For before there were Gospels, there was the gospel—the basic proclamation about the saving significance of the life, death, and resurrection of Jesus. . . . This proclamation . . . is in its essence a narrative."[11]

What Is Narrative Criticism?

In broadest terms, narrative criticism (NC) attends to the literary and storied qualities of a biblical narrative, like a Gospel.[12] This "storied" analysis is accompanied by a focus on the final form of the text rather than emphasis on issues of the text's production, which is characteristic of methods like source and redaction criticisms. By focusing on the final form, and so the entire story line, the interpreter attends to key storied elements that contribute to reading a Gospel with a wide-angle lens—following its narrative contours from beginning to end. Narrative features, such as story and discourse levels and the implied author and reader, have been key elements of NC that assist in reading the Gospels as stories.

Two Levels of the Narrative

An interpretive device regularly used in NC comes from Seymour Chatman's configuration of two narrative levels.[13] Chatman identifies these two as the story level and the discourse level. The **story level** consists of elements that most readers easily notice as they read a narrative: the settings, events, and characters that make up the plot. Since the Gospels center on

11. Terence L. Donaldson, "The Vindicated Son: A Narrative Approach to Matthean Christology," in *Contours of Christology in the New Testament*, ed. Richard N. Longenecker (Grand Rapids: Eerdmans, 2005), 100–121, here 104.
12. For a detailed discussion of this method, see Jeannine K. Brown, "Narrative Criticism," in *DJG*, 619–24.
13. Seymour B. Chatman, *Story and Discourse: Narrative Structure in Fiction and Film* (Ithaca, NY: Cornell University Press, 1978).

Jesus, it is the course of his life and interactions with his disciples, opponents, and the many who benefit from his public ministry that capture our attention (fig. 1.1).

Turning our focus toward the **discourse level** requires more of the wide-angle lens already mentioned, since the discourse is the author's (or narrator's) way of shaping the story elements to communicate key messages with the Gospel's audience. For narrative critics, the discourse level (alternately called the narrative's *rhetoric* by Rhoads and Michie) consists of various literary devices that organize the story's plot elements and orient the reader to the author's purposes. These include point of view, narration, event **sequencing** and **pacing, characterization,** irony, and a variety of structural patterns (fig. 1.2).

For example, in John's Gospel, irony is used to infuse various plot elements with symbolic meaning. Jesus offers living water to a Samaritan woman (John 4:13–14) and to all who come to him (7:37–38). Yet at his most vulnerable moment, Jesus cries out that he himself is thirsty (19:28). Another example involves John's repeated use of the language of Jesus being "lifted up" (Greek *hypsoō*), a term that can indicate spatial elevation: Jesus will be lifted up on a cross to die. But the term can also mean to be exalted to a place of honor.[14] John plays on both senses of the word to show how Jesus' death will ironically be his exaltation (3:14; 8:28; 12:32, 34).

Figure 1.1

A Narrative's Story Level: The "What" of the Story

Settings	Characters	Plot
Temporal: When?	Protagonist: The Lead Character Antagonist(s): Character(s) Who Oppose the Protagonist	Gospels: Episodes and Sayings
Locative: Where?	Character Types:* • Round • Flat • Stocks • Foils • Walk-ons	Exposition, Rising Action, Climax, Resolution

* These five types are explored by James L. Resseguie, *Narrative Criticism of the New Testament: An Introduction* (Grand Rapids: Baker Academic, 2005), 123–25.

14. BDAG, 1045.

An interesting example of sequencing and pacing occurs in Jesus' early Galilean ministry narrated in Matthew 4:17–9:38. After Jesus calls his first disciples (4:18–22), Matthew provides a summary statement of Jesus' Galilean ministry of healing, preaching, and teaching—all in the service of God's kingdom (4:23). The **evangelist** virtually repeats this summary at the conclusion of this section (9:35) to signal that what comes between these "bookends" (also called an *inclusio*) gives flesh to this healing and teaching ministry. And this is just what we see in Matthew 5–9: Jesus teaches about the kingdom in the Sermon on the Mount (Matt. 5–7) and then heals and performs other miracles as he embodies the kingdom's arrival (Matt. 8–9). Additionally, Matthew's sequencing of an extended sermon prior to narration of Jesus' healing activity functions to slow down the narrative to a "real time" pace. His pacing in the Sermon on the Mount (and the subsequent major discourses—five in all) invites the reader to hear Jesus' teachings as spoken quite directly to them (and not just to the storied audiences of disciples and crowds).[15]

Figure 1.2

A Narrative's Discourse Level: The "How" of the Story

Themes	Sequencing of Episodes	Point of View
Simple Repetition E.g., "repentance" in Luke/Acts	*Simple Linear Sequencing* E.g., the sequence of seven signs in John 2–11	*Assessing Characters in Light of the Authorial Perspective* E.g., Pharisees' (untrue) accusation of Jesus in Mark 3:22
Clustering E.g., work and Sabbath in John 5	*Story Clusters* E.g., healings and miracles in Matthew 8–9	*Listening for Authorized Character Voices in the Story* E.g., John the Baptist's authorized voice in Luke 3:7–18
Strategic Placement E.g., preaching on Isaiah 61 to inaugurate Jesus' ministry to the margins (Luke 4:14–30)	*Intercalation* (ABA pattern, sandwiching of one episode within another) E.g., cursing of fig tree episode (Mark 11:12–14, 19–25) surrounding clearing of the temple (11:15–18)	*Listening for Direct Authorial Assessments* E.g., the young Jesus as full of wisdom in Luke 2:40

15. Jeannine K. Brown, "Direct Engagement of the Reader in Matthew's Discourses: Rhetorical Techniques and Scholarly Consensus," *NTS* 51 (2005): 19–35. See chap. 2 for more on the issue of narrative pacing.

Themes	Sequencing of Episodes	Point of View
Inclusio *or* *Bookend* E.g., Jesus as "God with us"/"with you" (Matt. 1:23; 28:20)	*Interchange* (ABABABAB type pattern) E.g., alternating comparison of scenes involving John the Baptist and Jesus in Luke 1–2	*Listening for Other Authorized Commentary, Especially from the Jewish Scriptures* E.g., Matthew's commentary in Isaiah citation about Jesus as Servant of the Lord (Matt. 12:18–21; cf. Isa. 42:1–4)

To illustrate the connection between the story and discourse levels of a Gospel, we could refer to the "what" and the "how" of the narrative. If the story level illuminates the "what" of the story (e.g., events), the discourse level focuses on "how" the story is told via rhetoric and stylistics. The discourse level involves the ways "the implied author uses characters, settings, plot, and rhetoric to communicate meaning."[16] And even if these levels are not at every turn fully distinguishable, they provide an insightful interpretive lens for hearing what an author is communicating.

The Implied Author and Reader

Discussion of the discourse level points us toward another narrative-critical issue—namely, how to conceive of authorship from a narrative-critical perspective. In NC the concept of the **implied author** provides an important construct for interpreting any narrative. The implied author remains distinct from the empirical author of a narrative and may be defined as the author presupposed by the narrative itself. As such, the implied author is a textually derived construct.

A contemporary example might help for distinguishing the flesh-and-blood (empirical) author from the implied author of a text. Let's say you pick up a novel by an author you know nothing about. Presumably, you can read that novel and understand the story and its themes without researching the author. As you read, you may become curious about the author and search out biographical information. This information may even provide further insight into the significance of what you've read. Yet you will be able to understand the narrative you've read even if you lack

---

16. Elizabeth Struthers Malbon, "Narrative Criticism: How Does the Story Mean?," in *Mark and Method: New Approaches in Biblical Studies*, ed. Janice C. Anderson and Stephen D. Moore, 2nd ed. (Minneapolis: Fortress, 2008), 23–49, here 47.

this authorial information. (It does help greatly to know the general setting in which a book is written; e.g., a two-hundred-year-old novel may require certain additional reading strategies as compared to a contemporary novel.) The reason you can understand the novel is because you have discerned (whether you are fully aware of it or not) the implied author as you've read the novel—the author who has been communicating with you throughout the story.

Now suppose you read something quite different from that same author—say, a letter from the author to her daughter. While written by the same empirical author, the implied author of this letter could be quite distinct from the implied author of the novel. In fact, when reading the novel, you may have had no inkling that the author is a mother. Yet now, reading this personal letter, you find yourself aware of a *quite different writing persona*—that is, a distinct implied author. The implied author of the letter may seem quite warm and personable in ways not evident in the novel. The same empirical author will almost by necessity bring a different implied author to each of her compositions.

So how does the concept of the implied author help us interpret an almost two-thousand-year-old Gospel? First, it proves helpful because each of the four Gospel compositions are anonymous. Although associated with particular persons in their titles and in church tradition, they originally almost certainly circulated without titles (which were probably added to distinguish one from the other: "According to Matthew," "According to Mark," etc.). While we may trust these early titles and traditions, it is not necessary to reconstruct the empirical Matthew to understand the Gospel associated with his name. If it were, then anyone hearing or reading this Gospel apart from that association would be doomed to misunderstand it.

Second, a Gospel's internal cues provide us with plenty of assistance for understanding the author's communicative purposes. For example, the implied author of Mark begins his Gospel with an Old Testament composite to illuminate who Jesus is in relation to Israel's hopes (Mark 1:2–3). The author cites Malachi 3:1 and Isaiah 40:3, with an allusion to Exodus 23:20, to provide an opening frame to his story of Jesus. With these Old Testament texts, the implied author communicates the "coming presence" of Israel's God as well as Israel's lack of covenantal loyalty, so that both promise and warning are signaled from these scriptural

connections.[17] This same implied author of Mark's Gospel portrays the
disciples as hard-hearted and lacking understanding—a portrayal that
functions to press the reader toward greater insight about Jesus' mission
and toward fidelity to him.

Corresponding to the implied author, NC also highlights the concept
of the **implied reader**. For some narrative critics, the implied reader, like
the implied author, is a textually derived construct—namely, the reader
presupposed in the text. For example, in his narrative work on John's
Gospel, R. Alan Culpepper understands the implied reader as "defined by
the text as the one who performs all the mental moves required to enter
into the narrative world and respond to it as the implied author intends."[18]
Others who practice a narrative approach also include in their definition
what empirical readers inevitably contribute to textual meaning, so that
the implied reader is some combination of textual cues and the different
ways real readers respond to those cues.[19]

These two concepts—the implied author and the implied reader—offer
a reading strategy for a Gospel, with the goal of understanding its communicative intention. In NC this goal might be often referred to as ap-
proximating the response of the implied reader. For instance, if we can
understand the kind of disciple Luke, as implied author, is shaping through
his narrative, then we might actively choose to live out that vision of discipleship. Let's say we come to a (partial) sketch of the implied reader of
Luke as *someone who participates in God's reign by following Jesus and
renouncing preoccupation with status to instead embrace those who are
on the margins of society*. Living out the communicative intention of Luke
will then involve participating in the kingdom in these ways.[20]

The Evolution of Narrative Criticism

A significant strength of NC as a methodology has been its ability to adapt
and change in response to critiques. For example, since its inception NC

17. Rikki E. Watts, *Isaiah's New Exodus in Mark* (Grand Rapids: Baker, 1997), 87.
18. R. Alan Culpepper, *Anatomy of the Fourth Gospel: A Study in Literary Design* (Philadelphia: Fortress, 1983), 7.
19. E.g., David Howell, *Matthew's Inclusive Story: A Study in the Narrative Rhetoric of the
First Gospel*, JSNTSup 42 (Sheffield: JSOT Press, 1990), 210–11.
20. Brown, "Narrative Criticism," 621.

has broadened in scope to acknowledge and address the importance of historical realities in the reading of the Gospels. Early on, practitioners of NC made it a practice to bracket out historical concerns. This choice was an intentional divergence from the various criticisms that had focused on historical questions of a Gospel's production (source criticism), its prewritten forms (form criticism), and the editing done by its author to meet the needs of its particular audience (redaction criticism). As this bracketing of historical questions received substantive critique, narrative critics like Mark Allan Powell responded by affirming the importance of sociohistorical information for understanding the Gospels as stories. According to Powell, rather than being a blank slate, the implied reader has the linguistic and contextual knowledge that the implied author expects his reader to know.[21] This makes great sense, since the Gospels themselves are "cultural products."[22]

So while NC brackets out questions of composition history, it does recognize the importance of the sociohistorical contexts of the storied features of a Gospel. For instance, understanding Jesus' reference to a child as he responds to the disciples' question about kingdom greatness (Matt. 18:1–4) should take into account the relative lack of status of children in the first-century Greco-Roman world. Jesus is critiquing the disciples' preoccupation with status by teaching that the kingdom should not be understood in terms of status acquisition and social ranking.[23]

Let's think through another example of the adaptability of NC. An ongoing critique of the method has been that it takes categories from narratology that were developed to analyze modern fiction and applies them to the Gospels—ancient compositions that claim historicity (Luke 1:1–4). To assess this critique, it is helpful to notice that the primary differences between fictional narratives and historical ones have less to do with their formal features (e.g., plot, characterization) and more to do with different *stances* of author and audience toward the narrative. The

21. Mark Allan Powell, "Expected and Unexpected Readings of Matthew: What the Reader Knows," *AsTJ* 48 (1993): 31–51, here 32.
22. The term comes from Joel Green, *Gospel of Luke*, NICNT (Grand Rapids: Eerdmans, 1997), 19. P. Merenlahti and R. Hakola go further to argue that narrative analysis should be an integral part of historical study (and vice versa). Merenlahti and Hakola, "Reconceiving Narrative Criticism," in *Characterization in the Gospels: Reconceiving Narrative Criticism*, ed. D. Rhoads and K. Syreeni, JSNTSup 184 (Sheffield: Sheffield Academic Press, 1999), 13–48, here 48.
23. Brown and Roberts, *Matthew*, 166–67.

author of a narrative claiming some level of historicity functions as the guarantor of the truth of the narrative.[24] And the audience of a historical narrative will attempt to fill in the inevitable gaps in the story with historical information rather than with fictional material. For instance, the violent actions of the character of King Herod in Matthew 2 can be helpfully understood in light of what we know from other primary sources about this Rome-appointed king ruling over the Jewish people. Josephus, for example, corroborates and fills out a portrait of Herod as a despotic ruler, sometimes acting violently toward those he perceived as rivals or threats to his reign.[25]

In response to the critique of the use of modern narrative categories in NC, narrative critics have sought to determine the formal features of ancient narratives to expand their understanding of the Gospels. For example, when studying characterization in any particular Gospel, it is valuable to determine the parameters, tendencies, and techniques of ancient characterization more broadly. Are characters fairly dynamic or more static in narratives that are essentially contemporaneous with the Gospels? And how do these characters function? There is evidence that characters could serve a representative role—as types of various qualities or ethical categories. We will explore these questions and ideas in chapter 3, but my point here is to note that ancient narrative practices can inform and expand our understanding of the Gospels as stories. Modern categories derived from the analysis of fiction are not inappropriate starting points for analysis, and these can be augmented by the study of first-century conventions.

All in all, NC has proved to be an adaptable methodology and finds itself at home in conversation with a variety of other methods for Gospel study, including such diverse reading strategies as historical criticism, feminist criticism, postcolonial criticism, and theological interpretation.[26] Eclectic approaches often include NC as a way to attend to the subtle and complex storied features of a Gospel while also bringing other interpretive lenses to Gospel study.

---

24. Merenlahti and Hakola, "Reconceiving Narrative Criticism," 34–35.

25. Josephus, *Jewish Antiquities* 16.11.1–8. For examples of Roman rulers who used despotic power to protect their reigns, see Eugene Eung-Chun Park, "Rachel's Cry for Her Children: Matthew's Treatment of the Infanticide by Herod," *CBQ* 75 (2013): 473–85, here 476–77.

26. For some specific examples, see Brown, "Narrative Criticism," 623.

Gospels as Stories: Diving Deeper

Now that we have surveyed some of the key ways scholarship and the church have read the Gospels and have introduced NC as a beneficial and developing methodology, we turn to an exploration of the particulars of narrative analysis. The rest of this book is organized by chapter pairs, alternating theory and practice. As subsequent chapters (2, 4, 6, 8) give a detailed account of various key facets of narrative analysis, they will be accompanied by a chapter that fleshes out these methodological areas of analysis in one of the four Gospels. The methodological chapters include plotting (chap. 2), characterization (chap. 4), intertextuality (chap. 6), and narrative theology (chap. 8). I explore how each of these might contribute to a narrative reading of the Gospels and help to illuminate their central themes and purposes. In the alternating chapters, I illustrate these theoretical categories by exploring narrative plotting in Luke (chap. 3), the disciples as character group in Matthew (chap. 5), intertextuality in John (chap. 7), and the narrative theology of Mark (chap. 9).

By focusing on Matthew, Mark, Luke, and John in each of four discrete chapters, we'll be able to see more clearly how these four storytellers develop complex and compelling portraits of Jesus the Messiah in the interest of captivating and transforming their readers.

Part Two
Plot and Plotting

"No, no! The adventures first," said the Gryphon in an impatient tone: "explanations take such a dreadful time."

So Alice began telling them her adventures.

Lewis Carroll, *Alice's Adventures in Wonderland*

2

The Selection, Sequence, and Shape of the Story

The plot of a story is so basic to narrative that it might, at first glance, seem hardly necessary to give attention to the crafting of any particular plot. Isn't it enough to read a plot straightforwardly from beginning to end? Yet authors give careful attention to the **plotting** of their stories, as we will explore in this chapter. So it makes sense to investigate how and why they plot their stories as they do.

Consider a familiar story with a well-known plotline: William Shakespeare's *Romeo and Juliet*. A pair of star-crossed lovers from feuding households meet, instantly fall in love, and are secretly married. The enmity between their families is brought to a crisis point when Romeo murders Juliet's cousin, Tybalt, in vengeance for killing Romeo's close friend. When Romeo is banished, Juliet fakes her own death and waits in the tomb for Romeo to return in hopes of being reunited with him. The tragic turn of the story comes when Romeo isn't given the message about the plan. Instead, he finds Juliet and thinks she really is dead. He drinks poison so he can die with her, and he does so just before she awakes from her drugged state. When she sees her true love dead, she kills herself with his dagger. The tragedy of their deaths brings an end to the feud.

In tragedies like this one, we often ask "What if?" questions. What if Romeo hadn't flown off the handle when his close friend was killed by Tybalt? Then the lovers might have come through unscathed. If only Romeo had received the message about the plan, then no one would have had to die. Or what if Juliet had awakened just minutes sooner, before Romeo ingested the poison? Then they could have lived happily ever after. But Shakespeare has shaped the plot to lead to its fatal conclusion, as if it were inevitable. His plotting "works" (his sequencing has a logic to it), and its movement has a driving sense of cause and effect. As we will see, these are key elements of the plotting of any story.

In this chapter, we explore the value of investigating the plotting of the four Gospels. After introducing key terms and essential aspects of plot and plotting, we address the plotting issues of selection and sequencing, as well as a variety of stylistic and pacing techniques that contribute to the shape of each Gospel story. As we will see, although the Gospels draw upon a common set of events from the life of Jesus, they each offer a distinctive plotline of his life and ministry.

The Basics of Plot and Plotting

We focus on plotting and plot in this first set of chapters (chaps. 2 and 3) because plot is usually considered to be the most basic element of a story. We can go back to Aristotle for this idea. He describes plot as the arrangement of incidents or actions in a story, and he subsumes characterization to plot.[1] In this prioritization, he considers plot to be the primary principle of narrative,[2] what James Resseguie calls the narrative's "designing principle."[3]

Behind the plot—what we might call the architecture of the story—lies an author's plotting activity. Plotting refers to *the way* the story is framed and told. It is "the active work of structuring revealed or dramatized in the text."[4] In NC, this activity occurs on the discourse level of a narrative, where the implied author communicates with the reader through the story's arrangement (see chap. 1).

1. Aristotle, *Poetics* 1450a.
2. We will note the influence of this prioritization when we discuss characterization (chap. 4) and the tendency in ancient storytelling to subsume character to plot.
3. James Resseguie, *Narrative Criticism in the New Testament: An Introduction* (Grand Rapids: Baker Academic, 2005), 197.
4. Peter Brooks, *Reading for the Plot: Design and Intention in Narrative* (New York: Knopf, 1984), 34.

Cause-Effect Arrangement

The emphasis in the definition of plot on *arrangement* and not simply on *action* is famously and wonderfully illustrated by E. M. Forster: "We have defined a story as a narrative of events arranged in their time-sequence. A plot is also a narrative of events, the emphasis falling on causality. 'The king died and then the queen died' is a story. 'The king died, and then the queen died of grief' is a plot. The time-sequence is preserved, but the sense of causality overshadows it."[5]

It is this combination of sequence and **causality** that informs a narrative plot. Peter Brooks defines it in this way: "Plot is the principle of interconnectedness and intention."[6] The sense of intentionality or causation is what propels the story forward toward its conclusion and makes the conclusion feel, in some sense, inevitable. Aristotle referred to this combination of sequence and causality in his definition of plot: "A sequence of events which follow one another either inevitably or according to probability."[7] Paul Goodman explains the reader's experience of causality like this: "In the beginning anything is possible; in the middle things become probable; in the ending everything is necessary."[8]

An example of plotted causality from all four Gospels involves the driving momentum toward Jesus' execution by Roman crucifixion. If we were to read Mark from beginning to end, we would discover a cluster of agents, motivations, and causes for Jesus' death.

Early in the story Jewish leaders in Galilee react to a Sabbath debate with Jesus by plotting to kill him (Mark 3:6). When Jesus arrives in Jerusalem, he clears the temple and calls for a return to its true purpose as a place of prayer for all nations. The temple leaders look "for a way to kill him" (11:18). Soon after, Jesus tells a parable indicting these Jewish leaders for their poor leadership and violent intentions (12:1–11). They want to arrest him but delay because of their fear of the crowds (12:12). Finally, as Passover nears, these leaders plan how they might arrest Jesus secretly and then kill him (14:1–2). They arrest him during the night

5. E. M. Forster, *Aspects of the Novel* (New York: Harcourt, Brace, 1927), 86.

6. Brooks, *Reading for the Plot*, 5.

7. Aristotle, *Poetics* 1451a, in *Poetics*, ed. and trans. by Stephen Halliwell, Loeb Classical Library 199 (Cambridge, MA: Harvard University Press, 2014), 23.

8. Paul Goodman, *The Structure of Literature* (Chicago: University of Chicago Press, 1954), 14, quoted in Resseguie, *Narrative Criticism*, 198.

(in secret), with the help of Judas and a mob they've assembled (14:43–46), and then they turn Jesus over to Pilate for trial and crucifixion (15:1).[9]

Judas' betrayal of Jesus to the Jewish leaders provides another part of the equation. He arranges to do so for the promise of money (Mark 14:10–11) and then identifies Jesus to the authorities by giving him a kiss of greeting in the dark of night (14:43–46).

Pilate's central role in Jesus' death becomes clear when the Gospel's story line is informed by its historical context. Pilate, as a Roman official, has the power to enact capital punishment (in contrast to his Jewish subjects, including their leaders), and he decides to crucify Jesus to pacify the crowds (Mark 15:15a). Only he can officially condemn Jesus to death and crucify him. After an ineffectual attempt to release him, Pilate hands Jesus over to his soldiers for crucifixion (15:15b).

An interrelated and complicating causative factor in Jesus' death is the "divine necessity" that contributes to this part of the plotline. We hear this from Jesus himself as he begins his journey to Jerusalem (Mark 10:32). He predicts his coming death three times, mentioning the agents in each case as the Jewish leaders (8:31; also 10:33), all humanity (i.e., both Jew and gentile; 9:31), and gentiles (along with the Jewish leaders; 10:33–34). In the first of these "passion predictions," Jesus speaks of the "must" (Greek *dei*) of this mission, and later we hear of its ultimate purpose: "To give his life as a ransom for many" (10:45).[10]

Elements of a Plot

In chapter 1 (fig. 1.1) I distinguish three aspects of the story level of a narrative: *settings*, *characters*, and *plot*. In that representation, plot refers to the action of the story line with its sense of causality: episodes and dialogue moving through turns of situation and conflicts toward the story's final climax and resolution. Although some define plot as inclusive of

9. The identification of specific groups of leaders differs across the narrative, with, e.g., Pharisees being more prominent in Jesus' Galilean ministry and chief priests and Sadducees more coming into play in Jerusalem.

10. Resseguie suggests the importance of differentiating causality from correlation (*Narrative Criticism*, 199–200). To continue with our example, Peter's denials are correlated with but are not the cause of Jesus' arrest and death, as they happen concurrently and are clearly associated with Jesus' death.

character and setting,[11] I find a distinction between plot and these other aspects of a story to be helpful for narrative analysis. As the authors of *Mark as Story* define plot (as distinct from characters and settings), "*Plot* involves events—their order in the narrative, sequential relations, turning points and breakthroughs, and the development and resolution of conflicts."[12]

As we consider these movements of a story, Gustav Freytag's well-established categories—exposition, rising action, climax, and resolution—prove helpful for tracing the contours of a plot.[13]

Exposition—description and backstory crucial for understanding a story—is usually front-loaded in a narrative to help the reader understand the characters and events that will prove to be central. Matthew's opening genealogy, for instance, sets Jesus in the context of his Jewish ("son of Abraham"; Matt. 1:1–2, 17) and kingly ("son of David"; 1:1, 6, 17) identities to help the reader get up to speed for the narrative to follow.

Rising action refers to the early stages of narrative activity, which signal the direction the plot will take and build its tension. Rising action introduces the central conflict(s) of the story, often stemming from decisions and actions of key characters. **Conflict** is a crucial plot mechanism and can take many different forms. Resseguie identifies a range of potential narrative conflicts, including "clash[es] of actions, ideas, points of vie[w], desires, values, or norms."[14] In Mark, for instance, conflict forms around three key subplots of the story. Jesus comes into conflict with the forces of evil, with Jewish and gentile authorities, and even with his own disciples.[15]

11. E.g., Mark Allan Powell, *What Is Narrative Criticism?*, GBS (Minneapolis: Fortress, 1990), 23. This broader view of plot makes sense, in that characters and settings are important contributors to plot, and as Resseguie notes, "plot and character are . . . inseparable in a narrative" (*Narrative Criticism*, 198). Yet for analytical purposes, it is helpful to look at these three narrative elements distinctively even while acknowledging their interdependence.

12. David Rhoads, Joanna Dewey, and Donald Michie, *Mark as Story: An Introduction to the Narrative of a Gospel*, 2nd ed. (Minneapolis: Fortress, 1999), 6 (emphasis original).

13. Gustav Freytag, *Technique of the Drama: An Exposition of Dramatic Composition and Art*, trans. and ed. Elias J. MacEwan (Chicago: Scott, Foresman, 1894). Freytag further delineates what I've called "resolution" as "falling action" and "denouement" (a final resolution of the conflict).

14. Resseguie, *Narrative Criticism*, 201.

15. Rhoads, Dewey, and Michie, *Mark as Story*, 77. "These three lines of conflict interweave and overlap at significant points, yet each conflict has its own direction, content, ambience, and resolution" (77).

Jesus' conflict with his disciples is primarily an ideological conflict over his own mission focused on service rather than status and his expectations for similar commitments on their part (e.g., Mark 10:35–45).

The **climax** of a story occurs when the plot reaches the height of its tension, right before final resolution. In the case of the Gospels, the climactic point comes at the death of Jesus on the cross, as all plotlines lead to this moment in the story. Yet we are also able to identify other lesser climactic peaks in the plotline of a Gospel. For example, in John 11 Jesus raises Lazarus from the dead, with this event foreshadowing Jesus' own death and resurrection to come. This miracle is the seventh and final "sign" Jesus performs in his public ministry (cf. John 2:11; 4:54) and so provides a penultimate climax in John.[16]

The **resolution** comes on the heels of the climax of the story and involves the narrative solutions to the story's conflicts, along with the tying up of other loose ends of the plot. For example, in Matthew women who have followed Jesus in his ministry and have held vigil at his cross and tomb find the tomb empty and hear from an angel the news of Jesus' resurrection (Matt. 28:1–7). Almost immediately they encounter the risen Jesus and worship him (28:8–9), and he commissions them to spread the news to the apostles (28:10). Their encounter with Jesus provides a keen sense of resolution in the narrative, coming after the seeming finality of Jesus' death and burial. Other subplots of the story are resolved in Matthew 28, including the previous desertion of the disciples at Jesus' arrest. Now, in an act of restoration, Jesus meets them (now eleven) in Galilee and commissions them to disciple the nations, with the promise of his abiding presence (28:16–20).

Selection for the Story

A first major area where we can see the evangelists being attentive to plotting relates to their selection of material. Even a quick comparison of the four Gospels reveals not only numbers of shared vignettes across two or more Gospels but also episodes and sayings that are unique to a single Gospel. While the rationale for what's included or omitted by particular

---

16. For a delineation of the seven signs and for textual connections between the seventh sign and Jesus' death and resurrection in John, see fig. 7.3 and discussion there.

evangelists is not always apparent, what is clear is that their selection of material impacts the plot.[17]

At the very end of John's Gospel, we read "Jesus did many other things as well. If every one of them were written down, I suppose that even the whole world would not have room for the books that would be written" (John 21:25). Even if we understand John to be using hyperbole here, the abundance of Jesus' actions and words during his life and ministry required the evangelists to consider carefully the question of selection.[18]

By closely comparing the Gospels, we can see that not many episodes cross all four of them. The following are shared in common:

- The recounting of John the Baptist's ministry and imprisonment
- Jesus' calling of the disciples
- One miracle, the feeding of the five thousand
- Jesus' public entry into Jerusalem
- The clearing of the temple
- Peter's denial (and Jesus' foretelling of it)
- Some key episodes during Jesus' passion (e.g., his arrest, trials, and crucifixion)
- Jesus' resurrection

In the Synoptics—Matthew, Mark, and Luke—the shared episodes and teachings increase significantly.

Yet there are quite a number of episodes or teachings unique to each of the four, and these give different casts to the individual Gospels (see fig. 2.1). Even in shared accounts there are often differences on a smaller scale that may contribute to an evangelist's special points of emphasis. For example, while Matthew and Luke both include the account of a centurion who asks Jesus for his servant's healing, Luke alone mentions

---

17. Redaction criticism involves hypothesizing about the rationale for selection to suggest the unique purposes of each evangelist. For example, Luke alone has the account of the healing of a Samaritan with leprosy who returns to thank Jesus (Luke 17:11–19). This story fits well with Luke's particular interest in Samaritans (and other non-Jews).

18. The same necessity of selection is true if we grant that the evangelists are drawing upon oral traditions of Jesus' words and deeds, since the earliest church would have thoughtfully selected traditions to pass along and the evangelists would have chosen from among these traditions for their written narratives.

that the request comes through intermediaries—a group of Jewish elders who plead on the centurion's behalf (Luke 7:3). This inclusion fits Luke's more positive portrait of at least some Jewish leaders (e.g., also 13:31) when compared to Matthew.

Figure 2.1
**Unique Episodes and Teachings
in the Gospels: A Selection**

Matthew	Mark	Luke	John
Visit of the Magi	Reference to wild beasts at temptation	Birth of John the Baptist	Jesus as the Word "in the beginning"
The "antitheses"	Jesus' family thinks he is out of his mind	Shepherds hear of Jesus' birth and visit him	Water-into-wine miracle
Blessing on Peter	Parable: seed secretly growing	John answers tax collectors and soldiers	Healing of man by pool in Jerusalem
Temple tax episode	Blind man healed at Bethsaida—partial, full	Woes to the rich	Raising of Lazarus
Parable: unforgiving servant	Includes Aramaic words/phrases: four times	List of women who minister to Jesus	Jesus washes his disciples' feet
Parable: sheep and goats	Sayings: "salted with fire" and "[having] salt among yourselves"	Healing of ten lepers	Jesus' priestly prayer
Warning from Pilate's wife	Young man who fled naked at Jesus' arrest	Zacchaeus episode	Doubting Thomas
The commissioning to disciple the nations	Women's fear concludes the Gospel	Road to Emmaus appearance	Jesus provides a miraculous catch of fish after his resurrection

These differences among the Gospels—both on the level of the plot and in the smaller details of an episode—contribute to the reality that in the Gospels we encounter four distinctive plotlines. "Each of the evangelists tells essentially the same story, but the plots and emphases of the gospels differ greatly."[19]

19. R. Alan Culpepper, *Anatomy of the Fourth Gospel: A Study in Literary Design* (Philadelphia: Fortress, 1983), 85.

Sequencing of the Story

As we noted in chapter 1, the turn in biblical studies to redaction criticism brought an increased interest in the arrangement of a Gospel's pericopes. Form criticism—the predecessor to redaction criticism—understood these series of stories and sayings to be virtually without implicit connections, like individual pearls on a string that could easily be "unstrung" and rearranged. Redaction critics began to look for and notice greater intentionality by the evangelists. The Gospel writers connected pericopes into sequences that seem to have a logic to their ordering and that made sense in light of the evangelists' theological interests and particular audiences.

Narrative criticism took this observation a step further to suggest that each Gospel has a narrative logic—a distinctive plot in which the sequencing of episodes, dialogue, and sayings contributes to a coherent story line.[20] A Gospel's distinctive plot can be traced and appreciated as it accents key themes and is intended to lead the reader to particular kinds of responses to who Jesus is and what he does. Literary theorist Mieke Bal refers to the multifaceted role of sequencing when she writes, "Playing with sequential ordering is not just a literary convention; it is also a means of drawing attention to certain things, to emphasize, to bring about aesthetic or psychological effects, to show various interpretations of an event, to indicate the subtle difference between expectation and realization, and much else besides."[21]

How Does Sequencing Work in the Gospels?

It is fair to ask the question, Does literary theory on sequencing, intended to address modern fictional narratives, really "work" when applied to the Gospels? At first glance, studying a story's sequence may seem an odd thing to do in a historical narrative, where we might expect an author to give us the events in simple chronological order. A helpful angle for

20. This is true in spite of the fairly episodic nature of the Gospels. "To some extent, the Gospels, especially Mark, appear to reflect episodic plots. But redaction critics have shown that, in most instances, there is a narrative logic, controlled by a theological vision, to the arrangement of pericopes." Frank J. Matera, "The Plot of Matthew's Gospel," *CBQ* 49 (1987): 233–53, here 240.

21. Mieke Bal, *Narratology: Introduction to the Theory of Narrative*, trans. Christine van Boheemen (Toronto: University of Toronto Press, 1985), 52–53.

answering this concern comes from the study of the genre of the Gospels.[22] As noted in chapter 1, the Gospels most resemble another kind of writing of the time—Greco-Roman biography. A key feature of such biographies was their anecdotal nature—they were arranged more topically than chronologically to emphasize the teachings of the biography's subject.[23]

For example, Suetonius, the Roman biographer of emperors and poets, describes his biographical writing in this way: "Having given as it were a summary of his life, I shall now take up its various phases one by one, not in chronological order, but by categories [*per species*], to make the account clearer and more intelligible."[24] Duane Stuart describes the biographies of Suetonius as broadly chronological but topical in the body of the work: "Normally the body of each biography consists in a record of deeds and a description of all manner of characteristics, thematically organized, and forming a huge parenthesis, as it were, [enclosed] between chronological narratives treating the preliminary stage of a career and its closing phases."[25]

Similarly, each Gospel follows chronology for its basic structure, beginning with Jesus' early years (Matthew and Luke) and then narrating his baptism, public ministry, and passion and resurrection. In the body of a Gospel, the arrangement of individual episodes and sayings often tells us more about the evangelist's thematic interests than about chronology.

Knowing this genre tendency for thematic sequencing over chronological ordering can help us see the contours of a Gospel in a new light. For example, in Matthew 8:1–9:34 the evangelist narrates nine healing episodes in fairly quick succession. Parallels to these healing accounts in Mark and Luke occur in different locations for the most part and sometimes in different orders.[26] Attending to the genre of Matthew means considering

---

22. Richard Burridge highlights the connection between literary or narrative criticism and genre: "Literary analyses inevitably . . . raised the issue of the genre of the gospels and their place in first century literature." Burridge, "Gospels: Genre," in *DJG*, 335–42, here 336.

23. Burridge notes that "lives of generals, politicians or statesmen tend to be more chronologically ordered, depicting their great deeds and virtues, while accounts of philosophers or writers are more anecdotal, arranged topically around collections of material to display their ideas and teachings" ("Gospels: Genre," 337–38).

24. Suetonius, "Life of Augustus" 2.9, in *Lives of the Caesars*, trans. J. C. Rolfe, Loeb Classical Library 31 (Cambridge, MA: Harvard University Press, 1998).

25. Duane Reed Stuart, *Epochs of Greek and Roman Biography* (New York: Biblo and Tannen, 1967), 185.

26. For example, Mark has a reversed order for Jesus healing a man with leprosy and healing Peter's mother-in-law (1:40–44 and 1:30–31, respectively) from Matthew (8:1–4 and 8:14–15,

the evangelist's thematic interests in sequencing these healing stories in close proximity. He does so as part of the two-prong focus on the Messiah's *words* in the Sermon on the Mount (Matt. 5–7) and the Messiah's miraculous *deeds* in subsequent chapters (Matt. 8–9). Jesus' actions of healing highlight his compassion and authority, as well as identify him as Isaiah's servant of the Lord who bears the illnesses of his people (8:17). Matthew also repeats the theme of faith across these chapters as the appropriate response to Jesus' healing power (e.g., 8:10; 9:2, 22, 29).

The Primacy Effect: The Starting Point for Jesus' Ministry

An interesting exercise for exploring the sequencing of the Gospels involves comparing how each evangelist begins Jesus' public ministry. This taps into the literary notion of the **primacy effect**, which suggests that material occurring first in a plot has a high impact on readers—initial impressions stick with us.[27] Since each Gospel offers a distinctive starting point for Jesus' public ministry—a hallmark event—the reader's initial impressions will be shaped differently for each. Matthew begins narrating Jesus' ministry with a long "sermon" (Matt. 5–7), a choice that fits well with his emphasis on Jesus' teaching ministry.[28] Alternatively, in Mark Jesus begins his ministry by driving out a demon (Mark 1:21–28), aligning with Mark's keen interest in showing Jesus' power over the forces of evil (see also 1:34; 3:11, 15, 22; 5:1–20; 7:24–30; 9:14–29).[29]

Turning to Luke, we see Jesus' first action of his public ministry occurring in his hometown. In the synagogue on the Sabbath, he reads from Isaiah (Isa. 61:1–2), accenting a focus on the poor and the captives as a hallmark of his ministry (Luke 4:16–21). Based on the primacy effect, the reader will not be surprised that this theme of God's concern for the poor and marginalized follows Jesus across Luke's narrative. Finally, John

---

respectively). Additionally, Mark has quite a bit of intervening material between these healings and the healing of a demoniac (Mark 5:1–20), while in Matthew these fall within the same chapter (Matt. 8:1–4, 14–15, 28–34).

27. Resseguie, *Narrative Criticism*, 209–10. Resseguie also describes the recency effect, which involves material that comes later in the narrative that might confirm, adjust, or even override the primacy effect.

28. This long sermon comes after a brief summary of Jesus' Galilean ministry (Matt. 4:17, 23–25) and his calling of disciples (4:18–22), a necessary precursor for Jesus teaching his disciples (5:1–2).

29. In Mark (as in Matthew), Jesus calls four disciples prior to his first ministering action.

indicates that Jesus' first action of his public ministry involves turning water into wine at a wedding (John 2:1–12), the first of seven signs in John 1–12 that point to Jesus as Messiah and Lord. Each evangelist begins his narration of Jesus' ministry with an episode that emphasizes particular themes of that Gospel.

Structural Patterns for Sequencing

As we consider strategies of sequencing, we can explore some common structural patterns of narratives, patterns that include literary conventions such as **chiasm, intercalation**, and *inclusio*.[30] In ancient writings like the Gospels, which didn't have paragraphing or even word spacing or punctuation, these kinds of patterns would signal to readers and hearers the organization of a written work.[31]

Chiasm is a sequencing pattern in which repetition occurs, but in reverse order in its second half. While the sequence may be of variable length (e.g., ABCDCBA), the following illustrates the arrangement of the repetition, with the final element being similar to what comes first.

| A | B | C | B' | A' |

An example of a chiasm that structures part of a Gospel comes in the five controversy stories of Mark 2:1–3:6.[32] This narrative unit begins and ends (the A terms) with a *healing* by Jesus that proves controversial to teachers of the law and Pharisees (2:6 and 3:6, respectively). The B terms (second and fourth pericopes) both involve controversies of *eating*—Jesus eating with tax collectors and sinners and his disciples gleaning and eating grain on the Sabbath. This connection is enhanced by a concluding proverb in each case (2:17, 27–28). The C term at the center is a controversy about *fasting*—with a concern expressed that Jesus' disciples do

---

30. David Bauer lists these and other structural and rhetorical devices (what he refers to as "compositional relationships"). We will explore another of these, called interchange, in the next chapter, since Luke features this device in his early chapters. Bauer, *The Structure of Matthew's Gospel: A Study in Literary Design*, BLS 15 (Sheffield: Sheffield Academic Press, 1988), 13–19.

31. John Dart, "Scriptural Schemes: The ABCBAs of Biblical Writing," *SBL Forum*, accessed March 20, 2019, http://sbl-site.org/Article.aspx?ArticleID=296.

32. For an extended argument for this chiasm, see Joanna Dewey, "Literary Structure of the Controversy Stories in Mark 2:1–3:6," *JBL* 92 (1973): 394–401. For the often-controversial nature of identifying chiasm, especially on the macrolevel of biblical narratives, see Dart, "Scriptural Schemes."

not fast. This controversy provides opportunity for Jesus to teach on fasting and about the new time of the kingdom that calls for a different way of living.

A	B	C	B′	A′
Controversial healing (Mark 2:1–12)	Eating with "sinners" (2:13–17)	Fasting and the time of "new wineskins" (2:18–22)	Eating grain on Sabbath (2:23–28)	Controversial healing (3:1–6)

In addition to providing structural clues for the reader or hearer, a chiasm also offers to its readers or hearers a pleasing sense of a return to the beginning—with a story arc wrapping up as it had started.[33]

Intercalation is a narrative pattern in which one episode interrupts another, producing a kind of storied ABA pattern. A key feature of intercalation is that the two stories are intended to be interpreted in light of each other. Although Matthew and Luke do have a few intercalations, Mark is the Gospel that is characterized by this particular structural device. This is so much the case that intercalations are often called "Markan sandwiches."

   A Commencing of first story
      B Second story
   A′ Completion of first story

We read an example in Mark 5:21–43, where the evangelist narrates Jesus' raising to life the daughter of a synagogue leader (5:21–24, 35–43) interrupted by an account of the healing of a woman suffering from ongoing bleeding of an unspecified nature (5:25–34). We can observe a number of literary links between the two accounts in addition to the intercalation structure. Both recipients of healing are women and both have an association with the number twelve—the daughter is twelve years old (5:42)[34] and the woman has been suffering with her condition for twelve years (5:25). The narrator refers to Jairus' "daughter" (5:23, 35), and Jesus calls the

---

33. This sense of return to the beginning also characterizes intercalation and *inclusio*. Some argue that the center of a chiasm provides the key for interpretation, although this is a debated point.

34. In the first-century world, this would put her on the cusp of adulthood and marrying age.

woman "Daughter" (5:34). Both receive healing from Jesus, and in both cases physical contact is involved (5:27–31, 41–42).

A Request by Jairus for Jesus to come and heal his dying daughter
 B Woman approaches Jesus and is healed by him
A′ Jesus raises the daughter back to life

If Mark uses intercalation to guide his reader toward meaning, then we should focus on the shared motifs between the two intertwining episodes. First, Mark shows Jesus to be a powerful and compassionate healer. In compassion, he willingly goes with Jairus to help his daughter (5:24) and grants peace and freedom from suffering to the woman with a hemorrhage (5:34). In power, he heals without even knowing it (5:27–29) and restores the young woman from the grip of death itself (5:41–42).

Second, Mark highlights faith in both episodes. Jairus expresses faith that Jesus can heal his dying daughter if he will only come to see her (5:23). When his daughter dies, Jesus presses him to continue in faith: "Don't be afraid; just believe" (5:36). The woman in need of healing believes in Jesus' power so much that she trusts that simply touching his garment will make her well (5:27–28), and Jesus commends her for that trust (5:34).

Inclusio is a structural feature that bookends a section of narrative, with a repeated word, phrase, or theme placed at the front and at the end of a passage or story segment.

Word, phrase, or theme
 Narrative segment (of any length)
Word, phrase or theme

Matthew provides an example in his theme of Jesus' presence "with" his people. This motif occurs in the Gospel's very first narrative passage (Matt. 1:23) and in its very last line (28:20). The evangelist shows the importance of this theme by its strategic placement as an *inclusio* for the whole Gospel (cf. also 18:20). As R. T. France puts it, "The phrase 'God with us' . . . will have its arresting counterpart at the end of the gospel, where Jesus himself declares, 'I am with you always.'"[35]

35. R. T. France, *The Gospel of Matthew*, NICNT (Grand Rapids: Eerdmans, 2008), 49.

"They will call him Immanuel (which means 'God with us')." (1:23)
The entire narrative of Matthew 1–28
"I am with you always." (28:20)

"Out of Order" Sequencing

A final set of considerations that prove helpful for plot analysis involves events that are out of sequence. These arise from a narrative displacement, in which "the order of events *referred to by* the narrative" is not aligned with "the order of events *presented in* the narrative discourse."[36] Sometimes a narrator will introduce an event that happens later in the story at an earlier point in the narrative sequence. This "flash-forward" occurs out of sequence in the narrative, since it introduces a part of the story that has not yet occurred in the story's chronology. Literary critics call this "flash-forward" a **prolepsis**.[37] An example occurs in John 11:2, where the narrator refers to Mary's anointing of Jesus: "This Mary . . . was the same one who poured perfume on the Lord and wiped his feet with her hair." Yet this episode will not be fully narrated until the next chapter of John (12:1–11).

A "flashback," or **analepsis**, is "the narration of an event *after* its ordinary chronological order in the narrative world."[38] Mark 6:17–29 provides an example with its flashback to the account of Herod's execution of John the Baptist. In the story time up to this point, Mark has been narrating Jesus' healing ministry and, at 6:7–13, the ministry of the twelve apostles patterned after his own. He then describes the reaction of Herod Antipas to Jesus' ministry. He and others think that John has been raised from the dead (6:14, 16). Mark then proceeds in a flashback to narrate John's death at Herod's command: "For Herod himself had given orders to have John arrested" (6:17). After recounting this past episode, the narrator returns to his story line, with the twelve apostles reporting to Jesus about their itinerant ministry (6:30).

---

36. Brooks, *Reading for the Plot*, 12 (emphasis added). These are his definitions of the *fabula* and *sjužet*, respectively, terms used in Russian Formalism to express the ideas we've referred to as *story* and *discourse* (see chap. 1). This displacement is sometimes referred to as a disjunction between story time and narrative time (Culpepper, *Anatomy of the Fourth Gospel*, 53).

37. Prolepsis is defined as "the narration of an event *before* its logical order in the narrative world." Janice Capel Anderson and Stephen D. Moore, eds., *Mark and Method: New Approaches in Biblical Studies* (Minneapolis: Fortress, 1992), 165. Although language of foreshadowing is sometimes applied, a prolepsis is not simply a reference to a later event but a narration or partial narration of it.

38. Anderson and Moore, *Mark and Method*, 162.

The Shape of the Story

The sequencing of a story contributes in significant ways to the shape of its plot. As we step back from the particulars of the ordering of episodes and sayings, we can notice on a macrolevel how each Gospel has something of a distinctive shape to it. This is the case even though all four share the key climactic events of Jesus' crucifixion, death, and resurrection. The distinctive shape of each Gospel arises from a confluence of factors, including sequencing, style, and pacing (along with the way the author uses key settings and characters). In this final section of the chapter, we look at style and pacing as key ways (along with sequencing) that the evangelists shape their plotlines.

A Matter of Style

A frequently replayed description of the Gospels comes from Martin Kähler: "To state the matter somewhat provocatively, one could call the Gospels passion narratives with extended introductions."[39] This is a comment about the shape of the Gospels. It has been popular to ascribe Kähler's observation to Mark in particular, especially since Mark is the Gospel that gives the most attention proportionately to Jesus' passion. Mark's narrative covers the terrain of Jesus' Galilean ministry in its first half (Mark 1–10) and his time in Jerusalem leading to his crucifixion in the second (Mark 11–16).[40] This weighting of attention to Jesus' passion (close to 40 percent of the Gospel) is a stylistic and theological distinctive of Mark when compared to Matthew (who spends about 30 percent on Jesus' passion) and Luke (about 20 percent). John, in his own unique way (and so with distinctive shaping), has a pronounced focus on Jesus' passion, especially if the extended Upper Room Discourse of John 13–17 is included as part of the passion narrative.

As we consider Mark on the microlevel, we notice that its unique shape also derives from its author's stylistic habit of narrating lengthy episodes with colorful details. Both Matthew and Luke, who likely used Mark as

---

39. Martin Kähler, *The So-called Historical Jesus and the Historic, Biblical Christ*, trans. Carl E. Braaten (Philadelphia: Fortress, 1964), 80n11. The book was originally published in German in 1896.

40. The emphasis is only increased if we see a shift toward the passion already at Mark 8:31, when Jesus first predicts to his disciples his coming death.

their primary source,[41] tend to shorten these episodes, inevitably omitting in the process some of the lively details. They seem to do so because it provides them additional space to add to Mark's basic format more episodes and especially more sayings of Jesus. A striking example of Mark's fondness for details involves the woman who has been subject to bleeding for twelve years and comes to Jesus for healing (Mark 5:24b–34). Mark includes quite a number of interesting details, all of which Matthew omits (cf. Matt. 9:20–22):

- She had spent all her money paying doctors who didn't help her get better (Mark 5:26).
- She feels in her body that she has been healed (5:29).
- Jesus realizes that power has left him but doesn't know who has been healed (5:30–31).
- The woman fearfully admits that it was she who touched Jesus (5:33).[42]

On the other hand, Matthew adds a few details that fit well with his stylistic and thematic interests. First, he adds that the woman touched "*the edge of* [Jesus'] cloak" (Matt. 9:20), adding the word *kraspedon* (Greek for "edge" or "tassel") to Mark's reference to Jesus' "cloak" (Mark 5:27). According to Numbers 15:37–39, Jewish men were required to wear these tassels on the corners of their garments to remind themselves to be faithful to God's commands. Matthew's inclusion of this detail (also at Matt. 14:36) fits his pronounced emphasis on Jesus as fully torah observant.[43] Second, Matthew concludes his brief account by noting that the woman's healing happened "at that moment" (9:22), a stylistic turn of phrase that Matthew uses elsewhere in accounts of healing and that highlights Jesus' authority (8:13; 15:28; 17:18).

When we take a closer look at the style of John's Gospel, we note that it differs in shape from the other three Gospels (the Synoptics) in a number of ways. Even Mark's longer episodes cannot compete in length with some

---

41. See chap. 1 on the questions of the Gospels' sources and of their literary dependence.

42. Luke omits the first two details and retains the last two (cf. Luke 8:42b–48). Luke is roughly 70 percent of the length of Mark in this account; Matthew's episode is only about 30 percent as long as Mark's.

43. Jeannine K. Brown and Kyle Roberts, *Matthew*, THNTC (Grand Rapids: Eerdmans, 2018), 511–13.

of John's extended episodes, such as Jesus' engagement with a Samaritan woman and her village (forty-two verses long). John also structures the middle section of his Gospel with a series of narrative-dialogical cycles. These cycles arise out of a particular Jewish festival setting, often revolve around a sign or miracle, and involve extensive dialogue between Jesus and Jewish leaders or disciples.

- Healings and dialogue about work—set during the Sabbath (John 5:1–47)
- Feeding sign, walking on water, and dialogue about bread and Jesus' identity—set during Passover (6:1–71)
- Dialogue about water, light, and Jesus' identity—set during the Festival of Tabernacles (7:1–8:59)[44]
- Dialogue with his disciples (Upper Room Discourse) the night before he is crucified—just before Passover (13:1–17:26)

These lengthy episodes and narrative-dialogue cycles contribute to the Gospel's shape—as *Jesus in dialogue* typifies much of John's story line.

The Pacing of the Story

Each of the Gospels has a sense of pace to it. We've already begun exploring this facet of a story's shaping in our comparison of Mark's longer episodes to those in Matthew and Luke and in the description of John's even longer and more dialogical episodes and cycles. As we consider this idea of pacing further, Gérard Genette's description of "the speed of a narrative" is a helpful notion.[45] According to Genette, "the speed of a narrative will be defined by the relationship between a duration (that of the *story*, measured in seconds, minutes, hours, days, months, and years) and a length (that of the *text*, measured in lines and pages)."[46] Narratives inevitably have a certain sense of rhythm, moving along with variations in tempo. And "the time it takes [to read a nar-

---

44. For more about the festival settings of John 5–10, see chap. 8.

45. Culpepper introduces these ideas from Genette in *Anatomy of the Fourth Gospel*, 71.

46. Gérard Genette, *Narrative Discourse: An Essay in Method*, trans. Jane E. Lewin (Ithaca, NY: Cornell University Press, 1980), 87–88 (emphasis added). Similarly, Bal compares the text, which is a "series of sentences," with the story (or *fabula*), which is a "series of events" (*Narratology*, 52).

rative], to get from beginning to end . . . is very much part of our sense of the narrative."[47]

The pacing of Matthew's Gospel, for instance, is quite variable given the inclusion of five large discourses consisting of Jesus' teachings. Matthew's choice to arrange his Gospel in this way results in long, uninterrupted sections in which the reader or hearer tracks with Jesus' teachings in something like "real time."[48] Alternatively, as each discourse concludes, the pace picks up in a subsequent narrative section, in which actions, episodes, and interactive dialogue among characters take a front seat. This alternation of slowing down and speeding up across the first Gospel impacts the shape of the story (see fig. 2.2). And it impacts the reader's involvement by drawing the reader into Jesus' teachings in the discourses in a more immediate and direct way. As Janice Capel Anderson suggests, "It is as if Jesus speaks in the implied reader's present."[49]

Figure 2.2
The Pacing of Matthew's Gospel: Alternation of Narrative (N) and Discourse (D)

N	D	N	D	N	D	N	D	N	D	N
1:1– 4:25	5:1– 7:29 Sermon on the Mount	8:1– 9:38	10:1– 11:1 Mission discourse	11:2– 12:50	13:1–53 Parables discourse	13:54– 17:27	18:1–35 Community discourse	19:1– 23:39	24:1– 25:46 Eschatological discourse	26:1– 28:20

Pacing is also impacted by an author's use of **summaries** and **scenes**. Genette distinguishes these two features of a plot. A summary is "the narration in a few paragraphs or a few pages of several days, months, or years of existence, without details of action or speech."[50] Scenes, however, involve more extended "periods of action" that often play a decisive role in

47. Brooks, *Reading for the Plot*, 21.
48. Jeannine K. Brown, "Direct Engagement of the Reader in Matthew's Discourses: Rhetorical Techniques and Scholarly Consensus," *NTS* 51 (2005): 19–35, here 26. Although all five begin with a narrative introduction (e.g., 5:1–2), only two of the five discourses include (brief) narrative interruptions (13:10–11a, 24a, 31a, 33a, 34–37a, 51b–52a; and 18:21–22a).
49. Janice Capel Anderson, "Matthew: Gender and Reading," *Semeia* 28 (1983): 3–27, here 25.
50. Genette, *Narrative Discourse*, 95–96.

the plot.[51] We see an example of Matthew's use of summaries and scenes in a narrative unit involving the pairing of the Sermon on the Mount (Matt. 5:1–7:29) and the narration of Jesus' healing ministry (8:1–9:34). This discourse-narrative pair, which fits the category of *scene*, is bookended by two virtually identical *summaries* of Jesus' ministry that mention Jesus teaching in synagogues, preaching "the good news of the kingdom," and healing "every disease and sickness" (4:23; 9:35). What we hear in brief summary form at the beginning and end of this unit (via an *inclusio*) we then see detailed out in the scene that comes between the two summaries.

Conclusion

In this chapter, we've explored the plotting and plots of the Gospels in conversation with literary theory. We have focused attention on how the evangelists craft their plotlines by means of selection, sequencing, and the shaping techniques of pacing and their individual styles of storytelling. Our examples from the Gospels in this chapter have focused on Matthew, Mark, and John. In the next chapter, we turn to Luke's Gospel and its own distinctive plotline for the story of Jesus. By investigating Luke's plot and plotting at greater length, we will be able to elaborate on some of the theoretical aspects of plotting introduced in this chapter. As we will see, Luke plots his Gospel both to communicate how Jesus the Messiah accomplishes the divine plan and to prepare readers and hearers for his second volume, the book of Acts.

---

51. Genette, *Narrative Discourse*, 109–10. Genette also identifies the use of ellipsis in a plot, which is a time lapse either mentioned or implied (106–8). See discussion of this feature in chap. 3.

3

Narrative Plotting
in the Gospel of Luke

In this chapter, we take theory related to the plotting of a story (chap. 2) and employ it for understanding the contours of Luke's Gospel. Because the third Gospel is the first of the two-part work Luke-Acts, we will be able to see Luke's intentionality in plotting more clearly at times by comparing how Acts is plotted. For example, Luke's lengthy **travel narrative** (9:51–19:27) parallels the extensive missionary travels of Paul and company in the middle section of Acts (13:1–21:16).

The structure of Luke that will provide the parameters of our discussion follows a typical outlining of the book.

1:1–4	Preface
1:5–2:52	Births of John and Jesus
3:1–4:13	Jesus' ministry preparation
4:14–9:50	Jesus' Galilean ministry
9:51–19:27	Jesus' movement toward Jerusalem (travel narrative)*
19:28–24:53	Jesus' arrival in Jerusalem, passion, and resurrection

* The end point of the Lukan travel narrative is a matter of debate, with its conclusion at 19:27, 28, 44, or 48, given the multiple references to Jerusalem and its environs in the chapter (e.g., 19:28, 29, 41).

Drawing on this outline of Luke, I summarize how each section furthers the plot of the Gospel before addressing some key features of Luke's plotting in that section. This plan will allow us to get a feel for the shape of the Third Gospel from beginning to end, despite the necessary selectivity for discussing issues of sequencing, selection, style, and pacing in each section.

Luke's Preface (Luke 1:1–4): Paving the Way for the Plot

Luke begins his Gospel with a brief preface that is unique among the four Gospels but has affinities with prefaces from other ancient writings, including Greek and Roman biographies.[1] What can we learn about the plot of Luke from this preface?

First, we learn that Luke identifies his Gospel as an "account" or "narrative" (*diēgēsis*) of similar type to the ones he has consulted for his own writing (Luke 1:1). The preface is one continuous sentence in Greek, with the first line providing this identifying term for what Luke and others before him have written (so implied in 1:3). "Seeing that many have taken up the task of writing a narrative [*diēgēsis*] . . . it seemed good to me also . . . to write [a narrative] in orderly fashion" (1:1, 3 AT).

As we have already noted in chapter 1, Mark is quite likely one of the narratives Luke refers to in his opening sentence. He has investigated such narratives (Luke 1:3), along with oral traditions of "the things that have been fulfilled among us" (1:1).[2] With that phrase, Luke implies his narrative will address the whole sweep of God's covenantal fulfillment through Jesus. And as the opening of Acts makes clear, he is interested in his Gospel to write "about all that Jesus began to do and to teach until the day he was taken up to heaven" (Acts 1:1–2a).

Luke's commitment to writing a narrative means he gives us a plot to follow. It is a plot both about Jesus' words and actions (Acts 1:1) and

1. Charles H. Talbert provides a catalogue of seven commonplace components of ancient prefaces to histories and biographies. Comparing Luke's preface to them, he notes that it fits well within this genre, sharing six of the seven. Talbert, *Reading Luke: A Literary and Theological Commentary on the Third Gospel*, rev. ed. (Macon, GA: Smyth & Helwys, 2002), 10. Although there is some debate about whether Luke, in distinction from the other three Gospels, is more like ancient historiography than biography, Talbert concludes that Luke's preface has greater affinities with biographical and other prefaces than with historical prefaces (11). Richard Burridge suggests that Luke conforms his Markan source even more closely to the genre of ancient biography ("Gospel: Genre," in *DJG*, 335–42, here 338).

2. The phrase "handed down" (*paradidōmi*) is used to describe these oral traditions in v. 2 and is a technical term routinely used for passing on oral tradition, here referring to traditions about Jesus' life and teachings.

about the divine meaning of his life and ministry (Luke 1:1). Joel Green highlights the latter dimension when he writes, "For Luke, 'narrative' is proclamation. Luke has in mind the use of history to preach, to set forth a persuasive interpretation of God's work in Jesus."[3]

Luke, in his preface, also draws attention to his plotting of the Gospel. He depicts his narrative as written "in orderly fashion" (*kathexēs*; Luke 1:3 AT), or as the CEB renders it, "a carefully ordered account."[4] As we saw in chapter 2, the Gospels, like Greco-Roman biographies, are not consistently chronologically arranged. Instead, they are often ordered more topically, especially in their middle sections. And while Luke is certainly interested in placing his life of Jesus with reference to historical events, especially Roman political realities (see 2:1; 3:1), he deliberately sequences some of the episodes of Jesus' public ministry according to themes and topics. Luke has carefully organized his Gospel. And our explorations in this chapter will bear out the intentionality of his plotting.

Births of John and Jesus (Luke 1:5–2:52)

In the opening narrative frame of his Gospel, Luke introduces not only Jesus but also John the Baptist, the one who will prepare Israel for their Messiah. This section is expositional—it provides the audience with a sense of the identities of both John and Jesus and, prophetically, what they will do. Both are destined to play their part in the divine plan of salvation, which is a key thematic focus in these early chapters. Jesus is at the center of the divine plan to fulfill God's covenantal promises to Israel and to bring their longed-for salvation of peace and joy. In this way, this expositional section also encompasses God—who orchestrates the arrival of the Messiah in line with covenant promises to Israel—as a character in the story.[5] Even at this expositional stage the narrative tension to come is intimated (Luke 2:34–35), as some in Israel will not welcome Jesus as Messiah: "This child is destined to cause the falling and rising of many in Israel" (2:34).

3. Joel B. Green, *The Gospel of Luke*, NICNT (Grand Rapids: Eerdmans, 1997), 38.
4. The Greek *kathexēs* can refer to logical sequencing or to temporal ordering (BDAG, 490).
5. The Holy Spirit also emerges with qualities of a character in the story line, especially as the agency of the Spirit is highlighted across the birth narratives (Luke 1:15, 35, 41, 67; 2:25–26).

Sequencing: Jesus and John the Baptist in Comparison

The first two chapters of Luke move along through a series of alternating scenes between the early lives of John the Baptist and Jesus. This sequencing arrangement has been referred to as **interchange** (e.g., ABABABA)[6] and coheres with the ancient category of comparison, or *synkrisis*, taught as part of a rhetorical education in the Greco-Roman world.[7] According to one first-century rhetorical handbook, such comparisons could highlight differences between people, though the strategy was not used for people who were strikingly different.[8]

Luke's comparison of John and Jesus offers a positive portrait of John and shows the unity of purpose they share, while also highlighting Jesus as greater than John.[9] The alternation of focus between John and Jesus begins almost immediately at 1:5, where we are introduced to Zechariah and Elizabeth, the soon-to-be parents of John. The parallels between the two children involve their birth announcements (1:5–25, 26–38); songs or hymns by Mary and Zechariah (1:46–55, 67–79); their birth accounts (1:57–66; 2:1–21); and a brief comment in each case on their maturation (e.g., growing in strength; 1:80; 2:40; see fig. 3.1). These parallels are not set out in exact alternation (e.g., ABABABA; for their sequencing, see fig. 3.2). Nevertheless, Luke clearly arranges parallel episodes for both John and Jesus across Luke 1–2, with a couple of singular events narrated—the meeting of Mary and Elizabeth (1:39–45) and the presentation and purification of the infant Jesus in the temple (2:22–39).

Figure 3.1
Parallel Accounts in the Lukan Birth Narrative (Luke 1–2)

John the Baptist	Angelic announcement of birth to father (1:5–25)	Zechariah's song (1:67–79)	Birth account and naming (1:57–66)	Comment on maturing/growth (1:80)
Jesus the Messiah	Angelic announcement of birth to mother (1:26–38)	Mary's song (1:46–55)	Birth account and naming (2:1–21)	Comment on maturing/growth (2:40; cf. 2:52)

6. David Bauer, *The Structure of Matthew's Gospel: A Study in Literary Design*, BLS 15 (Sheffield: Sheffield Academic, 1988), 18.

7. Graham N. Stanton, *A Gospel for a New People: Studies in Matthew* (Edinburgh: T&T Clark, 1992), 77–84. Stanton describes this common rhetorical strategy and its use in Matthew.

8. Stanton, *Gospel for a New People*, 78.

9. Robert C. Tannehill, *The Narrative Unity of Luke-Acts: A Literary Interpretation*, vol. 1, *The Gospel according to Luke* (Philadelphia: Fortress, 1986), 19–20.

Figure 3.2
Sequencing of Vignettes in Luke 1–2

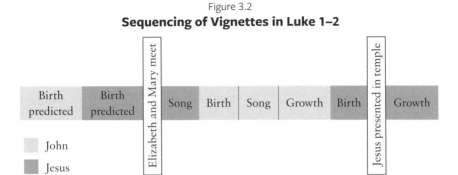

A central purpose of this extended comparison is to show God at work in the lives of both John and Jesus, even prior to their conceptions, bringing redemption for Israel. In John as prophet (1:76) and Jesus as savior (2:11), God is fulfilling covenant promises made to Israel (1:54, 72). "Luke self-consciously begins his narrative in the middle of the story. . . . The God who has been working redemptively *still is*, now, and especially, in Jesus."[10]

The point of the comparison is also to distinguish Jesus from John. Although John is a crucial agent in God's restoration work, Jesus is unrivaled as "Son of the Most High," Savior, Messiah, and Lord (Luke 1:32; 2:11). As Simeon celebrates when he takes the infant Jesus into his arms, "my eyes have seen your salvation . . . a light for revelation to the Gentiles, and the glory of your people Israel" (2:30–32).

Songs in the Birth Narratives

Luke has included in the birth narratives songs from various characters: Zechariah, Mary, and Simeon.[11] These are spread across the story line of Luke 1–2, interspersed within the narrative action (1:46–55, 67–79; 2:28–32). The shift in genre from narrated events to poetry also shifts the story's pacing, as the reading experience slows down from the quicker pace of plotted action to a poetic pause that offers added insight into what is happening.

This poetic commentary helps us hear in more explicit ways themes that have already been emerging in the plot. For example, the announcement of

10. Green, *Gospel of Luke*, 52 (emphasis original).
11. These are variously identified by commentators as songs, hymns, canticles, poems, or prophetic/praise responses.

the Messiah's birth implicitly signals that God is now showing covenant mercy in fulfilling divine promises to Israel (Luke 1:32–33). Mary's and Zechariah's songs provide an extended and explicit focus on celebrating God's covenant mercy (1:50, 54–55, 72, 78).[12] Salvation and forgiveness for God's people is coming about because of "God's merciful compassion" (1:78 CSB).[13]

While all three songs point to God's salvific work now coming to a climax in Jesus, each of the three songs also has its own unique features. Mary's song celebrates the God who raises up the humble in status and brings down rulers, the proud, and the rich (Luke 1:48, 51–53). This sense of reversal upon the arrival of God's salvation in Jesus will pervade the rest of Luke.[14] Zechariah's song focuses on John specifically, with his words highlighting John's prophetic and preparatory role (1:76–77).

And Simeon's song, with its allusions to Isaiah 49:5–6, signals how the Messiah will be a light to the gentiles as well as the glory of Israel (Luke 2:31–32).[15] Simeon's role in the plot also differs from that of Mary and Zechariah, who, as parents of Jesus and John (respectively), are key characters in moving the plot forward in this part of the narrative. Simeon has a more incidental plot function, yet in his persistent waiting "for the consolation of Israel" (2:25) and in his prophetic words he represents the people of Israel in this part of Luke's story. "Mary and Zechariah sing of Israel's story; Simeon embodies that story. He is faithful Israel waiting for the advent of God."[16]

A Note on Selection

Virtually every part of the birth narratives is unique to Luke's Gospel. There is a slight overlap between Luke and Matthew regarding the return

---

12. Suzanne Nicholson notes that Luke understands God's mercy to include faithfulness to promises made. Nicholson, "Mercy," in *DJG*, 584–88, here 587.

13. Luke uses here two Greek nouns (*splagchnon* and *eleos*) that can both be translated as "mercy" to emphasize the deep well of God's compassion. Luke also mentions the Lord's mercy toward Elizabeth in giving her a son in her old age (1:58).

14. E.g., Luke 4:18; 5:30–32; 6:20–21; 7:22, 34; 14:12–14, 15–24; 15:1, 7, 10; 16:19–31; 19:7–10; 21:1–4.

15. For Luke's use of this Isaiah text across his two-volume work, see Jeannine K. Brown, "Jesus Messiah as Isaiah's Servant of the Lord: New Testament Explorations," *JETS*, forthcoming.

16. Gail R. O'Day, "The Praise of New Beginnings: The Infancy Hymns in Luke," *Journal for Preachers* 14 (1990): 3–8, here 7.

of Jesus' family to Nazareth in Galilee (Luke 2:39; cf. Matt. 2:22b–23, where the reference is to relocation in Nazareth). Yet Luke's material has a pronounced focus on Mary, while Matthew narrates the birth and infancy accounts from Joseph's perspective (Matt. 1:18–2:23). And while in Matthew Magi find out about the Messiah's birth from a star and visit him, in Luke shepherds are the recipients of an angelic announcement and go to see the child. The material revolving around John's birth, Jesus' presentation at the temple, and his family's visit to Jerusalem when he is twelve years old (Luke 2:41–52) also occurs only in Luke.

Jesus' Ministry Preparation (Luke 3:1–4:13)

This section of Luke focuses on preparation for ministry. After an eighteen-year hiatus in the story's narration, Luke situates the inauguration of John's ministry in terms of both Roman and Jewish rule (Luke 3:1–2). John's ministry, which has already been a matter of prophetic testimony (1:76–79), focuses on calling his people to repentance and to baptism. John's warning against presuming upon one's covenantal status without requisite repentance hints at the mixed reception ahead to the ministries of John and Jesus. Jesus comes to John for baptism and receives God's commendation (3:21–22), setting up the testing of Jesus in the wilderness and his faithfulness to God with each temptation (4:1–13).

Narrative Pacing: Jesus from Twelve to Thirty

A feature of Luke's Gospel is the ellipsis, or time lapse, of Jesus' middle years. Luke alone narrates an episode from Jesus' life when he was twelve (2:41–51) and uniquely identifies Jesus' age at the onset of his public ministry—about thirty years old (3:23). These age markers highlight the ellipsis, which impacts the pacing of the story[17] and heightens the sense of the story leaping ahead between Luke 2 and Luke 3. This time gap is also accented by Luke's intentional setting of Jesus' birth and his ministry

---

17. Gérard Genette, *Narrative Discourse: An Essay in Method*, trans. Jane E. Lewin (Ithaca, NY: Cornell University Press, 1980), 106–8. In this case, the ellipsis is explicit. Genette also identifies the category of implicit ellipses, "whose very presence is not announced in the text . . . infer[red] only from some chronological lacuna or gap in the narrative continuity" (108). Matthew's gap between Jesus' infancy (Matt. 2) and his public ministry (and John's preaching; Matt. 3) creates an implicit ellipsis.

(which immediately follows John's) within the political realities of the day. Herod the Great is king of Judah at the time of Jesus' birth (1:5), and Tiberius is emperor (Caesar) when John and Jesus begin their ministries (3:1). To fill in this gap, the reader is given a summary statement of what transpires in Jesus' life from age twelve to thirty: "And Jesus increased in wisdom and in years, and in divine and human favor" (2:52, Joel Green's translation).[18]

Sequencing for Chronology and for Theme

We can observe Luke's careful sequencing (cf. 1:3) at a number of points in this section of the Gospel. For example, in contrast to Mark, who narrates as a flashback Herod's imprisonment of John because of John's criticism of his marriage to Herodias (Mark 6:17–18; cf. 1:14), Luke includes this information prior and closer to its actual occurrence and provides an explicit evaluation of this action as "evil" (Luke 3:19–20).

Luke also locates Jesus' genealogy between Jesus' baptism and his temptation, thereby creating narrative emphasis and effect. First, the narrative pause created by the genealogy provides exposition of the Old Testament backstory, as many of the names recall particular stories (e.g., Abraham as the father of the nation). Second, by extending the genealogy all the way back to Adam, Luke intimates the universal reach of God's salvation in Jesus (cf. 2:30–32). Finally, the reference to Adam as "son of God" (3:38) resonates with the angelic announcement that Jesus "will be called the Son of God" (1:35) and connects to the same title used of Jesus in the temptation narrative ahead (4:3, 9). Jesus is the faithful Son of God who, unlike Adam, resists temptation.

Another lens for discerning Luke's sequencing comes by comparing his account of Jesus' temptation with Matthew's narration of it (Matt. 4:1–11). They differ in the order of the final two temptations; Luke concludes with the temptation for Jesus to throw himself down from the temple precipice (Luke 4:9–12; the second temptation in Matthew). Given Luke's keen interest in including the temple at key junctures in his story line (e.g., he begins and ends his Gospel at the temple), it is not surprising that he might include the temptation connected to the temple at the climax of this account.

---

18. Green, *Gospel of Luke*, 153. For Green's discussion of "years" for *hēlikia*, see 157–58.

A Note on Selection

We've already noted Luke's longer genealogy of Jesus that goes back to Adam (3:34b–38), in contrast to Matthew's genealogy, which begins with Abraham. Other material unique to Luke in this section includes his longer quotation from Isaiah 40. Each of the Gospels includes a quotation of Isaiah 40:3 (at Matt. 3:3; Mark 1:3; Luke 3:4; John 1:23). Only Luke cites the additional verses (Isa. 40:4–5), which fit well with his own emphasis on the universal scope of salvation: "All people will see God's salvation" (Luke 3:6; cf. Isa. 40:5).

Luke is also more expansive in his narration of John's prophetic ministry to Israel. When the crowd asks how they should respond to his call for repentance and his warnings, John the Baptist commends specific actions of mercy and justice: to the crowds he calls for sharing of food and clothing (Luke 3:11), to tax collectors he calls for honest dealings in their work (3:13), and to soldiers he rules out extortion and false accusation (3:14). This fits Luke's keen interest in the practice of mercy and justice (10:37; 11:42; 12:33; 18:1–8, 22; 19:8).

Jesus' Galilean Ministry (Luke 4:14–9:50)

In Luke 4:14–30 Jesus begins his ministry to Israel in his hometown of Nazareth. His sermon in the synagogue there announces his forthcoming ministry of mercy and justice to Israel, which plays out in his teachings, healings, and other miracles that are key to the plot in this section of Luke.[19] Jesus' preaching centers on "the good news of the kingdom of God" (4:43; 8:1). Jesus also chooses and gathers disciples around himself, both men and women, who will participate in his ministry in significant ways.

The opening hometown account also portends the rejection Jesus will experience. Already foreshadowed in the opening scene (Luke 4:28–30), opposition arises, especially from Pharisees and teachers of the law, and is focused on Jesus' claims of authority (5:21), his practice of associating

---

19. Green notes that there is a balance between Jesus' teachings and actions across Luke 4:14–9:50. He also identifies the episodic nature of the material, anchored by repeated narrative summaries (Luke 4:14–15, 44; 5:15; 7:17; 8:1–3) that "serve as a précis, reorienting Luke's audience to the thread holding the various scenes together" (*Gospel of Luke*, 199).

with tax collectors and sinners (5:30–31; 7:39), and what seem to be Sabbath transgressions by him (6:1–11). We hear of the beginnings of a plan to thwart what Jesus is doing and even to harm him (6:7, 11). This conflict forms the rising action of the plot. Jesus' Galilean ministry concludes with a midstory climactic declaration by Peter that Jesus is "God's Messiah" (9:20), followed by two predictions Jesus makes about his coming death (9:22, 44; for the plot of the entire section, see fig. 3.3).

The Pairing of Accounts about Women and Men in Jesus' Ministry

Across his Gospel, Luke often recounts a story about a woman alongside a story of a man.[20] In Luke 4:14–9:50 we see such intentional pairing of accounts about men and women, specifically as they are recipients of or participants in Jesus' ministry. A side-by-side sequencing pattern emerges at the following points:

Men	Women
Jesus heals a demon-possessed man (4:31–37)	Jesus heals Peter's mother-in-law (4:38–39)
Jesus heals a centurion's servant (7:1–10)	Jesus raises a widow's son from the dead (7:11–17)

Other pairings are spread across the narrative (they are nonadjacent), yet they are clearly connected by theme or action:

Men	Women
Jesus offers forgiveness to a paralyzed man (5:17–26)	Jesus offers forgiveness to a woman with a sinful life (7:36–50)
Jesus calls twelve (male) apostles, who are "with him" (6:12–16; 8:1)	Many women are "with him," supporting Jesus from their means (8:2–3)

20. We could note this pattern already in the birth narratives, where accounts featuring Zechariah and Mary are paired as part of Luke's comparison of John and Jesus. Additionally, Simeon and Anna are paired as prophetic voices about Jesus in 2:25–35, 36–38, respectively. For a list of such pairings across Luke, including within the teachings of Jesus (e.g., 4:25, 26–27), see Mark Allan Powell, *Introducing the New Testament: A Historical, Literary, and Theological Survey*, 2nd ed. (Grand Rapids: Baker Academic, 2018), 174.

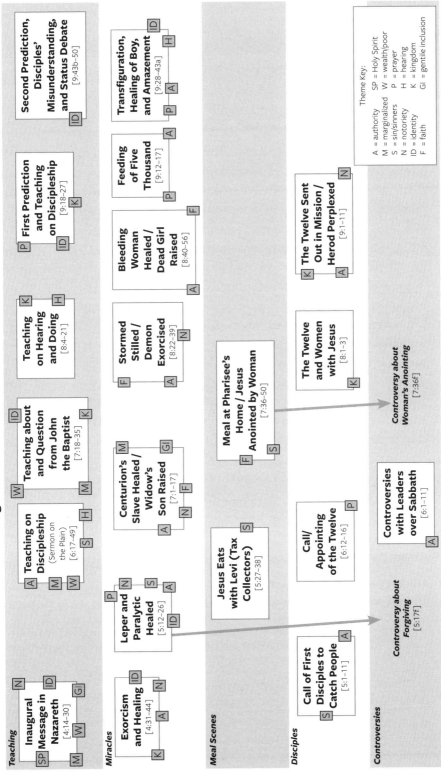

Figure 3.3.
Diagram of Plot and Themes for Luke 4:14–9:50

Teaching

Inaugural Message in Nazareth [4:14-30] — [N] [SP] [ID] [W] [GI] [M]

Teaching on Discipleship (Sermon on the Plain) [6:17-49] — [A] [M] [W] [S] [H]

Teaching about and Question from John the Baptist [7:18-35] — [ID] [W] [M] [K]

Teaching on Hearing and Doing [8:4-21] — [K] [H]

First Prediction and Teaching on Discipleship [9:18-27] — [P] [ID] [K]

Second Prediction, Disciples' Misunderstanding, and Status Debate [9:43b-50] — [ID]

Transfiguration, Healing of Boy, and Amazement [9:28-43a] — [P] [A] [H] [ID]

Feeding of Five Thousand [9:12-17] — [P] [A]

Miracles

Exorcism and Healing [4:31-44] — [ID] [A] [N] [K] [M]

Leper and Paralytic Healed [5:12-26] — [P] [N] [S] [A] [ID]

Centurion's Slave Healed / Widow's Son Raised [7:1-17] — [M] [GI] [F] [N] [A]

Stormed Stilled / Demon Exorcised [8:22-39] — [F] [A] [N]

Bleeding Woman Healed / Dead Girl Raised [8:40-56] — [F] [A]

Meal Scenes

Jesus Eats with Levi (Tax Collectors) [5:27-38] — [S]

Meal at Pharisee's Home / Jesus Anointed by Woman [7:36-50] — [F] [S]

Disciples

Call of First Disciples to Catch People [5:1-11] — [S] [A]

Call/Appointing of the Twelve [6:12-16] — [P]

The Twelve and Women with Jesus [8:1-3] — [K]

The Twelve Sent Out in Mission / Herod Perplexed [9:1-11] — [K] [A] [N]

Controversies

Controversy about Forgiving [5:17f]

Controversies with Leaders over Sabbath [6:1-11] — [A]

Controversy about Woman's Anointing [7:36f]

Theme Key:
A = authority   SP = Holy Spirit
M = marginalized W = wealth/poor
S = sin/sinners   P = prayer
N = notoriety   H = hearing
ID = identity   K = kingdom
F = faith   GI = gentile inclusion

This feature of Luke's narrative coheres with the greater number of named women in his Gospel and, in general, contributes to the greater prominence of women in his story line.[21]

Shared Ministry of Disciples in Luke

Luke's accent on women can also be seen in the ongoing subplot related to Jesus' disciples. Luke's earliest accounts of the emerging group of Jesus' disciples concentrate on the commissioning of some fishermen (5:1–11) and then of the wider group of the twelve apostles, who are listed by name (6:12–16). A few chapters later, Luke ties the twelve with a group of women who are also a part of Jesus' entourage of disciples (8:1–3). Both groups are "with Jesus" as he travels and proclaims the gospel of the kingdom. Three members of this larger group of women are named by Luke: Mary Magdalene, Joanna, and Susanna, with the first two reappearing in the resurrection narrative as witnesses to the empty tomb (24:10). The group of female disciples are described as helping to support the larger group—men and women—as they travel about with Jesus.

Luke's attention to a mix of male and female disciples (as in 6:12–16 and 8:1–3) recurs when Jesus sends out the twelve for ministry (9:1–6) and soon after sends out seventy-two disciples (10:1–24).[22] Given his introduction of women disciples at 8:1–3, it is natural to read the seventy-two as inclusive of women and, specifically, the named and unnamed women of Luke 8.[23] We'll return to this subplot below when we look more closely at the role of women in the resurrection narrative.

A Note on Selection

Luke draws primarily from his Markan source in this segment of his Gospel and follows for the most part Mark's order of events (cf. Mark 1–6). Unique to Luke, however, are a few episodes or expansions. Luke chooses

21. In Luke there are ten named women in his story (and at least seven unnamed women), as compared to four named women in Mark and John and three in Matthew. For Richard Bauckham's lists of named and unnamed persons in the Gospels, see Richard Bauckham, *Jesus and the Eyewitnesses: The Gospels as Eyewitness Testimony* (Grand Rapids: Eerdmans, 2006), 56–64.

22. At Jesus' entry into Jerusalem, Luke even describes a large group of disciples: "The whole crowd of disciples began joyfully to praise God" (19:37).

23. Richard Bauckham, *Gospel Women: Studies of the Named Women in the Gospels* (Grand Rapids: Eerdmans, 2002), 112.

to begin the account of Jesus' public ministry in his hometown of Naza-reth (Luke 4:14–30)—an important sequencing choice. As the front story of Jesus' ministry, this account expands significantly on Mark 6:1–6. Two features of the story especially help to propel the plot forward. First, Jesus preaches from Isaiah in the local synagogue, choosing to read Isaiah 61:1–2, which highlights a Spirit-empowered ministry to those on the margins.[24] Luke will emphasize across the rest of the Gospel that Jesus embodies this kind of ministry (Luke 4:21). Second, Jesus' hometown rejects him after he indicates that he will have a better reception among the gentiles (as Elijah and Elisha did; 4:24–30). This rejection presages the rejection Jesus will experience at the hands of the Jewish leadership, especially in Jerusalem.

Luke also expands the call narrative of the fishermen who will become his disciples by narrating a large catch of fish that Jesus provides and by accenting Simon Peter's role (5:1–11; cf. Mark 1:16–20). Peter responds to Jesus' display of authority by acknowledging his own sinfulness (Luke 5:8). This is the first of a series of stories that elaborate on Jesus' practice of associating with "tax collectors and sinners" (on the latter, see 5:30–32; 7:34), a Lukan motif. Other stories unique to Luke that highlight this social practice include Jesus' interactions with a woman known to be a sinner (7:36–50) and with Zacchaeus, who fits both categories (19:1–10).

Luke alone narrates the account of Jesus raising to life a widow's only son (7:11–17). As already noted, this story pairs with an account of a man—a centurion—whose servant is healed by Jesus (7:1–10). Luke's ac-count of the widow fits a wider interest in highlighting the plight and the value of widows (e.g., 2:37; 20:47; 21:1–4), a category of people accented in the torah for particular care (e.g., Deut. 27:19).

Luke's emphasis on the good news preached to those who are poor is quite pronounced. This theme is underscored in the opening narrative in Nazareth, where Jesus' Isaianic mission includes proclaiming "good news to the poor" (Luke 4:18; also 7:22). It finds unique emphasis in Luke's form of the beatitudes, with their corresponding woes (6:20–26):

"Blessed are you who are poor, for yours is the kingdom of God" (6:20).

"But woe to you who are rich, for you have already received your com-fort" (6:24).

---

24. The rendering in Luke adheres closely to the Septuagint of Isa. 61:1–2, except for a line that seems to be drawn from Isa. 58:6 ("to set the oppressed free").

Jesus' Movement to Jerusalem (Luke 9:51–19:27): The Travel Narrative

The travel narrative (TN), as it is routinely called, follows on the heels of Jesus' two passion predictions and is clearly marked by Luke with its destination in view: "Jesus resolutely set out for Jerusalem" (Luke 9:51). The reiteration of this destination across the TN propels the plot forward toward Jesus' coming crucifixion, even more than his conflict with the Jewish leadership. The latter is narrated only sporadically in the TN (11:53–54; 13:17; 14:1; 15:1–2). The plotting effect of such minimal attention to the central antagonists is to heighten Jesus' own agency in his coming suffering and death. He *willingly* moves toward Jerusalem, where he will be crucified.

The pacing and progress of this section of Luke emerges from a combination of episodes focused on Jesus' teaching—often in parables but also including frequent narrative markers noting Jesus' movement toward Jerusalem as well as actions of healing and sharing meals. Unlike Matthew, Luke's inclusion of Jesus' teachings does not occur in extended, virtually uninterrupted discourses. Instead, the evangelist narrates a mixture of actions and teachings, keeping the story moving at a fairly steady pace.[25]

The Travel Motif

Jesus' journey to Jerusalem provides a unifying motif for the TN. Luke uses the Semitic idiom "setting one's face" to communicate Jesus' resolve to go to Jerusalem (9:51; cf. KJV). This resolve is reaffirmed by Luke through repeated references to Jesus' journey from Galilee to the capital city.[26] At key junctures within the TN, Luke provides a summary of Jesus' traveling ministry or shows the progression of his movement:

"Then Jesus went through the towns and villages, teaching as he made his way to Jerusalem" (13:22).

"Now on his way to Jerusalem, Jesus traveled along the border between Samaria and Galilee" (17:11).

"Jesus entered Jericho and was passing through" (19:1).

25. This is also true of the section on Jesus' Galilean ministry (Luke 4:14–9:50).
26. Indications of journeying and/or reference to Jerusalem occur at 9:51–53, 56, 57; 10:38; 13:22, 31, 33; 14:25; 17:11; 18:31, 35; 19:1, 11 (also 19:28–29, 36–37, 41, 45).

At the end of the TN, as the story setting transitions to Jerusalem, we read, "After Jesus had said this [a parable], he went on ahead, going up to Jerusalem" (19:28).

Part of the theological rationale for Jesus' resolute journeying is provided at Luke 13:33, where Jesus speaks of the necessity of pressing on, "for surely no prophet can die outside of Jerusalem." This fits the message of the passion predictions (see 9:22, 44), the third of which occurs as Jesus nears Jerusalem and further underscores that destination: "We are going up to Jerusalem, and everything that is written by the prophets about the Son of Man will be fulfilled" (18:31).

Luke's Penchant for Meal Scenes and Parables

Luke sets many of Jesus' actions and teachings in homes where meals are taking place. Meal scenes are not unique to the TN, but they are important in the flow of the story (see fig. 3.4).[27] They also are vehicles for communicating important Lukan themes, including women following Jesus in discipleship, status renunciation, justice for the poor, and salvation for those who are "lost." While these meal scenes illuminate an important setting across Luke, they provide more than setting alone. They are also in themselves a signal of what is happening in the arrival of God's reign. Jesus' ministry is characterized by deep welcome in the invitation to eat together that is extended to all people and is particularly offered to those at the margins.

Figure 3.4
Meal Scenes in the Travel Narrative

Reference	Meal Location	Themes
10:38–42	Martha and Mary's home	Women following Jesus in discipleship
11:37–54	Home of a Pharisee	Warnings to Pharisees and torah experts
14:1–24	Home of a prominent Pharisee	Sabbath controversy and status renunciation
19:1–10	Zacchaeus' home	Salvation to the "lost" and justice for the poor

27. Eugene LaVerdiere identifies ten meal scenes in Luke; those outside the TN occur in 5:27–39; 7:36–50; 9:10–17; 22:7–38; 24:13–35; and 24:36–53. LaVerdiere, *Dining in the Kingdom of God: The Origins of the Eucharist in the Gospel of Luke* (Chicago: Liturgy Training Publications, 1994), 12.

Luke has the greatest number of parables of the four Gospels, with many of these showing up in the TN. While the range of themes in the parables of the TN is broad, they are quite often focused on discipleship themes like wealth, faithfulness, prayer, and humility. This is especially the case for parables that are unique to Luke (see fig. 3.5).

Figure 3.5
Unique Lukan Parables in the Travel Narrative*

Reference	Parable	Themes
10:25–37	Good Samaritan	Love of neighbor and enemy
12:13–21	Rich fool	Critique of wealth
13:6–9	Barren fig tree	Faithfulness
14:28–33	Tower builder and warring king	Counting the cost of discipleship
15:8–10	Lost coin	God's love for "the lost"
15:11–32	Lost son	God's love for "the lost"
16:1–8	Dishonest steward	Wealth, faithfulness
16:19–31	Rich man and Lazarus	Critique of wealth
17:7–10	Humble servant	Faithfulness
18:1–8	Unjust judge	Prayer
18:9–14	Pharisee and tax collector	Humility

* See Garwood Anderson, "Parables," in *DJG*, 651–63, here 655.

The Travel Narrative: A Comparison with Acts

Luke has carefully arranged his Gospel to have important connections to his second volume, Acts.[28] The presence of the extended travel section in Luke finds its counterpart in the mission travels of Paul in Acts, as the gospel moves from the Jewish world to include gentile communities (Acts 13:1–21:16). Both journeys conclude in Jerusalem (Luke 19:28; Acts 21:17), with Paul's time in Jerusalem followed by his imprisonment in Rome at the end of Acts (28:16–31).

A Note on Selection

Much of the material in the TN is unique to Luke, including those episodes already identified: his frequent references to Jesus' journey to Jerusalem as well as the many parables and meal scenes. Additionally,

28. For other comparisons, see discussion below of the trials of Jesus and of Paul.

Luke has incorporated a number of healings in the TN that occur only in his Gospel. These include the healing of a woman with a bent back (Luke 13:10–17), a man with abnormal swelling (14:2–4; as part of a Sabbath controversy), and ten men with leprosy (17:11–19). Jesus' authority and compassion to heal continue to be on display in these episodes.

Jesus' Arrival in Jerusalem, Passion, Resurrection (Luke 19:28–24:53)

The final section of Luke's Gospel has Jesus entering Jerusalem, being acclaimed as king by a "whole crowd of disciples" (19:37–38), and clearing the temple of its sellers (19:45–46). The Jerusalem leaders plot against him and question his authority (19:47; 20:1–2, 19; 22:2), while the people are captivated by his teaching (19:48; 20:19, 39). Then Judas, one of Jesus' disciples, offers to give Jesus up to the leaders, which he does after Jesus celebrates the Passover with the twelve apostles. After Jesus' arrest, the plot comes to its penultimate moments in his multiple trials (before the Sanhedrin, Pilate, and Herod) and in Pilate's decision to crucify Jesus (23:24). The climax of the story comes in Jesus' crucifixion and death. But Jesus is raised from the dead, appears to his followers, and is taken up to heaven, providing resolution to the plot and concluding the Gospel on notes of worship, joy, and praise (24:52–53).

Multiple Trials in Luke and Acts

Luke fosters a connection between the series of trial scenes in his two volumes by adding the trial of Jesus before Herod (Luke 23:6–12), which is not found in his primary source, Mark, or in any other Gospel. Jesus' trials before the Sanhedrin (the Jewish council), Pilate, and Herod find a counterpart in Paul's trials before the Sanhedrin, Felix, Festus, and Agrippa (Acts 23–26). In both cases, Luke emphasizes the innocence of the one accused—Jesus, Paul—as well as the overarching divine plan that is at work in the midst of human opposition.

An Analepsis: Women and the Lukan Passion Predictions

In the previous chapter, we explored some features of sequencing, including analepsis, or flashback, in which an event is narrated after the fact. We can observe an example in Luke's resurrection account, when the angelic figures speak to the women who have come to Jesus' tomb but find it empty.[29] They remind the women of what Jesus had told them in Galilee (Luke 24:6b–8): "'Remember how he told you, while he was still with you in Galilee: "The Son of Man must be delivered over to the hands of sinners, be crucified and on the third day be raised again."' Then they remembered his words."

This passage provides a summary of Jesus' earlier predictions of his coming passion, which have occurred at 9:22; 9:44; and 18:33.[30] In the first two cases Jesus' "disciples" are present; in the third case it is the twelve who are expressly mentioned (18:31). Although Luke has indicated that women have followed Jesus in his public ministry (8:1–3; see discussion above), it has not been fully apparent in each case whether "the disciples" in Luke are a mixed group, including both men and women. Here, in this analepsis, the women are clearly "written in" to the earlier story. Or to put it differently, the reader learns that the women have been privy to Jesus' prediction of his passion only at this late point in the story, after Jesus' resurrection.[31] Through this flashback, the reader receives confirmation that "the disciples" in Luke do include both men and women. The fact that the women listed in Luke 24:10 include Mary Magdalene and Joanna, two women already listed among the women who are with Jesus in his public ministry (8:1–3), provides additional attestation.

With these narrative cues in hand, the reader will be prone to perceive both men and women as part of the group of Jesus' followers mentioned at the end of the Gospel: "The Eleven and those with them" (24:33). It is to this mixed group that Jesus appears and so it is both women and men he commissions as witnesses (Luke 24:48; cf. Acts 1:12–14).

A Note on Selection

We've already noted that Luke is unique in narrating Jesus' trial before Herod. He also includes a unique (and extended) post-resurrection

---

29. Robert J. Karris, "Women and Discipleship in Luke," *CBQ* 56 (1994): 1–20, here 10.

30. The language of 24:7 seems something of a composite of the second and third passion predictions.

31. As Karris notes, "If we used narrative analysis to express what Luke is doing in Luke 24:7, we would say that Luke is making the women present in situations where the reader initially was led to believe they were absent" ("Women and Discipleship," 15).

appearance of Jesus to two disciples on a journey to Emmaus (Luke 24:13–35). They come to recognize Jesus only when they sit down to eat a meal together and Jesus breaks bread (24:30–31) in a way reminiscent of the Passover meal he has shared with his apostles (22:19). This account provides Luke an opportunity to highlight themes of Jesus' fulfillment of the Old Testament (24:25–27) and of hiddenness and recognition (24:16, 31–32).

Peace is a theme that Luke adds to and enhances in the Jerusalem and passion narratives. In each of the Synoptics when Jesus is acclaimed as he enters Jerusalem, those greeting him celebrate him with words from Psalm 118, "Blessed is he who comes in the name of the Lord!" (Matt. 21:9; Mark 11:9; Luke 19:38). Only Luke adds the exclamation, "Peace in heaven" (Luke 19:38), complementing the angelic announcement of "peace on earth" at Jesus' birth (2:14 AT). Luke is also the only evangelist who includes in the prediction of Jerusalem's future destruction Jesus' unfulfilled yearning: "If you, even you, had only known on this day what would bring you peace" (19:42).[32]

The Ending of Luke

The ending of Luke reminds the reader of key plot elements and themes that have been a part of the Gospel from the beginning. Luke's ending also points ahead to the beginning of Acts in its key episodic elements. Robert Tannehill refers to this bidirectional nature of the end of the Gospel as its dual sense of closure (connecting backward) and openness (preparing for Acts).[33]

In Jesus' resurrection appearance to his followers (Luke 24:36–49), Luke narrates that Jesus "opened their minds so they could understand the Scriptures" about the Messiah's suffering and rising from the dead (24:45–46). This action of Jesus provides a narrative resolution to the disciples' lack of understanding recorded after the final two passion predictions of Jesus. Luke notes in each case that the disciples didn't understand because the meaning of Jesus' words "was hidden from them" (9:45; 18:34). Now, after the resurrection, Jesus makes it possible for them to comprehend.

---

32. Cf. Jesus' post-resurrection greeting, "Peace be with you" (24:36), with three occurrences in John (20:19, 21, 26).

33. Tannehill, *Narrative Unity of Luke-Acts*, 1:298–301.

This appearance account also points ahead to Acts by giving a brief summary of what will be expanded in Acts 1–2 related to the commissioning of the disciples to be witnesses (Luke 24:48; Acts 1:7–8) and the coming of the Holy Spirit upon them (Luke 24:49; Acts 2:1–13). The final pericope of the Gospel (Luke 24:50–53) also provides a foretaste of Acts by narrating briefly Jesus' ascension, which will be told in more detail in Acts 1:6–11.

Finally, this concluding paragraph connects backward to the very first chapter of Luke—the Gospel begins and ends in Jerusalem and, more specifically, in the temple (1:8–9; 24:53). This final location provides a fitting setting for the thematic praise, worship, and joy that attends the resurrection community (24:52–53).[34]

Conclusion

Luke has carefully shaped and crafted his story of Jesus to communicate with his readers. We have explored some of the Gospel's key structural and stylistic indicators that lead us toward Luke's messages—about Jesus, about God's coming kingdom, and about discipleship. Luke's Jesus proclaims and enacts God's inclusive kingdom, one that welcomes all people—Jew and gentile, male and female, "righteous" and "sinner"—and invites each one to follow Jesus in repentance, trust, and worship.

34. The themes of praise and joy appear across Luke: (1) praise (e.g., 1:68; 2:28; 5:26; 7:16; 13:13; 17:18; 18:43; 19:37; 23:47; 24:53); and (2) joy (e.g., 1:14, 44, 58; 2:10; 10:17, 21; 19:37; 24:41, 52). Worship is usually tied to the temple and frames the Gospel: 1:10; 2:37; 24:52–53.

Part Three
Character and Characterization

Avoid depicting the hero's state of mind; you ought to try to make it clear from the hero's action.

Anton Chekhov, *Letter to Alexander Chekhov*
(his brother), May 10, 1886

4

The People in the Story

One of the most arresting features of a story is its characters. This may not be surprising given "the predilection of people to be interested in people."[1] As readers we are often drawn into a story because of a connection we feel with a central character, whether a link based on admiration or sympathy or some combination of these kinds of positive responses.

Or we might experience the opposite. We might experience a sense of distance from a character if they exhibit qualities we disapprove of. Ebenezer Scrooge provides a good example. Charles Dickens tells *A Christmas Carol* in such way that his readers take Scrooge's behavior through much of the book as a foil—he behaves precisely how they are not to behave. It is only at the end of the book that the reader might feel drawn to emulate Scrooge in his newfound generosity. Dickens has created this memorable character to teach his readers a moral lesson about the spirit of giving.

In this example, we can see the two narrative levels we have been exploring in previous chapters—the story and discourse levels of *A Christmas Carol*. On the story level, we are engaged in reading a character—specifically, Ebenezer Scrooge. When we step back to explore what the **narrator** (or implied author) is doing with Scrooge, we have entered the realm of characterization. Characterization is the art of bringing to life the characters in a story through what they say and do and in relation

1. R. Alan Culpepper, *Anatomy of the Fourth Gospel: A Study in Literary Design* (Philadelphia: Fortress, 1983), 101.

to other characters in the story.[2] In *A Christmas Carol*, Dickens paints Scrooge's portrait with words and employs Scrooge and other characters to communicate with and, hopefully, shape his reader. Dickens, at the discourse level of his narrative, uses Scrooge first as a foil and then as an exemplar for his readers—all in the service of characterization.

What does this have to do with the Gospels, especially since they are historical narratives and not fiction like *A Christmas Carol*? While there are certainly significant differences between fictional and historical stories, narrative authors always *characterize* the persons in their stories. Authors who write narratives about historical personages have somehow "made a living person live on paper."[3] In other words, through selection, focus, and amplification they have shaped these persons in particular ways for specific purposes. The Gospel writers have historical purposes as they pursue characterization, and they also have theological purposes. In fact, the Gospels can be helpfully described as *theological history*, in the sense that both sets of intentions are important to them.

Let's take the example of Christology to consider characterization in the Gospels more closely. Each Gospel has at its center a portrait of Jesus; each has characterized Jesus in specific ways. And while there is significant overlap in these portraits, there are also some important differences (see fig. 4.1). These differences align with key emphases that each writer is making about Jesus and his messianic work.

Figure 4.1
Key Christology Emphases in the Gospels

Matthew	Mark	Luke	John
Messiah	Messiah	Messiah	Messiah
God's Son	God's Son	God's Son	God's Son
Lord	Lord	Lord	Lord
Son of Man	Son of Man	Son of Man	Son of Man
Faithful Israel	Faithful Israel	Faithful Israel	
Servant of the Lord	Servant of the Lord	Servant of the Lord	
Son of David		Son of David	
		Savior	Savior

2. Jack Dean Kingsbury, *Conflict in Luke: Jesus, Authorities, Disciples* (Minneapolis: Fortress, 1991); cf. Culpepper, *Anatomy of the Fourth Gospel*, 103.
3. Culpepper, *Anatomy of the Fourth Gospel*, 103.

Matthew	Mark	Luke	John
Wisdom			Word (*logos*)
Immanuel			
		Prophet	
			Passover lamb
			The "I Am"

For example, Matthew identifies Jesus as embodying God's Wisdom by drawing a parallel between Jesus' messianic deeds ("the deeds of the Messiah"; Matt. 11:2) with Wisdom's deeds (11:19) and by narrating that Jesus gives an invitation (in 11:28–30) similar to the one that Wisdom offers in Proverbs 9:3–6.[4] Matthew implicitly continues this portrait of Jesus as God's Wisdom by showing Jesus speaking truth in riddles (e.g., Matt. 12:39–42; 22:41–46) and amazing those who hear him, and by characterizing him as profoundly wise as he answers his opponents (21:23–22:46). While John hints at the connection between Jesus and Wisdom in his prologue through his use of "the Word" (John 1:1–18), Mark and Luke do little with this category. Matthew's characterization is unique in its ongoing, though mostly implicit, attention to this part of Jesus' identity.[5]

And although Jesus is the primary focus of the evangelists' use of characterization, these writers show intentionality in their portrayal of each person who shows up in the Gospels—from Mary, Jesus' mother, to Mary Magdalene, and from John the Baptist to John, the brother of James.[6] To help us better understand what the evangelists are doing with their characters, let's listen in to the conversation about characterization in biblical studies, drawn from a wider conversation in literary circles.

The Conversation about Characterization

The conversation concerning the role of characters in narrative reaches all the way back to Aristotle, who understood characters to be subsumed

4. It is also helpful to compare Jesus' words with the Jewish books of Sirach and Wisdom, which share similar vocabulary with Matt. 11:28–30 (Sir. 24:19; 51:26–27; Wis. 6).

5. For more on Matthew's Wisdom Christology, see Jeannine K. Brown and Kyle Roberts, *Matthew*, THNTC (Grand Rapids: Eerdmans, 2018), 388–91.

6. Additionally, a character group—like the disciples or the Pharisees—may function as a single entity for character analysis. For a discussion of character groups and for an extended look at the characterization of the disciples in Matthew, see chap. 5.

to a narrative's plot[7]—a view that has proven to be influential. Such a minimization of the role of characters might explain why Mieke Bal, a literary critic, could write just thirty years ago that "in the course of the long history of Western criticism and poetics, characters have never been described in a satisfactory way theoretically."[8]

The question of whether characters, especially in the ancient world, are simply types in support of the plot, or whether they assume more individuality, continues to inform theoretical discussions today.[9] In response, most theorists perceive characters along a spectrum from simple type to more complex individuality. In fact, classifying where any particular character falls along a spectrum is a key facet of the conversation around characterization. The other primary area of discussion is the method or process of characterization: *How* does an author portray her characters? We will take a look at each of these issues—classification of characters and method of characterization—in order to help us read characters in the Gospels more thoughtfully.

Classification of Characters

Early analysis of characters and characterization in the Gospels tended to highlight two features: (1) their primary role as plot functionaries and types and (2) their nature as static rather than dynamic. We've already noted that Aristotle accented the first feature: the use of characters as types—as examples of either positive or negative traits. In fact, sometimes a character will possess a single trait, relegating that character almost entirely to a function of the plot. Examples from the Gospels include many of the minor characters, such as the two blind men of Matthew 9:27–31. This character pair, like others that appear for just a few lines and then exit the story line, are usually used to exemplify a single characteristic—in this case, faith in Jesus as Messiah ("son of David"; 9:27). Jesus commends them for their faith: "According to your faith let it be done to you" (9:29). And it is this trait that Matthew encourages his readers to emulate.[10]

---

7. Aristotle, *Poetics* 6.19.

8. Mieke Bal, *Lethal Love: Feminist Literary Readings of Biblical Love Stories* (Bloomington: Indiana University Press, 1987), 105.

9. Petri Merenlahti contends, "As far as biblical characterization is concerned, perhaps the most central question of all concerns the *representation of individuality*." Merenlahti, *Poetics for the Gospels? Rethinking Narrative Criticism* (New York: T&T Clark, 2002), 77.

10. Cornelis Bennema helpfully notes that many of even the minor Gospel characters exhibit more than one trait and so sit on a continuum somewhere between "flat" and "round."

The view that characters do not undergo change finds support in ancient characterization generally, which focused less on psychological development (an admittedly modern notion) and more on characters as static or unchanging.[11] In this view, any perceived character development could be attributed to the notion, common in the ancient world, that the reader is seeing merely the "progressive revelation of [a character's] latent characteristics."[12] Given the assumption of a person's fixed nature, character development would actually be a gradual revealing of who the person is and had always been. Mark's characterization of Jesus could be understood to fit a static framework, since the identity of Jesus as Messiah and his mission to preach and enact the good news about the kingdom of God undergo no change as the narrative progresses. Any perceived shift—as at Mark 8:31 where Jesus first predicts his coming death—is better understood as a progressive revealing of his person and mission.

Despite these tendencies of ancient characterization, they do not give a comprehensive picture of how the evangelists portray the people in their narratives. Recent work on characterization has offered increasing nuance to the question of the individuality of characters in the Gospels. Using E. M. Forster's language, many scholars have argued that quite a number of characters in the Gospels are **round**—in other words, they are complex with numerous traits and may very well show signs of development. These are contrasted with other characters who are **flat**—that is, those who are simple types, often demonstrating a single attribute. Other biblical scholars have expanded this two-part distinction to include additional character categories. For example, James Resseguie also identifies characters as stocks, foils, or walk-ons, each expanding further the category of and spectrum beyond flat characters.[13] An example of walk-ons are the soldiers who appear across John's passion narrative and simply do the bidding of either the Jewish leaders or Pilate.

Bennema, *A Theory of Character in New Testament Narrative* (Minneapolis: Fortress, 2014), 75.

11. Outi Lehtipuu, "Characterization and Persuasion," in *Characterization in the Gospels: Reconceiving Narrative Criticism*, ed. David Rhoads and Kari Syreeni, JSNTSup 184 (Sheffield: Sheffield Academic, 1999), 75.

12. D. A. Russell, "On Reading Plutarch's *Lives*," GR 13 (1976): 139–54, here 146, 146n2.

13. James L. Resseguie, *Narrative Criticism of the New Testament: An Introduction* (Grand Rapids: Baker Academic, 2005), 123–25.

An important insight in the discussion about characterization is the recognition that classifying characters is best done on a continuum rather than in either/or fashion. While we can ask whether a specific character is flat or round, the better question might be, Where on a spectrum between flat and round does the character fall? In this task, key questions are

- How complex is the character's portrayal?
- How much change or development, if any, does the character undergo?[14]

How does this theoretical discussion about classification help us read characters in the Gospels more thoughtfully? First, it helps us hold in check our own modern sensibilities to "psychologize" biblical characters. If we are a product of our culture, we will have been trained to "get into the heads" of the persons who inhabit the stories we read and view (e.g., in movies). Yet the evangelists do not provide us with much fodder for this kind of psychologizing, since they seldom explore in much detail their characters' motivations. A tantalizing moment in Matthew's portrayal of Peter occurs when he asks to join Jesus in walking on the lake (Matt. 14:25–28). What is Peter's motivation? To be with Jesus? To experience something extraordinary? To share in Jesus' authority over the sea? And does this request arise from faith (cf. 14:31)? Or from the rashness that seems to typify Peter elsewhere (17:4; 26:33)? As much as we might like to explore the mind of Peter in this narrative moment, we are given virtually nothing from which to reconstruct what he is thinking or his motivations.

Even when motivations are hinted at—as in the case of the chief priests and elders turning Jesus over to the Roman governor—the motivational details are maddeningly slim. According to Matthew, Pilate knows "it was out of self-interest that they handed Jesus over to him" (Matt. 27:18). How does Jesus' arrest and execution serve their interests? Does it pay him back for his verbal besting and shaming of them just days before (21:23–27; 22:41–46)? Does it remove a potential revolutionary who could upset the

---

14. Bennema suggests viewing characters along a three-pronged spectrum of complexity, development, and penetration into the inner life (*A Theory of Character*, 72–82). I consider inner life to be a part of complexity and do not suggest this as a separate category, since in the Gospels it's often difficult to distinguish inner life (i.e., thoughts and feelings) from outer (what someone says and does).

status quo, which is in their best interest to maintain? Or are they jealous of his popularity ("because of jealousy"; CEB)?[15]

By reminding ourselves that the evangelists often portray characters with less rather than more detail, especially about their inner life, we might avoid overinterpretation.

Second, learning character theory helps us to recognize the significance of character development when we do see it in the Gospels. If we know that not every character is complex or experiences development, we may recognize the significance of those who are (complex) and do (experience development and change). The Samaritan woman of John 4 is a good example. Her conversation with Jesus is one of the longest in the Gospels, which should encourage us to see her as a complex, round character. John also highlights her progress from misunderstanding to comprehension. She changes as a result of her encounter with Jesus. She moves from inquisitor of Jesus to a believer and then to a witness, engaging in what Harold W. Attridge calls "successful apostolic outreach to her fellow Samaritans."[16]

Method of Characterization

In addition to classification of characters, the other primary area of theoretical discussion involves the *method* of characterization authors employ in their narratives. How do authors go about characterizing the people in their stories? An important initial observation is that ancient authors seem to prefer indirect over direct characterization. In other words, ancient authors (the evangelists included) tend to *show* rather than *tell* their readers about their characters. And they do this *showing* routinely through what their characters say and do.[17]

We can see this tendency toward showing over telling in John's characterization of the Samaritan woman, who encounters Jesus in Sychar (John 4:5). The only information the narrator gives in his introduction about her is that she is a Samaritan coming to draw water (4:7). Later, John directly

15. The Greek term *phthonos* can have either sense.
16. Harold W. Attridge, "The Samaritan Woman: A Woman Transformed," in *Character Studies in the Fourth Gospel: Narrative Approaches to Seventy Figures in John*, ed. Steven A. Hunt, D. Francois Tolmie, and Ruben Zimmerman (Grand Rapids: Eerdmans, 2016), 268–81, here 268.
17. Jeannine K. Brown, *The Disciples in Narrative Perspective: The Portrayal and Function of the Matthean Disciples*, SBLAB 9 (Atlanta: Society of Biblical Literature, 2002), 53.

narrates that many of her fellow Samaritans in Sychar believe "because of the woman's testimony" (4:39). The rest of his characterization of this Samaritan woman is accomplished by indirect means:

- From what she says and does—for example, she misunderstands Jesus' symbolic language (4:11), and she goes to her townspeople and invites them to consider Jesus to be the Messiah (4:28–29)
- From what Jesus says and does—for example, he indicates that she has had five husbands (4:18), and he pursues a conversation with her about the nature of true worship (4:21–26)

As readers, we are left to put together these and other moments of indirect characterization to create a coherent portrait of this woman. As we'll see below, this portrait has been sketched quite variably in the history of interpretation.

Considering the techniques of characterization as comprehensively as possible in conversation with various theorists, we can generate the following list.[18] Authors portray their characters through

- What a character says
- What a character does
- What other characters say in relation to that character
- What other characters do in relation to that character
- The narrator's (implied author's) more direct characterization
    - Through explicit identification of a character's attributes or motivations
    - Through explicit identification of a character's social status, gender, vocation, appearance
    - Through comparison with other characters[19]

---

18. Drawing from, for example, Susan E. Hylen, "The Disciples: The 'Now' and the 'Not Yet' of Belief in Jesus," in Hunt, Tolmie, and Zimmerman, *Character Studies in the Fourth Gospel*, 214–27, here 217–23; Mark Allan Powell, "Characterization on the Phraseological Plane in the Gospel of Matthew," in *Treasures New and Old*, ed. David R. Bauer and Mark Allan Powell, SBLSymS 1 (Atlanta: Scholars Press, 1996), 161–77; Elizabeth Struthers Malbon, *Characterization as Narrative Christology* (Waco: Baylor University Press, 2009).

19. For example, Luke invites a comparison between John the Baptist and Jesus across Luke 1–2, as we've seen in chap. 3 (see, e.g., Luke 1:80; 2:52). This form of characterization via comparison is less explicit than other narrator-focused means.

- Social realities outside the narrative relevant to the character, construed by readers[20]
- Other potentially relevant points of comparison or illumination: settings, plot, themes

What emerges from this list is the reality that characterization routinely happens as characters are in relation to other entities—whether other characters, the narrator, other features of the narrative (i.e., plot and theme), or even its readers. The rest of the chapter will explore and illustrate these various relationships for understanding characterization in the Gospels.

Characters' Relationships

Characters and the Narrator

The most important relationship for understanding characterization is a character's relationship to the narrator—the one who shapes the story and paints the character within the narrative framework. The narrator, at least in ancient storytelling, has an utterly reliable perspective on any character.[21] In narrative analysis, the evaluative **point of view** of any particular character in a Gospel is judged to be true or untrue by a comparison with the reliable viewpoint of the narrator.[22] While characters may assess other characters, the narrator's perspective is the pivotal one for a full understanding of any particular character. Elizabeth Struthers Malbon comments on the centrality of the narrator by noting that, in a narrative, "all words are not created equal."[23]

In the Gospels, Jesus provides a straightforward example. Each evangelist makes clear early on that Jesus' perspective is fully trustworthy, being

20. We'll discuss this area more below when addressing the relationship between readers and characters.

21. While some narrative critics distinguish the implied author from the narrator (e.g., Malbon, *Characterization*, 16), I follow Mark Allan Powell's approach. He describes the relationship between the two in this way: "The implied author guides the reader through the use of a narrator—the voice that the implied author uses to tell the story." Powell, *What Is Narrative Criticism?*, GBS (Minneapolis: Fortress, 1990), 25.

22. See Powell, *What Is Narrative Criticism?*, 54.

23. Malbon, *Characterization*, 13.

consistently aligned with the narrator's point of view.[24] This alignment emerges from what the narrator says about Jesus. Mark, for example, introduces his narrative with these words: "The beginning of the good news about Jesus the Messiah, the Son of God" (Mark 1:1). Already Mark has authorized Jesus—his forthcoming words and actions—by affirming his identity as Messiah, Son of God. Mark continues to establish Jesus as a trustworthy character by words of affirmation from God's authorized prophet, John the Baptist (1:7–8; cf. 1:2–6), and from the very voice of God (1:11).

By viewing the narrative and its characters from the perspective of the author or narrator, we are able to hear a coherent perspective on the various words, actions, and (when they are apparent) motivations of the story's characters. The narrator's point of view is so central that we, as readers, are encouraged to take on that perspective and evaluate the characters in the story just as the narrator does. For example, when Matthew narrates that Galilean Pharisees accuse Jesus of casting out demons by the prince of demons (Matt. 9:34), the reader knows that this is exactly wrong from Matthew's point of view. Matthew has already made it clear that it is by the Spirit of God that Jesus does his healing work (3:16–17; cf. 12:18, 24–28).

And while the Pharisees and other Jewish leaders are most often portrayed as wrong in their assessments about Jesus, other characters are portrayed more ambivalently in the Gospels. The Matthean disciples, for example, are sometimes portrayed as exemplars for the reader, as when they leave their livelihoods to follow Jesus (Matt. 4:18–22; 9:9). Other times, however, they provide the foil to true discipleship, as when they desert Jesus and flee from danger at his arrest (26:56). In both cases the narrator aligns the reader's perspective with his own to show that the disciples function as either an example or a foil.

Returning to John's portrayal of the Samaritan woman, we have already noticed that one of the more direct ways John contributes to her characterization comes at the conclusion of the account, where we hear that many from her town believe in Jesus "because of the woman's testimony"

24. Gary Yamasaki speaks of this as a "concurrence of points of view," in which "a character in the story world acts as the filter through which the audience 'sees' and 'hears' the elements of the story." Yamasaki, *Watching a Biblical Narrative: Point of View in Biblical Exegesis* (New York: T&T Clark, 2007), 182.

(John 4:39). In fact, her testimony leads to the Samaritans of Sychar asking Jesus to stay in their town, which Jesus does. This then leads to many more becoming believers (4:41) and confessing that Jesus is "the Savior of the world" (4:42). This high note at the story's conclusion shapes the reader's perspective on this woman. Whatever ambiguity occurs in her portrait at the beginning of the account, by the end she is portrayed as a believer in Jesus and a witness to the universal salvation he brings.

Characters and Other Characters

Our understanding of a character is also influenced by what other characters say and do in relation to that character. Connections with and assessments by other characters clarify the portrait of any specific character. For example, Luke records a centurion's request for Jesus to heal his valued servant (Luke 7:2–3). In spite of a good possibility that this character—a soldier in the service of Rome—would be negatively perceived and portrayed within a Jewish context, the story takes an unusual turn. The centurion sends his request through a group of Jewish elders, who offer Jesus these words of commendation: "This man deserves to have you do this, because he loves our nation and has built our synagogue" (7:4–5). This evaluation of the centurion suggests that Jesus will be responsive to his request, and this suggestion is confirmed as Luke narrates that Jesus goes with the elders (7:6) and heals the servant before ever reaching the centurion's house (7:10). Luke, as a reliable narrator, confirms the elders' assessment, giving a uniformly and surprisingly positive portrayal of this character.

In this example, we can see the importance of the narrator's point of view for guiding our reading of characters. While what the elders say about the centurion is important for shaping our understanding initially, it is Luke who confirms this positive portrait by narrating Jesus' actions toward (he goes with the elders) and words about (he commends the man's faith; 7:9) the centurion. And since we know that Jesus is an utterly reliable guide for Luke's point of view, we hear the narrator's commendation in Jesus' tribute to the centurion.

On other occasions the perspectives of the narrator and characters sit at odds—a signal to the reader to bring a critical lens for character analysis. For example, Pharisees in John describe the Jewish crowd as ignorant of the law and cursed precisely because this "mob" is showing signs of believing in Jesus (John 7:47–49). But because John has been consistently characterizing Pharisees and other Jewish leaders as misguided about Jesus, readers will hear these negative words by the Pharisees as potentially contributing to a more positive portrayal of the crowds in comparison. The key here is that the narrator's point of view shapes whether we hear any particular character's voice at any specific moment as reliable.

Returning to John's portrayal of the Samaritan woman, an important way she is characterized comes through Jesus' interactions with her. Jesus' perspective, fully authorized by the narrator, contributes to the portrait of her persona. This means that following their conversation—their emerging relationship—gets us to the heart of John's characterization of her.

The conversation begins with Jesus' request for a drink (John 4:7), which the woman, unsurprisingly, takes literally.[25] The Greek word (*zōn*) translated "living" can also refer to "running" (i.e., fresh) water, and the dialogue progresses with Jesus referring to the former and the woman assuming the latter. She first responds with her own question about the propriety of a Jewish man making a request of a Samaritan woman (4:9a). We learn from a narrative aside that Jews and Samaritans avoided such interactions (4:9b; cf. 4:27 for the disciples' surprise that Jesus has been conversing with a woman). This aside fits the first-century reality of animosity between Jews and Samaritans, an animosity fostered by centuries of conflict.[26]

Jesus continues to offer her living water as he begins to intimate to her his unique identity ("If you knew . . . who it is that asks you for a drink"; John 4:10). The woman asks another question—this time about how he will draw water without a bucket (4:11). She seems to pick up on Jesus' intimations of his identity by questioning whether he thinks he is greater than Jacob, at whose well they are speaking (4:12).

Jesus persists in his offer of living water, now making it clear(er) that the water he speaks of is symbolic of something else and results in eternal life and the full removal of thirst (John 4:13–14). The woman now moves from asking questions to requesting the water Jesus is offering, although

25. This fits with a tendency of Johannine characters to misunderstand Jesus, especially when he speaks symbolically (e.g., John 3:3–4; 6:32–34).

26. For a brief rehearsal of this conflict, see Teresa Okure, "Jesus and the Samaritan Woman (Jn 4:1–42) in Africa," *Theological Studies* 70 (2009): 401–18, here 407.

she continues to think of physical water (4:15). This seems a significant turn in the conversation, and Jesus' response seems to affirm the shift. He tells the woman to return with her husband, and she replies that she has no husband (4:16–17). Jesus, in a prophetic word, affirms that she speaks the truth and tells her that she has had five husbands and her current "man" is not her husband (4:17–18). It is at this point in the conversation that interpreters move in two quite distinct directions in understanding the portrait of the Samaritan woman, illustrating how readers are involved in characterization.

Characters and Readers

The relationship of readers to characters may at first seem like an unnecessary detour for determining how authors characterize the people in their stories. Aren't readers irrelevant to how and what an author writes? In reality, the presence of gaps in the creation of characters invites readers to "get involved" in filling out any particular person in the narrative.

It may be surprising (at least for contemporary readers) how little detail is provided in ancient narration, even for those characters deemed "round" or more complex. Petri Merenlahti refers to this phenomenon in the Gospels as "the mystery of biblical characters" and asks, "how does so much come out of so little? How do figures who are sketched with only a few harsh strokes manage to give an impression of individuality and personhood?"[27]

Part of the answer to these questions is that readers are expected to fill in the gaps that are left between these "few harsh strokes." As noted in chapter 1, authors of historical narrative rely on their readers to be knowledgeable about certain features of their shared cultural context. This applies to the particulars of characters as well as to other narrative gaps around plot and setting. The first readers and hearers of the Gospels, for instance, will have known something of Roman governors (or prefects, as they were called), and some may have had particular knowledge about Pilate, the Roman prefect governing Judea at the time of Jesus' public ministry. As they encountered the portrait of Pilate in any of the Gospels, they would have brought such information to their reading to fill in details about Pilate at Jesus' trial before him. They may have known, for example,

---

27. Merenlahti, *Poetics for the Gospels?*, 77.

about Pilate's poor track record in navigating Jewish concerns and sensibilities.[28] If so, they would have brought this kind of information to bear in their assessment of Pilate, say in John's Gospel, and his dealings with the Jewish leaders and crowds at Jesus' Roman trial (John 18:28–19:16).

Reading the characters of the Gospels today, we will be better interpreters if we fill in narrative gaps as much as possible with relevant historical information. Cornelis Bennema, in his model for New Testament character analysis, refers to this reading strategy as "a plausible historically informed modern reader."[29] Reading in line with this construct means reading any particular character primarily from textual cues, but also with relevant cultural information from the first-century world, which most ancient readers or hearers would have possessed.[30]

How does attending to the reader side of the equation help us understand John's characterization of the Samaritan woman? In the previous section, we left our analysis of Jesus' conversation with the woman just at the point where interpreters begin to disagree significantly about her portrayal. Jesus has just confirmed the truth of her statement that she has no husband and has revealed that he knows she has had five husbands and is currently with a man who is not her husband (John 4:17–18).

What does this revelation about the woman's marital history status tell us about her? This is where interpretive paths diverge. Does her past indicate that she is a prostitute, as Protestant Reformer Wolfgang Musculus thought?[31] Is she an adulteress (and so serially divorced by her husbands), as others have assumed? Or are there other ways to construe five previous husbands in that social context?

Josephus, a first-century Jewish historian, tells of Berenice, daughter of Agrippa I, who had been widowed twice by the time she was twenty-two years old.[32] Given the young age of matrimony for women and a typically

28. For example, Josephus indicates that Pilate brought his army with their military standards into Jerusalem, flaunting (or at least ignoring) that the standard's images would have transgressed Jewish law against images from Exod. 20:4 (*Jewish Antiquities* 18.55–62).

29. Bennema, *A Theory of Character*, 68.

30. Bennema, *A Theory of Character*, 69. He asserts, "Knowledge of the social and cultural environment of the New Testament is essential for understanding the personality, motive, and behavior of ancient characters" (62).

31. Wolfgang Musculus, *Commentariorum in evangelistam Ioannem, Heptas prima* (Basel, 1545), 225, as quoted in Craig S. Farmer, "Changing Images of the Samaritan Woman in Early Reformed Commentaries on John," *CH* 65 (1996): 365–75, here 371.

32. Josephus, *Antiquities* 18.132.

later marrying age for men, the likelihood of the Samaritan woman losing more than one husband to death is quite high.[33] Additionally, historical evidence suggests that Jewish men had legal recourse to divorce that few Jewish women possessed. All of this presses us to reconstruct the Samaritan woman as someone who is less morally responsible for her five past husbands than we might initially think using modern Western social categories.

Her current situation should also be understood from a first-century social perspective. While it is possible she may simply be cohabitating with her current partner, there are other scenarios that also make sense. For example, she might be a second wife of this man, who is married to his first wife but could not be legally married to a second.[34] Polygamy was practiced in some (including some Jewish) circles, even though it was illegal under Roman law.[35]

While there is no way to know the precise configuration of this woman's marital past, if we as readers take our cues from the first century rather than the twenty-first century, we will be less likely to hear the woman as patently immoral. This more generous reading is confirmed by the lack of any clue from John (as narrator) that Jesus calls her out as a sinner. The language of sin, in fact, is absent from the entire account.

Instead, Jesus continues to press her to understand *who he is*. She responds to his statement about her past and present relationships by acknowledging that he must be a prophet (John 4:19). Then she asks a question that most any Samaritan might ask of a prophet: Who has it right in the worship dispute between Jews and Samaritans (4:20)? Is worship to happen on Mount Gerizim (as Samaritans believed and practiced) or in Jerusalem (as Jews believed and practiced)?[36] As the early church leader

33. Lynn Cohick, "The 'Woman at the Well': Was the Samaritan Woman Really an Adulteress?," in *Vindicating the Vixens: Revisiting Sexualized, Vilified, and Marginalized Women of the Bible*, ed. Sandra Glahn (Grand Rapids: Kregel, 2017), 249–55, here 253.

34. Lynn Cohick, *Women in World of the Earliest Christianity* (Grand Rapids: Baker Academic, 2009), 123; for a fuller discussion, see 122–28.

35. Cohick, "'Woman at the Well,'" 252. Cohick draws this conclusion about the Samaritan woman: "The Samaritan woman is a woman of her times, living with fairly simple marriage traditions, relatively easy divorce laws, and haunted by the threat that death might at any time steal away a husband or child" (*Women*, 128).

36. The often-expressed view that the woman is trying to evade Jesus' words about her immoral lifestyle comes from the Reformer Musculus. It is only in the Reformation period that the theme of the woman's sin and guilt becomes part of the interpretive tradition of the

Chrysostom suggested, she could have taken this moment with a prophet to ask about her own future concerns. Instead, she turns away from earthly matters and in doing so grows "more exalted in mind."[37]

Jesus answers her question about worship by pointing to the time that is arriving when true worship will not be tied to location but to worshiping "in the Spirit and in truth" (John 4:24). Then the woman speaks of that same end time when the Messiah will come and "will explain everything to us" (4:25). Jesus tells her that he is the Messiah. The conversation has moved from questions and misunderstanding to illumination and comprehension. As Teresa Okure notes, "At each point [in the dialogue] Jesus uses her concerns (of water-fetching, marital life, and the right place to worship) to reveal to her his true identity and convey to her the gift he offers."[38] The next thing we will hear about the Samaritan woman is her "testimony" to her fellow villagers about this one who could very well be the Messiah (4:28–30).

Characters and Other Narrative Features

Characters are defined by their relationships not only with the narrator, with other characters, and with the reader, who fills in inevitable gaps in characterization (ideally with appropriate and relevant historical information). Characters are also defined by their relationships with other narrative features, like plot, setting, and theme.

CHARACTERS AND SETTING

Sometimes particular characters are associated with specific settings, such that their characterization is significantly informed by the setting. For example, the man who is demon possessed and receives healing from Jesus (Mark 5:1–17) is described as living "in the tombs" (5:3). This setting functions to heighten the man's dire situation—his habitat is death itself. Another example comes from John's portrait of Jesus, which is connected to and elaborated by various festival settings. John carefully delineates festival settings in chapters 5–10 and then highlights Jesus' claims to be the

---

church. Farmer highlights how the early and Medieval church writers had a much more positive view of the woman's movement toward spiritual understanding ("Changing Images," 373).

37. John Chrysostom, *Commentary on St. John the Apostle and Evangelist: Homilies 1–47*, The Fathers of the Church 33, trans. Sister Thomas Aquinas Goggin (New York: Fathers of the Church, 1957), 316–18, as summarized by Farmer, "Changing Images," 367.

38. Okure, "Jesus and the Samaritan Woman," 414.

culmination of these festivals. For instance, during the Festival of Passover (John 6:4) with its key motif of (unleavened) bread, Jesus claims to be "the bread of life" (6:35). And during the Festival of Tabernacles (7:2), which celebrated God's provision of water and light in Israel's wilderness journeys, Jesus offers himself to all who are thirsty (7:37) and claims to be "the light of the world" (8:12).[39]

In the account of the Samaritan woman, John mentions that she comes to a well and that she comes at noon (John 4:6). Both of these settings are significant for the story and potentially contribute to the woman's characterization. The location of a well evokes similar scenes from the Old Testament in which a man and a woman meet at a well (Gen. 24:10–28; 29:1–11) and may intimate that something life changing is occurring. The temporal note that the Samaritan woman comes to the well at noon also seems significant, especially in contrast to the previous chapter in which Nicodemus—a Jewish (male) leader and "insider"—approaches Jesus "at night" (John 3:2), a setting associated with misunderstanding.[40] In chapter 4 an "outsider"—a Samaritan and a woman—approaches Jesus at midday, a setting associated with illumination (see fig. 4.2). While Nicodemus continues to lack understanding, even after his encounter with Jesus (3:10), the Samaritan woman moves from misunderstanding to a posture of understanding, trusting, and testifying.

Figure 4.2

Comparison between Episodes of John 3 and 4

Nicodemus (John 3)	Samaritan Woman (John 4)
Jewish	Samaritan
Man	Woman
Pharisee, member of ruling council	Status not mentioned
Comes to Jesus at night	Meets Jesus at noon
Misunderstands symbolism ("born again" or "born from above")	Misunderstands symbolism ("living water" or "running water")
No arrival at understanding	Comes to understand, believe, and testify

39. For a fuller discussion of the latter, see Craig R. Koester, *Symbolism in the Fourth Gospel: Meaning, Mystery, Community*, 2nd ed. (Minneapolis: Fortress, 2003), 157–59. See also chap. 8 below.

40. Some have suggested that the woman comes to the well at an unusual time of day, since women likely came to draw water in the morning when it was cooler. Yet we simply do not know enough about such patterns and their exceptions to draw this conclusion.

CHARACTERS AND PLOT

Characters may be assessed by how they do or do not contribute to the plot of a story. Some characters appear for a short narrative span and have little to do with the momentum of the plot (e.g., any single individual whom Jesus heals). More major characters or character groups are essential to the plotline, like the Jewish leaders or the disciples.[41] Some minor characters do, however, contribute to the forward movement of the plot. And the Samaritan woman fits in this latter category.

Even though she appears only in this single chapter of John, the account about this woman contributes to John's story line—signaling the movement of salvation from the Jews to the Samaritans. As John begins his Gospel, the story focuses on Jesus as the Jewish Messiah who comes to his own people (cf. John 1:11). With the story of the Samaritan woman and her impact on her village, we hear that salvation extends now even to Samaritans (4:39–42). Later, Greeks attending the Festival of Passover in Jerusalem will express a desire to see Jesus (12:20–21), with this episode intimating the movement of salvation to the gentiles. As the Samaritan woman's neighbors confess of Jesus: "We know that this man really is the Savior of the world" (4:42).

CHARACTERS AND THEME

A final narrative feature that may be connected to characterization is theme. As we've already noted, the Gospel writers communicate their themes at the discourse level of the narrative (see fig. 1.2). And sometimes they tie quite closely a particular character to one of their themes, so that the character functions as something of a vehicle for that theme, as with Nicodemus and his connection to the theme of being born again or born from above.[42] Alan Culpepper suggests, "Character and theme are at times closely interrelated so that a theme is developed or extended through a particular character, and a character illustrates or even personifies one of

---

41. Bennema suggests attending to where a particular character falls along the plotline of a Gospel to help determine their role in the plot (*A Theory of Character*, 103).

42. R. Alan Culpepper, "Nicodemus: The Travail of New Birth," in Hunt, Tolmie, and Zimmerman, *Character Studies in the Fourth Gospel*, 249–59, here 249. Culpepper concludes from analysis of Nicodemus' three appearances in John that he is "identified with the complexity of becoming one of the 'children of God,' for whom both belief in [Jesus'] name and birth from above are required" (259).

the Gospel's themes. . . . At the same time, the character is never merely a cipher for the statement about a theme."[43]

Returning for a final time to the Samaritan woman, her characterization is connected to John's themes of mis/understanding, witness, and salvation. She begins in a state of misunderstanding, as do a number of characters in John's Gospel (e.g., Nathaniel [1:46], Nicodemus [3:1–4], Mary [20:14–16], and Thomas [20:24–25]), but moves to an understanding of Jesus as Messiah by the conclusion of the account. In fact, she becomes a witness to Jesus as Messiah so that many in her village believe in him as well (4:39). In this act she is an exemplar of the theme of testifying/witness that pervades the fourth Gospel (e.g., 1:7; 3:32–33; 5:36, 39; 15:26; 19:35; 21:24). Finally, the exclamation of the villagers that Jesus is "the Savior of the world" (4:42) fits well with John's theme of salvation (3:17; 4:22; 5:34; 10:9; 12:47).

Conclusion

In this chapter, we've taken a look at how the Gospel writers characterize the people in their stories. We've seen that character analysis can be a fairly complex task, and we've used the lens of relationships to consider characterization: the relationship of a character to the narrator, to other characters, to the reader, and to narrative features like plot, setting, and theme. Across the chapter, we've turned to John 4 to see how discussion of character theory works itself out in the specific instance of the Samaritan woman. In the next chapter, we take an extended look at the character group of the disciples in Matthew's Gospel—following them from their first appearance to the final scene of the Gospel, where they figure prominently.

43. Culpepper, "Nicodemus," 249.

5

Matthew's Characterization of the Disciples

The disciples in Matthew's Gospel provide an interesting test case for characterization, since parts of their portrayal have gained broad scholarly consensus and other facets have been cause for debate. Their portrait is also intriguing because readers often experience a deep sense of identification with the disciples, in spite of their shifting characterization.

In this chapter, we look at Matthew's characterization of "the disciples," whom the evangelist identifies as the small band of twelve (then eleven) apprentices to Jesus who commit to following him in his Galilean ministry. In the process of this exploration, we will see at work the method of characterization described in the previous chapter. To conclude this exploration, we investigate briefly the function of the Matthean disciples, since the evangelist shapes these and other characters in order to form readers and hearers.

The Disciples as a Character Group in Matthew

To begin, we could ask the question of whether and how a group can be treated as a character—an entity that can be analyzed for characterization. As long as a group of people in a story shares a defined set of traits that are relatively stable, such "character groups" can be understood as a unified entity for the purpose of character analysis. Any group that routinely "speak[s] and act[s] in unison . . . may be viewed as a single character."[1] We hear the disciples "speaking in unison" much of the time in Matthew as they travel with Jesus through Galilee and to Jerusalem (e.g., Matt. 8:25; 13:10; 15:12; 18:1; 21:20; 26:8–9).

Another important issue to clarify is the composition of "the disciples" in Matthew. Almost without exception, Matthew uses "the disciples" in relation to Jesus (*his* disciples) to refer to the twelve apostles—those listed in 10:2–4.[2] There are disciples of other teachers mentioned in the first Gospel, including disciples of John the Baptist (9:14; 11:2; 14:12) and disciples of the Pharisees (22:16). Matthew also describes Joseph of Arimathea as one who "had himself become a disciple of Jesus" (27:57), yet the language here is distinct. The evangelist uses the verb rather than the noun form (*mathēteuō* rather than *mathētēs*), possibly to distinguish Joseph from the twelve disciples by noting he had "been discipled" by Jesus.

Finally, in noting that "the disciples" refers routinely to the twelve, I am not suggesting that no other characters follow Jesus in discipleship in Matthew's story. Quite the contrary. Matthew identifies and highlights a number of individuals or groups who possess qualities of authentic discipleship, sometimes in direct contrast to "the twelve disciples." An important example is the "many women" portrayed as standing vigil at Jesus' crucifixion who "had followed Jesus from Galilee to care for his needs" (27:55–56). Matthew uses two discipleship terms here: *akoloutheō* ("follow") and *diakoneō* ("serve" or "care for needs") to signal that these women are true followers of Jesus.[3] And their actions of staying near Jesus in his death and at his burial (27:61; 28:1), along with the actions of Joseph of Arimathea (27:57–60), provide a vivid contrast to the twelve, who desert Jesus at his arrest (26:56).

1. Susan E. Hylen, "The Disciples: The 'Now' and the 'Not Yet' of Belief in Jesus," in *Character Studies in the Fourth Gospel*, ed. Steven A. Hunt, D. Francois Tolmie, and Ruben Zimmerman (Grand Rapids: Eerdmans, 2016), 214–27, here 216.

2. "The disciples" translates the plural *mathētai* preceded by the Greek article. When referring to Jesus' disciples, the phrase often includes the pronoun ("his") as well. The singular *mathētēs* (without an article) is usually used in Jesus' teaching to portray what an "ideal" disciple looks like (e.g., Matt. 13:52; 16:24; see also 10:42). For the would-be disciple mentioned at 8:21 (with the definite article), see Jeannine K. Brown, *The Disciples in Narrative Perspective: The Portrayal and Function of the Matthean Disciples*, SBLAB 9 (Atlanta: Society of Biblical Literature, 2002), 40.

3. Jesus himself sets the model for discipleship by "serving" rather than "being served," with *diakoneō* used in both cases in Matt. 20:28.

Matthew's Characterization of the Disciples—the Twelve

We could take on the task of exploring how Matthew characterizes the twelve disciples from a variety of angles. We might walk through the text sequentially from the beginning of the story to its end. Or we might explore key facets of the disciples' characterization trait by trait. Instead, in line with the last chapter, we will move through some of the various perspectives and relationships that inform a character's portrait in addition to their own words and actions: their relationship to the narrator, to other characters, and to readers, as well as to other narrative features.

We begin with the narrator's direct characterization of the Matthean disciples as he details the identity of the twelve, before moving to the disciples' own words and actions, as well as Jesus' interactions with them—a composite that provides much of the material for their portrait. We then turn to the narrator's few explicit references to their attributes, as well as to comparisons depicted between the disciples and other characters. We conclude by looking at the narrative relationship of the disciples to Matthew's settings, plot, and themes.[4] Along the way, I suggest areas where readers are invited to fill in gaps in the portrait of the disciples, illuminating the kinds of historical information relevant for their portrait.

The Identity of the Disciples according to the Narrator

We gain some basic information about the identities of the twelve disciples at a few key points fairly early in Matthew's Gospel. The first glimpse into this group comes when Jesus calls four fishermen—Peter, Andrew, James, and John (Matt. 4:18–22)—to leave their livelihood to follow him. Soon after, Jesus calls a tax collector, Matthew, to leave his work to follow as a disciple of Jesus (9:9). These five are woven into the list of the twelve "apostles" at 10:2–4, where the rest are also identified by name: "These are the names of the twelve apostles: first, Simon (who is called Peter) and his brother Andrew; James son of Zebedee, and his brother John; Philip and Bartholomew; Thomas and Matthew the tax collector; James son of Alphaeus, and Thaddaeus; Simon the Zealot and Judas Iscariot, who betrayed him."

---

4. In addressing plot, we will attend to the question of whether the disciples develop as characters during the course of the story.

These twelve men (all male names) are Jewish, as Jesus is. This part of the identification of the twelve, while not explicit, is discernable for a reader familiar with sociocontextual information from the first-century world,[5] including the identification of the majority of these names as Semitic[6] as well as the recognition of various features of the first Gospel as Jewish (e.g., references to the law, to Jewish sects like the Pharisees, to Jewish practices, and to locations inhabited by Jews in the first century). A competent reader will also make the connection between the twelve disciples and the twelve tribes of Israel (clarified at 19:28), understanding in Jesus' choosing of twelve disciples an implicit claim to be reconstituting God's people as a sign of the kingdom's arrival. "The Twelve exemplified the awakening of Israel and its gathering in the eschatological salvific community."[7]

A few of the twelve disciples are identified with two names or with an additional description, a common practice especially when someone had a popular name (like Simon and Judas in first-century Judaism).[8] The additions give us more information about Matthew (his vocation as tax collector; cf. Matt. 9:9), Simon "the Zealot" (known as a zealot in his antipathy toward Rome), and Judas "Iscariot" (likely a geographical tag referencing Kerioth in southern Judah).

In spite of these few distinguishing notes about individuals, the reader gets the sense that the twelve disciples function narratively more as a defined group than as distinct individuals. This sense comes from the on-going emphasis on Jesus interacting with "the/his disciples" even before they are all named (e.g., Matt. 5:1; 8:23; 9:10, 37) as well as the corporate commission the twelve receive in Matthew 10. They are, as a group, given authority by Jesus to heal and do exorcisms (10:1, 8) and are commissioned

5. Recall from the previous chapter Cornelis Bennema's "plausible historically informed modern reader," who would have such information. Bennema, *A Theory of Character in New Testament Narrative* (Minneapolis: Fortress, 2014), 68.

6. Richard Bauckham notes that the Greek name "Simon" was nearly identical to the Semitic, Simeon. *Jesus and the Eyewitnesses: The Gospels as Eyewitness Testimony* (Grand Rapids: Eerdmans, 2006), 74. He also suggests the possibility that the two remaining Greek names, Philip and Andrew, may have used in the Gospel traditions because the Semitic names of these two men were common enough that a more distinctive name was needed for their designation (107).

7. Gerhard Lohfink, *Jesus and Community: The Social Dimension of Christian Faith* (Philadelphia: Fortress, 1984), 10.

8. Bauckham, *Jesus and the Eyewitnesses*, 102.

to preach about the kingdom to Israel (10:5–7). They are also routinely characterized in particular ways as a group. Although later in the narrative Peter (see fig. 5.1) and then Judas will emerge as (somewhat) distinct from the other disciples, in the first half of the Gospel "the disciples" in aggregate are confirmed as a character group.

Figure 5.1
Peter and the Disciples: Distinctive or Similar Portraits?*

Peter's Portrait	Similar or Distinctive?	Disciples' Portrait
Leaves everything to follow (Matt. 4:18–22)	Both: Follow wholeheartedly	Leave everything to follow (4:18–22)
Impulsively exits boat and wavers when walking on water ("little faith") (14:22–33)	Both: Of "little faith" Unique: Peter as particularly impulsive	Routinely called those of "little faith" by Jesus (e.g., 8:26; 16:8; 17:20)
"Explain the parable to us" (15:15)	Both: Need Jesus to explain his teachings Peter: Emerges as spokesperson	"Explain to us the parable" (13:36)
Confesses Jesus to be the Messiah; future authority is conferred (16:13–20)	Both: Understand Jesus to be the Messiah; future authority is conferred Peter: Emerges as spokesperson	Jesus warns the twelve not to spread this confession (16:20); future authority is conferred (18:18–19)
Brashly renounces Jesus' prediction of his death (16:21–23)	Both: Misunderstand Jesus' mission to die Unique: Peter as impulsive	Disciples grieve and misunderstand Jesus' coming death (17:22–23; 20:17–24)
Answers for Jesus to collectors of temple tax (17:24–27)	Unique: Peter as impulsive	
Asks number of times to forgive (18:21)	Both: Set up Jesus' teachings with questions	Ask questions of Jesus (e.g., 18:1)
"What will we have?" (19:27 CEB)	Peter: Emerges as spokesperson	
"I will never disown you." (26:35)	Both: Protest Jesus' prediction that they'll desert him, but they all do	All the disciples agree (26:35) but all will flee (26:56)
Peter denies Jesus three times (26:69–75)	Disciples: Desert Jesus Peter: Follows Jesus at a distance (26:58) and denies him when questioned	Disciples desert Jesus (26:56)

* At 17:1–13 and 26:36–46, Jesus singles out Peter, James, and John for time alone with him.

The Characterization of the Disciples by Their Own Actions and Words

Much of what readers infer about the disciples comes from what this character group does and says within the narrative. The initial impression of any character group is important, and the disciples are no exception. When they first appear on the scene, represented by the four fishermen, their first action is to leave their nets and boats without hesitation ("at once . . . immediately") to follow Jesus (Matt. 4:18–22). This positive characterization is reaffirmed when Matthew, a tax collector, responds by leaving his work to follow Jesus (9:9).

An important narrative role that the disciples fulfill is their *presence with Jesus* as his closest followers. Shortly after the call of the first disciples, Jesus sets out to teach "his disciples" about his expectations for them as the kingdom arrives (Matt. 5:1–2). They remain with him after the conclusion to the Sermon on the Mount (7:28–29) as Jesus heals and performs other miracles (8:23–27; 9:10–11, 19, 37). And while they are often in the background, they are referenced across the narrative frequently enough to show that they remain with Jesus throughout his Galilean ministry.[9]

They move to a position of greater prominence in Matthew 16:21–20:28 (see discussion below regarding the disciples and Matthew's plot) and then remain with Jesus during his week in Jerusalem until the night of his betrayal, just before his death.[10] A key turning point in their characterization comes when all the disciples flee during Jesus' arrest, deserting him in his darkest hour (26:56). Given the role of a disciple to follow (cf. 16:24) and be "with Jesus" (26:71), their desertion is all the more poignant and disappointing. This climactic moment in the subplot about the disciples eludes resolution until the final lines of the Gospel. Only then do the "eleven disciples" (without Judas) reappear as they meet Jesus on a mountain in Galilee where he has directed them to go (28:16). As we will see, their restoration after desertion is a result not of their own words or actions but of Jesus' gracious reestablishment of relationship (26:32; 28:7, 10) and his promise of ongoing presence (28:20).

9. Jesus engages and reengages the disciples all along the way: Matt. 11:1; 12:1–2; 13:10, 36, 51; 14:15, 22; 15:1, 12, 23, 32; 16:5, 13.

10. They are present across the Jerusalem narrative: Matt. 20:29; 21:1, 6, 20; 23:1; 24:1, 3; 26:1, 8, 17, 20, 31, 35, 36, 45.

Another element of the disciples' portrayal that has both positive and negative facets is their role as helpers to Jesus in his ministry at various points in the story.[11] When Jesus feeds the five thousand, he gives the food to his disciples, who in turn pass the food to the crowd (Matt. 14:19). They similarly assist Jesus in the feeding of the four thousand (15:36). This helper role, with a focus on the disciples' obedience to Jesus' instructions, is also highlighted as they procure a donkey for Jesus' entry into Jerusalem (21:6–7) and arrange for their shared Passover meal (26:19).

Yet Jesus' expectations for a more significant helper role from his disciples are frustrated on a number of occasions. Although he has given them authority to share key facets of his ministry (Matt. 10:1, 7–8), they fall short in this role. When large crowds (five thousand) who follow Jesus are hungry, he seems to expect the disciples to provide in a miraculous way: "You give them something to eat" (14:16). In the feeding of the four thousand, the disciples seem to infer from Jesus' words that he wants *them* to act: "Where could we get enough bread in this remote place to feed such a crowd?" (15:33). As Dorothy Jean Weaver observes, the disciples "respond not with the self-assurance of those who know they have the 'authority' to carry out such 'deeds of power' but rather with the incredulity of those faced with an impossible task."[12] The clearest example of the disciples falling short of Jesus' expectation to participate in his mission comes when they prove unable to heal a boy who has a demon (17:16), although Jesus has already given them "authority to drive out impure spirits and to heal every disease and sickness" (10:1).

If we take a closer look at what the disciples say in the story, we again observe a mixed portrait of both the positive and the negative. The very first words of the disciples in Matthew come in response to their experience of a violent storm as they are in a boat with Jesus. The disciples rouse Jesus from sleep and exclaim, "Lord, save us! We're going to drown!" (Matt. 8:25). When Jesus responds by calming the storm, they are amazed and ask: "What kind of man is this? Even the wind and the waves obey him!" (8:27). As the disciples spend more time with Jesus and see other displays of his power, they come to answer the question of Jesus' identity with affirmation that he is the Messiah.

11. Brown, *Disciples in Narrative Perspective*, 99–101, 112.
12. Dorothy Jean Weaver, *Matthew's Missionary Discourse: A Literary Critical Analysis*, JSNTSup 38 (Sheffield: JSOT Press, 1990), 134.

"[They] worshiped him, saying, 'Truly you are the Son of God'" (14:33).[13]

"Simon Peter answered, 'You are the Messiah, the Son of the living God'" (16:16).[14]

These confessions align with the narrator's own affirmations about Jesus (1:1) and so demonstrate that the disciples have rightly understood who Jesus is. And their worship of him (14:33; 28:17)[15] confirms they truly grasp at key moments his identity as the Messiah and Son to whom God has granted all authority (28:18).

Yet Matthew also portrays the disciples as very often misunderstanding the teachings of Jesus. Their less-than-adequate comprehension surfaces in their frequent questions, requests for an explanation, and actions or statements that are subsequently corrected by Jesus (see fig. 5.2).

Figure 5.2
Disciples' Words Showing Their Inadequate Understanding

Disciples' Questions or Requests for Explanation	Reference	Jesus' Corrections
"Why do you speak to the people in parables?"	13:10	
"Explain to us the parable of the weeds in the field."	13:36	
Peter: "Explain the parable to us."	15:15	
"Where could we get enough bread?"	15:33	
"It is because we didn't bring any bread."	16:7	"You of little faith" (cf. 16:8–11)
Peter: "Never, Lord! . . . This shall never happen to you!"	16:22	"Get behind me, Satan!" (cf. 16:23–28)
"Why then do the teachers of the law say that Elijah must come first?"	17:10	

13. Language of God's "son" was often used in Judaism to refer to Israel's king (e.g., 2 Sam. 7:14; Ps. 2:7) and more specifically to the Messiah (2 Esd. 7:28–29). It is also the case that "Matthew's identification of Jesus as God's Son also points to a deeper, filial relationship that comes to be defined in Trinitarian categories—rightly so—in subsequent centuries." Jeannine K. Brown and Kyle Roberts, *Matthew*, THNTC (Grand Rapids: Eerdmans, 2018), 49.

14. Matthew often singles out Peter as the spokesperson for the twelve. Since Peter's characterization overlaps significantly with that of the twelve in other places, I treat Peter as an indicator of the disciples' characterization, at least until the passion narrative, where he is more distinctively portrayed at 26:33–35, 69–75.

15. While *proskyneō* can indicate a deep reverence (involving "falling down before" someone of higher rank; BDAG, 882), Matthew's frequent use of the term, and at key moments (2:2, 8, 11; 28:9, 17), signals that the sense of worship is likely intended on the discourse level.

Disciples' Questions or Requests for Explanation	Reference	Jesus' Corrections
"Why couldn't we drive [a demon] out?"	17:19	
"Who, then, is the greatest in the kingdom of heaven?"	18:1	
Peter: "Lord, how many times shall I forgive my brother or sister?"	18:21	
"If this is the situation between a husband and wife, it is better not to marry."	19:10	"Not everyone can accept this" (cf. 19:11–12).
They rebuke children coming to Jesus.	19:13	"Let [them] come" (19:14–15).
"Who then can be saved?"	19:25	
Peter: "What . . . will there be for us?"	19:27	
James and John: "We can [drink the cup]."	20:22	"not for me to grant. . . . Not so with you" (20:23, 25–28).
"How did the fig tree wither so quickly?"	21:20	
"Tell us . . . when will this happen, and what will be the sign of your coming?"	24:3	
"Why this waste? This perfume could have been sold."	26:8–9	"She has done a beautiful thing" (cf. 26:10–13).
"Where do you want us to make preparations for you to eat the Passover?"	26:17	
Each: "Surely you don't mean me, Lord?"	26:22	
Peter: "Even if I have to die with you, I will never disown you." (Matthew indicates the other disciples give the same assurance.)	26:35	They all flee at Jesus' arrest (26:56), proving Jesus' words true (26:31, 34).

Even if we as readers might consider one or more of these questions legitimate or even helpful, the cumulative effect of their questions and Jesus' frequent teachings to set them straight paints the disciples as prone to misunderstand Jesus' teachings. And while the disciples answer Jesus' question, "Have you understood all these [parables]?," with a straightforward "yes" (Matt. 13:51), their ongoing need to have Jesus explain parables to them (e.g., 15:15) causes the reader to doubt this confident assertion.[16] By the time we hear the final words of the disciples in 26:35, their protestations ring hollow. The claim that they would choose to die

16. Warren Carter, *Matthew and the Margins* (Maryknoll, NY: Orbis, 2000), 297.

with Jesus rather than disown him is almost immediately followed by all of them deserting Jesus at his arrest (26:56).

The disciples' propensity to misunderstand is especially apparent when Jesus teaches the disciples about his mission to go to Jerusalem, suffer, and be killed (Matt. 16:21; 17:22–23; 20:17–19). In spite of what Jesus teaches about his mission "to give his life as a ransom for many" (20:28), the disciples continue to think that Jesus will establish his kingdom by might and that they will be the ones most to benefit by association.[17] Their preoccupation with their own status in the coming kingdom (e.g., 18:1; 19:27; 20:20–24) provides a vivid contrast to Jesus, who renounces any status or power he could assert—he comes as a Messiah who serves (20:25–28). Andrew Trotter sums up this part of the disciples' characterization: "Virtually everything [the disciples] 'understand' in the Gospel is understood with a grain of salt; Jesus has taught them clearly and well, but their own dullness and especially their over-riding misunderstanding of the nature of his messiahship clouds their understanding."[18]

Words and Actions of Other Characters in Relation to the Disciples

While we learn much about the disciples from their own words and actions, we also gain crucial information about their portrait from how other characters relate to them. Jesus is by far the character who has the most interaction with the disciples, and we will turn to what he says and does in relation to them in just a moment. First, however, an interesting feature of their relationship with Jesus can be discerned from what other characters say about their association.

The words of various characters accent the relationship of Jesus as the teacher of the disciples and they as his followers. Pharisees, speaking to the disciples, refer to Jesus as "your teacher" (Matt. 9:11). Those who collect the temple tax do the same, asking Peter, "Doesn't your teacher pay the . . . tax" (17:24). Alternately, a number of characters, speaking to Jesus, refer to the twelve as "your disciples"—including John's disciples

---

17. This is a reasonable expectation given first-century messianic hopes that tended toward a leader with a comprehensive scope of authority over political, military, and religious life; see Brown and Roberts, *Matthew*, 294.

18. Andrew H. Trotter, "Understanding and Stumbling: A Study of the Disciples' Understanding of Jesus and His Teaching in the Gospel of Matthew" (PhD diss., Cambridge University, 1986), 284, quoted in Brown, *Disciples in Narrative Perspective*, 12.

(9:14), Pharisees (12:2; 15:2, along with scribes), and a man with a son who is ill (17:16). The effect of these repetitions of "your teacher" and "your disciples" is to connect Jesus with his disciples quite closely—to align their practices and interests and highlight their loyalty to one another.

Focusing our attention on Jesus in relation to the twelve disciples, Matthew highlights numerous facets of the disciples' portrayal through Jesus' words and actions. A first area for exploration involves the sheer amount of teaching that Jesus provides his disciples. Matthew is known for the five great discourses containing Jesus' teachings, and each of these has the disciples as its audience either exclusively (the Mission Discourse, Matt. 10; the Community Discourse, Matt. 18; the Eschatological Discourse, Matt. 24–25) or in concert with the Galilean crowds (the Sermon on the Mount, Matt. 5–7; the Parables Discourse, Matt. 13). As the primary recipients of Jesus' teaching, the disciples are portrayed as "insiders"—they receive revelation about the kingdom and about Jesus' mission that others do not (e.g., 11:25–27; 13:11, 36–43).

Yet as we've already seen, the disciples struggle to understand, and some of Jesus' words to them diagnose this lack of understanding. When asked by Peter to explain the parable about what defiles a person, Jesus asks, "Are you still so dull?" (Matt. 15:16). And when the disciples mistake Jesus' riddle about yeast to be about physical bread, Jesus chastises them: "You of little faith. . . . Do you still not understand? Don't you remember the five loaves for the five thousand, and how many basketfuls you gathered? Or the seven loaves for the four thousand, and how many basketfuls you gathered? How is it you don't understand that I was not talking to you about bread?" (16:8–11a). It seems clear that Jesus expects his disciples to have greater understanding after what they've seen and heard than what they exhibit.

In Jesus' reprimand we also hear another characterization of the disciples: "You of little faith" (Matt. 16:8). This is a consistent part of the disciples' portrayal—Jesus speaks of them exhibiting little faith five times in Matthew's Gospel (6:30; 8:26; 14:31; 16:8; 17:20).[19] Narratively, their little faith arises when they are anxious about daily provision (6:30; 16:8), when they fear for their safety in spite of Jesus' presence (8:26; Peter at 14:31), and when they cannot heal even though they have been granted

---

19. This is particularly Matthean, as the term "little faith" (as either a noun or adjective: *oligopistia* or *oligopistos*), apart from Luke 12:28, occurs only in Matthew.

that power (17:20; cf. 10:1). Through these various narrative moments, Matthew associates little faith with anxiety (6:30), fear (8:26), doubt or wavering (14:31), inadequate understanding (16:8), and unfulfilled mission (17:20). Little faith is narratively defined as an inadequate trust in the extent of Jesus' power.[20] As Donald Verseput concludes, little faith is "the unjustified incapacity of the disciple to grasp and rely upon Jesus' inexhaustible power."[21]

In spite of Jesus' critique of the disciples as slow to understand and inadequate in faith, there is also a strong strand of hope that accompanies the disciples' portrait in Matthew. This hope begins in Jesus' identification of the disciples as those of little faith, especially as this term is not only "used as a reproach . . . but also as an invitation [to the disciples] to develop their discipleship."[22] More pointedly, this sense of hope arises from Jesus' words of encouragement toward the disciples, and especially his forecasting of their future role in the ongoing mission of God. Jesus refers to this future mission, first in his authorizing of Peter and his promise that his (Jesus') church will persevere (Matt. 16:17–19) and then when this same future authority is promised to the twelve (and to the wider church; 18:18–20). These promises culminate in the final scene of the Gospel, where Jesus commissions the (now eleven) disciples to disciple others by baptizing and teaching obedience (28:19–20). Matthew's Gospel concludes on this note of future hope that the disciples will participate in the ministry of Jesus.

Another important anchor for the ups and downs of the disciples' portrait comes when Jesus redefines family around allegiances. When told that his family wants to speak to him, Jesus points to his disciples and says, "Here are my mother and my brothers. For whoever does the will of my Father in heaven is my brother and sister and mother" (Matt. 12:49–50). This relational loyalty beyond biological family foreshadows Jesus' commitment to the disciples, even when their loyalty to Jesus is tested and fails. We see this commitment in Jesus' words that come immediately after his prediction that all of the disciples will "stumble" when he is arrested

---

20. Brown, *Disciples in Narrative Perspective*, 106. For an extended analysis of "little faith" in Matthew, see 101–7.

21. Donald J. Verseput, "The Faith of the Reader and the Narrative of Matthew 13:53–16:20," *JSNT* 46 (1992): 3–24, here 23.

22. Carlos Olivares, "The Term ὀλιγόπιστος (Little Faith) in Matthew's Gospel: Narrative and Thematic Connections," *Colloquium* 47 (2015), 274–91, here 291.

(26:31).[23] He continues, "But after I have risen, I will go ahead of you into Galilee" (26:32). Jesus reiterates this promise of their reconnection to the women who see him first at his resurrection: "Go and tell my brothers to go to Galilee; there they will see me" (28:10; cf. 28:7). This promise of restored relationship, with Jesus calling the disciples his "brothers," provides something of a positive conclusion to their portrayal, and "the implied reader will derive hope from Jesus' gracious words toward his fallible followers."[24]

The Internal Responses of the Disciples according to the Narrator

For the most part we've been exploring the indirect characterization of the disciples through what they say and do and through what other characters say and do in relation to them. Although Matthew uses direct characterization less frequently than these indirect means, he does provide a few explicit characterizations of the disciples. These come almost exclusively through narration of the disciples' internal responses to various events and situations rather than through statements about static qualities that define them. In other words, Matthew does not give us explicit statements of *being* for the disciples (i.e., attributes), such as "they were people of great faith," or even *summations* of their state of mind, such as "the disciples routinely misunderstood Jesus and his mission." Yet we can infer from the narrative that the first of these generalizations is untrue while the second is quite accurate. We do so by following the contours of what the narrator reveals about how the disciples respond across the story—both in their words and actions (as already discussed) and in their more internal processes that the narrator reveals in the telling of his story.

More than once Matthew indicates that the disciples respond to Jesus with fear or astonishment. They are "terrified" at Jesus' appearance on the lake (they think he is a ghost; Matt. 14:26) as well as at his transfiguration (Peter, James, and John, specifically; 17:6). They are "greatly astonished" at Jesus' teaching about the difficulty of the rich entering God's kingdom (19:25) and are amazed at his ability to wither a fig tree with only his words (21:20). Given that the disciples are routinely privy to Jesus' miraculous

---

23. The Greek *skandelizō* may be rendered "fall away" (NIV) or "stumble" (NTE). For the stumbling motif in Matthew, see Brown and Roberts, *Matthew*, 164.

24. Brown, *Disciples in Narrative Perspective*, 131.

actions and countercultural words, it is not surprising that they exhibit these intense responses to him. We also hear their overwhelming grief at the prediction of his coming death (17:22–23) and their deep sadness at the thought that one of them will betray Jesus (26:22). And we hear twice in the story that the disciples doubt or waver. Jesus asks Peter why he wavers when he attempts to follow Jesus in walking on the water (14:31). The narrator also mentions that the eleven both worship and waver in faith when they see the risen Jesus (28:17).[25]

Each of these responses indicates that the disciples do not fully grasp who Jesus is, his mission, and what he is able to do. Though their reactions may certainly be understandable to the reader, these responses contribute to an overall portrait of the disciples as those who often misunderstand Jesus and his work.

Yet at two points Matthew makes explicit that the disciples "understand" something Jesus communicates. This direct characterization has led some scholars to suggest that the Matthean disciples possess understanding as a character trait, in spite of the opposite effect we have seen arising from the words and actions of the disciples themselves.[26] Let's take a closer look at these two moments of explicit commentary about the disciples' understanding:

> "Then they understood that he was not telling them to guard against the yeast used in bread, but against the teaching of the Pharisees and Sadducees" (16:12).
>
> "Then the disciples understood that he was talking to them about John the Baptist" (17:13).

Rather than generalize these two narrator comments, it makes more sense to notice that the disciples come to understand specific knowledge after Jesus has corrected or instructed them (Matt. 16:8–11; 17:10–12). Matthew indicates that the disciples come to understand, in particular, Jesus' riddle about yeast and his words about Elijah's return. Neither

---

25. For the translation "waver" (Greek *distazō*), see discussion below.

26. For example, Gerhard Barth, "Matthew's Understanding of the Law," in *Tradition and Interpretation in Matthew*, ed. G. Bornkamm, G. Barth, and H. J. Held (Philadelphia: Westminster, 1963), 58–164, here 106; and Michael J. Wilkins, *The Concept of Disciple in Matthew's Gospel*, NovTSup 59 (Leiden: Brill, 1988), 165.

instance translates to the disciples possessing understanding as a character trait. Instead, the disciples' own words and actions, as well as Jesus' descriptions of them, point to their ongoing misunderstanding of Jesus' teachings and his messianic mission.

The Narrator's Comparison of the Disciples with Other Characters

Another means of characterization occurs in the juxtaposing of characters, often to highlight contrasting portraits. For example, Matthew's disciples are typified by little faith, a trait illuminated in distinction from the greater or lesser faith of other characters. We learn from these comparisons that *little faith* (*oligopistia*; e.g., Matt. 17:20) is not a complete *lack of faith* for Matthew, since it is only Jesus' hometown (13:58) and Jewish leaders (21:32) who are characterized by the latter (e.g., *apistia* at 13:58). But Matthew makes it clear that the little faith of the disciples is inadequate by providing a narrative contrast in people who come to Jesus for healing and are commended by him for their faith (*pistis*; e.g., 9:2, 22, 29). Finally, the "great faith" of two gentiles who come to plead for healing for someone close to them amazes Jesus (*tosoutos pistis* at 8:10; *megalē pistis* at 15:28).[27] These comparisons also emphasize for the reader that true discipleship exists beyond the character group of the twelve disciples.

The Relationship of the Disciples to Other Narrative Features

To conclude our exploration of the disciples' portrait in Matthew, we turn to the key narrative elements of setting, plot, and theme in relation to the disciples' characterization.

THE DISCIPLES AND SETTINGS

In Matthew, mountains provide an important setting, especially in relation to the disciples. Jesus often guides them to mountain settings for important moments of teaching (e.g., Matt. 5:1–2; 17:1; 24:1–3; 28:16–20). Knowing that the Old Testament displays "widespread interest in the

27. This fits Matthew's theme of gentile inclusion and taps into a competent reader's knowledge that the Old Testament envisioned gentile blessing as part of Israel's identity and mission as a "kingdom of priests" (Exod. 19:5–6) and "a light for the Gentiles" (Isa. 49:5–6; cf. Gen. 12:1–3).

mountain as a religious site and theological symbol,"[28] the competent reader will be all the more alert to this setting in Matthew. We see across Matthew that key moments of revelation occur on mountains and that the disciples are recipients of this revelation about Jesus (e.g., 17:5) and from Jesus (e.g., 5:1–7:27; 28:16–20; cf. 11:25–27).

The Disciples and Plot

The disciples as a character group are essential to Matthew's plot. Initially, their presence is a necessary prerequisite for Jesus' discourses, which are spoken on the story level, either partly or exclusively, to disciples. And while the initial conflict of the Galilean ministry focuses on Jewish leaders as Jesus' antagonists,[29] once Jesus begins to tell his disciples of his coming death in Jerusalem it is *the disciples* who come into conflict with Jesus and propel the story forward. Jesus' three predictions of his coming death (Matt. 16:21; 17:22–23; 20:17–19) intensify the ideological conflict between Jesus and the disciples.[30] The disciples consistently misunderstand and resist Jesus' mission to give himself for his people (20:28) and its implications for their own status and commitments. They cannot comprehend that "servanthood is the essence of discipleship,"[31] a theme evident from Jesus' teachings and his own example.

Another important feature of the disciples' portrayal for Matthew's plot is their fairly static characterization. While the disciples affirm Jesus as the Messiah at the climax of his Galilean ministry (Matt. 16:16), it is not clear that this is a significant departure from their initial impetus to follow him (4:18–22; 9:9).[32] And, as I have suggested, they are routinely and consistently portrayed as misconstruing Jesus' messianic mission (what he has come to do as Messiah), misunderstanding their own role

28. Terence L. Donaldson, *Jesus on the Mountain: A Study in Matthean Theology*, JSNTSup 8 (Sheffield: JSOT Press, 1985), 81.

29. Primarily Pharisees and teachers of the law (e.g., Matt. 9:34; 12:1–14, 22–24, 38; 15:1–20; 16:1–4).

30. Jack Dean Kingsbury, *Matthew as Story*, 2nd ed. (Philadelphia: Fortress, 1988), 130.

31. Kingsbury, *Matthew as Story*, 130.

32. David Howell plausibly suggests that the disciples grow in their understanding of Jesus' identity between 8:27 and 14:33 but do not progress in understanding beyond that point. David B. Howell, *Matthew's Inclusive Story: A Study in the Narrative Rhetoric of the First Gospel*, JSNTSup 42 (Sheffield: JSOT Press, 1990), 142.

as his followers, and evidencing inadequate faith in Jesus and his messianic power.

While some scholars suggest that by the end of the Gospel the disciples have gained understanding as a character trait,[33] this conclusion is difficult to sustain from the sparse textual clues about the disciples' responses after they are reunited with the resurrected Jesus. We hear only that they go to meet Jesus as he had instructed and that "when they saw him, *they worshiped him, yet they also wavered*" (28:17 AT).[34]

It is telling that these same two responses—worship and wavering—have typified the disciples already at Matthew 14:31–33. Jesus refers to Peter there as "You of little faith" (14:31), as he has the whole group elsewhere (e.g., 8:26), asking Peter why he wavers (or doubts). Matthew uses the same Greek word at both 14:31 and 28:17: *distazō*, which can be rendered "waver" and which is closely tied to "little faith."[35] At the conclusion of that pericope, the disciples worship Jesus (14:33).

If wavering (closely aligned with little faith) and worshiping characterize the disciples at the end of Matthew's story as these traits have earlier, then the disciples have not progressed in understanding and faith.[36] Yet this does not halt the progress of God's mission, since the conclusion of the Gospel holds out the promise that, in spite of less-than-ideal disciples, Jesus' mandate to "make disciples of all nations" will succeed. The guarantee for the disciple-making task comes not from the disciples but from Jesus himself. It is *Jesus' presence* that assures the reader that God's mission of blessing to the nations will produce fruit (28:20). It is "Jesus' effective presence" rather than the disciples' understanding and faith that provides a sense of hope at the end of Matthew's narrative.[37] As Mark Allan Powell concludes, "The reader ultimately views these disciples as characters with tremendous potential . . . not derive[d] from any qualities the disciples evince on their own, but from what Jesus sees in them and is able to impart to them."[38]

33. E.g., Kingsbury, *Matthew as Story*, 145.

34. My translation in Brown and Roberts, *Matthew*, 259.

35. Given that this word occurs only at these two places in all the New Testament, it seems significant that Matthew uses it in both places to characterize the disciples.

36. Verseput, "Faith of the Reader," 21.

37. Brown, *Disciples in Narrative Perspective*, 123.

38. Mark Allan Powell, "Characterization on the Phraseological Plane in the Gospel of Matthew," in *Treasures New and Old*, ed. David R. Bauer and Mark Allan Powell, SBLSymS 1 (Atlanta: Scholars Press, 1996), 161–77, here 171.

THE DISCIPLES AND THEMES

Some key discipleship themes emerge from Matthew's characterization of the disciples. We've already noted how Jesus' description of them as those of little faith contributes to the theme of faith more broadly in Matthew. And since "little faith" is applied so specifically to the disciples, it becomes a vehicle for that motif in Matthew.

Another discipleship theme connected with the disciples' portrait is status renunciation. This theme emerges from the disciples' misunderstanding of Jesus' teachings around status in God's kingdom and their preoccupation with their own status and ranking in the coming kingdom. We see this clearly in the disciples' question seeking to determine who is greatest in the kingdom (Matt. 18:1), as well as in the request for James and John to have the highest of positions with Jesus when the kingdom arrives (20:20–21). Even Peter's question of what he and the other disciples will receive for leaving everything to follow Jesus (19:27) suggests a concern for status, especially given the status contours of Jesus' response (19:30–20:16).

Jesus' teachings in response to these questions and requests are telling. The competent reader will recognize in Jesus' use of the examples of children and slaves two groups with little or no status in the first-century world.[39] Jesus uses these examples to provide a countercultural discipleship paradigm, one that is devoid of any presumption of or claim to greatness.[40]

> "Whoever takes the lowly position of this child is the greatest in the kingdom of heaven" (18:4).
>
> "Whoever wants to become great among you must be your servant, and whoever wants to be first must be your slave" (20:26–27).

Jesus warns against presumption about status (cf. Matt. 19:30; 20:16) and calls all disciples to live in countercultural ways that prioritize serving

---

39. Brown and Roberts, *Matthew*, 166, 187.

40. Ulrich Luz suggests that Jesus' goal "is not to present a new way to greatness—a more noble way than that of authority and power; it is rather that the desire to be great is itself to be eliminated, since even the most subtle desire for greatness for oneself corrupts genuine service." Ulrich Luz, *Matthew 8–20*, trans. Helmut Koester, Hermeneia (Minneapolis: Fortress, 2001), 545.

over being served (20:25, 28; 23:8–12). The twelve disciples, in their pre-occupation with status, become a foil to status renunciation so that the reader is drawn not to the disciples' aspirations for high status but to Jesus' words and his own example of humble service.[41]

The Function of the Disciples' Portrait for Matthew's Readers

In this chapter, we've explored in depth Matthew's characterization of Jesus' twelve disciples. And since Matthew is interested in shaping his readers for discipleship, we conclude with a brief look at how the disciples' portrait contributes to that shaping process.

Early on Matthew encourages the reader to identify with the disciples. He does so by their initial positive characterization: they leave their liveli-hoods to follow Jesus (Matt. 4:18–22; 9:9). Readers will also align them-selves with the disciples if they identify with the disciples' commitments and situation. The implied (or ideal) reader will feel a shared set of com-mitments, since Matthew writes with believers in Jesus as his primary audience.

As the narrative moves along, the disciples' characterization becomes more varied, with positive qualities, such as commitment to and presence with Jesus, intermingling with negative traits, like frequent misunder-standing and little faith. This increasingly negative portrait has an effect on the reader—it creates distance between the reader and the disciples. The reader will evaluate more closely the disciples' words and behavior, especially as they contrast with the values of the narrator and of Jesus. The reader will be drawn toward the latter, with the disciples' negative qualities acting as a foil, "challenging the reader to follow Jesus more faithfully than the disciples do."[42]

Yet the disciples—even at their lowest points—are not abandoned by Jesus. So the reader can still feel some sense of identification with the dis-ciples, even when they are negatively portrayed, because of Jesus' positive

---

41. Matthew's Jesus routinely teaches about authentic discipleship and its qualities. These teachings form a portrait of an "ideal disciple" for the reader to emulate. For an extended dis-cussion of discipleship in Matthew, see Brown and Roberts, *Matthew*, 334–55; and Jeannine K. Brown, "Living Out 'Justice, Mercy, and Loyalty': Discipleship in Matthew's Gospel," in *Following Jesus Christ: The New Testament Message of Discipleship for Today*, ed. John K. Goodrich and Mark L. Strauss (Grand Rapids: Kregel Academic, 2020), 7–24.

42. Brown, *Disciples in Narrative Perspective*, 130.

stance toward them and toward their future. This continued experience of a certain level of identification creates hope in the reader. That hope finds its source, in part, in Jesus' presence with his followers (Matt. 28:20; cf. 1:23; 18:20). That hope also extends to readers themselves, who may find that Jesus' continued commitment to his fallible followers provides assurance that "the exalted Christ will likewise assist them in their own struggles."[43]

43. David Bauer, "The Major Characters of Matthew's Story: Their Function and Significance," *Int* 46 (1992): 357–67, here 363.

Part Four
Intertextuality

Thus I rediscovered what writers have always known (and have told us again and again): books always speak of other books, and every story tells a story that has already been told.

Umberto Eco, postscript to *The Name of the Rose*

6

The Stories behind the Story

In contemporary life, and in the Western world especially, great value is often placed on the new and the novel. Marketers know that products labeled "brand new" sell. People are regularly on the lookout for the newest fad or idea. In contrast, the Gospel writers consciously look backward; they draw from the deep well of Israel's Scriptures as they narrate the life of Jesus. They conserve as well as adapt these traditions as they interpret the arrival of the Messiah for the churches they are wanting to influence and encourage.

In a real way, the Old Testament forms the **backstories** for Matthew, Mark, Luke, and John. Their stories of Jesus are grounded by and interwoven with stories drawn from Israel's sacred Scripture. **Intertextuality** is the term most often used to describe the varied ways the evangelists engage the Old Testament as well as the study of these connections. Intertextuality as a subdiscipline of New Testament studies has burgeoned in the past four decades. And it stands as a helpful companion to a narrative approach to the Gospels. This is especially the case when the storied character of intertextuality is given attention.

In this chapter, we briefly review the emergence of intertextuality within New Testament studies before getting a sense of its current landscape, including efforts to highlight the storied dimensions of reliance on the Old Testament. Then we consider how and why the Gospel writers use the Old Testament, providing examples from each of the

Gospels to gain clarity on these issues. Along the way, we'll see that the evangelists are deeply interested in connecting the story of Jesus to Israel's story.

The Emergence of "Intertextuality": From Atomizing to Echoing

Earlier generations of scholars tended to hold a conviction that the New Testament authors used bits of the Old Testament without much thought for their wider contexts. While there were certainly exceptions to this conclusion,[1] it was commonplace to hear the observation that the evangelists atomized the Old Testament—they used scriptural texts without much care for their original settings and contexts.

We can take an example from Matthew 2:15, where the Gospel writer cites Hosea 11:1b—"Out of Egypt I called my son"—to comment on the flight of Jesus' family to Egypt and their subsequent return (Matt. 2:13–15a, 21). Has Matthew misused Hosea by taking the prophet's clear (past tense) referent to "son" for Israel (Hosea 11:1a) and applying it erroneously to God's Son, Jesus? One scholar, in an article titled "Matthew Twists the Scripture," came to this conclusion: "Matt 2:15 interprets the return of Joseph and Mary with the child Jesus from Egypt as fulfillment of Hos 11:1, 'Out of Egypt I called my son,' which in its original setting means the exodus of Israel from Egypt. As only Matthew records the flight to Egypt, there is a strong possibility that the entire episode is an inference from the misunderstood Hos 11:1."[2]

Yet this is not the only or even best interpretive possibility. What if Matthew uses Hosea with full acknowledgment that the prophet is referring to Israel when speaking of God's son? This would connect Israel's role as God's chosen offspring to an important role of the Matthean Jesus. As God's Son, he acts as representative Israel to stand in for his people, to bring about their restoration, and to fulfill their mission to be a light to the nations. As Klyne Snodgrass suggests, the New Testament writers assume the reality of corporate solidarity—that is, "the reciprocal relation between the individual and the community that existed in the Semitic

---

1. For example, C. H. Dodd, *According to the Scriptures: The Sub-structure of New Testament Theology* (London: Nisbet, 1952).
2. S. V. McCasland, "Matthew Twists the Scripture," *JBL* 80 (1961): 143–48, here 144.

mind."[3] By drawing on Israel's foundational story of redemption from Egypt, Matthew intentionally draws a parallel between their story and God's providential rescue of Jesus from Herod's clutches by taking Jesus' family to Egypt and back. These storied parallels continue into Matthew 3–4, where Jesus is baptized in solidarity with his people (Matt. 3:15)[4] and then proves victorious in the face of temptation, in contrast to Israel during their time of wilderness testing (4:1–11).

Old Testament Echoes: The Legacy of Richard Hays

This kind of interpretive practice, which brings with it an assumption of the importance of the Old Testament context for understanding the New Testament author's use of a **citation** or **allusion**, owes much to the work of Richard Hays. In his *Echoes of Scripture in the Letters of Paul*, Hays suggests that interpreters attend not only to Old Testament citations and allusions in the Pauline letters but also to scriptural echoes.[5] An **echo** refers to an implicit evocation of an earlier text. The idea is that an echo "evokes resonances of [an] earlier text *beyond those explicitly cited*."[6] In literary theory this notion of invoking entire contexts is called **metalepsis**.[7]

A potential Old Testament echo in John's Gospel comes as he narrates Jesus' trial before Pilate. When Pilate presents Jesus to the crowd, he utters the words, "Here is the man!" (John 19:5; "man" translates the Greek *anthrōpos*). Is this an echo of Gen. 1:26–27, where God creates humanity (*anthrōpos* in the **Septuagint**)? If so, John would be implicitly signaling to his readers that Jesus is the second *adam*—the center of new humanity. While this may seem a rather thin connective thread, I suggest the validity

3. Klyne Snodgrass, "The Use of the Old Testament in the New," in *The Right Doctrine from the Wrong Texts? Essays on the Use of the Old Testament in the New*, ed. G. K. Beale (Grand Rapids: Baker, 1994), 29–51, here 37.

4. I translate *dikaiosynē* at Matt. 3:15 as "to fulfill God's promised redemption," indicating that Jesus joins his people in baptism to inaugurate God's kingdom work. See Jeannine K. Brown and Kyle Roberts, *Matthew*, THNTC (Grand Rapids: Eerdmans, 2018), 43.

5. Richard B. Hays, *Echoes of Scripture in the Letters of Paul* (New Haven: Yale University Press, 1989).

6. Richard B. Hays, *The Conversion of the Imagination: Paul as Interpreter of Israel's Scripture* (Grand Rapids: Eerdmans, 2005), 2 (emphasis original).

7. Jeannine K. Brown, "Metalepsis," in *Exploring Intertextuality: Diverse Strategies for New Testament Interpretation of Texts*, ed. B. J. Oropeza and Steve Moyise (Eugene, OR: Cascade, 2016), 29–31.

of this and other potential Johannine echoes and allusions to Genesis 1–2 in the next chapter.

At this point, the relevant question is how we might affirm (or exclude) potential echoes as part of a New Testament author's communicative plan.[8] Hays answers this question by proposing seven criteria for discerning textual echoes. Although much has been made of these seven, including questions of whether all of them actually function as criteria, I will highlight here four that have gained broad consensus:

1. The availability of the precursor text to both author and audience (usually assumed for Old Testament use in the New Testament)
2. Verbal repetition between the text and its New Testament usage
3. Repeated use of the Old Testament text by the same New Testament author in other locations
4. Thematic coherence with the New Testament author's own emphases[9]

As more of these criteria apply in any particular potential echo, we are on better footing for suggesting that the echo really does fit the pattern of the New Testament author's communicative intentions. We can also note that the church audiences of the New Testament books would likely have been able to catch at least some of these echoes (along with citations and allusions), although the criteria mentioned here are author rather than audience focused. Even audiences that were primarily gentile (as in the case of 1 Corinthians or 1 Peter) would have viewed the Old Testament as their Scriptures (there was not a New Testament as of yet) and so would have been schooled in the stories and messages of Old Testament books. Additionally, Jewish believers in these churches "would have been able to draw ongoing attention to the scriptural allusions and echoes" of these letters for their gentile counterparts.[10]

In Luke's transfiguration scene (Luke 9:28–36), he narrates that Moses and Elijah "were speaking about [Jesus'] exodus, which he would soon

8. Jeannine K. Brown, *Scripture as Communication: Introducing Biblical Hermeneutics* (Grand Rapids: Baker Academic, 2007), 225–28.

9. These criteria are drawn from Hays, *Echoes of Scripture in the Letters of Paul*, 29–32; and Mark Allan Powell, *Chasing the Eastern Star: Adventures in Biblical Reader-Response Criticism* (Louisville: Westminster John Knox), 101–2.

10. Referring to 1 Peter particularly; Joel B. Green, *1 Peter*, THNTC (Grand Rapids: Eerdmans, 2007), 5.

accomplish in Jerusalem" (9:31 AT). The Greek *exodos* is unique to Luke in this scene (cf. Matt. 17:3; Mark 9:4) and may evoke the event of Israel's redemption from Egypt, as reflected in the Greek title of the second book of the Old Testament (*Exodos*).[11] Yet does the single Greek word really hold this kind of freight in Luke's story line? Using the criteria above, we can answer this question in the affirmative in spite of a lack of verbal repetition beyond this single Greek word.

First, the book of Exodus (and the tradition about its key redemptive event) was certainly available to Luke and his audience. We see this clearly in Luke 20:37, where Luke's Jesus refers to Moses' words in "the account of the burning bush" (Exod. 3).[12] Second, in addition to considering the issue of verbal repetition, it's important to take account of storied connections between Luke's transfiguration scene and the exodus narratives. Joel Green highlights quite a number of these to suggest that the exodus (and especially Exod. 24–34) is a key backdrop to Luke 9:28–36, including "the presence of companions, the setting on a mountain, the explicit mention of Moses, Jesus' change of countenance, reference to tents (or tabernacles), the cloud, [and] the motif of fear," in addition to the use of the term *exodos*.[13]

Although Luke does not use *exodos* elsewhere in his Gospel (cf. Heb. 11:22), the evangelist does evoke key events from the book of Exodus across his narrative, including Passover (Exod. 12), rescue through the Red Sea (Exod. 13–14), and provision while in the wilderness (Exod. 16–17):

- Exodus imagery in Zechariah's song (e.g., Luke 1:68–74)[14]
- Safety on [through] the waters (8:22–25)
- Provision of food in the wilderness (9:10–17)
- Jesus' celebration of the Passover with the apostles (22:14–20)

These storied allusions highlight Luke's own thematic interests for using exodus language and events: his readers should be thinking about the

11. For *exodus* as a reference to the event of Yahweh's redemption of Israel from Egypt, see, e.g., Exod. 19:1: "And three months after the *exodus* of the children of Israel from the land of Egypt . . ." (LXX).

12. Luke 2:23 also refers to the written account of firstborn consecration from Exod. 13:2.

13. Joel B. Green, *The Gospel of Luke*, NICNT (Grand Rapids: Eerdmans, 1997), 346.

14. Green, *The Gospel of Luke*, 126.

Israelite exodus from Egypt for understanding what Jesus will soon accomplish in Jerusalem. Through these echoes of the exodus, Luke evokes the foundational story of God's redemptive activity for God's people now recapitulated and magnified in the life, death, and resurrection of Jesus.

A Storied Intertextuality

As a new generation of scholars has built upon Hays' work, they have frequently emphasized the storied ways that authors draw upon the Old Testament (as in the Lukan example). Richard Beaton, for instance, has identified how the Jewish Scriptures function on two levels of a Gospel's narrative, what he refers to as the "bi-referentiality" of Old Testament citations in a Gospel.[15] In narrative-critical terms, Beaton is illuminating how quotations function on both the story level and the discourse level of a narrative.[16] Matthew 12—a text that is central to Beaton's work— provides a helpful example.

At Matthew 12:18–21 the evangelist cites Isaiah 42:1–4, the longest Old Testament citation in all of Matthew. It makes sense, then, to understand that Matthew is drawing on this text for multiple purposes. Applying Beaton's concept of "bi-referentiality," we can note that the Isaiah citation provides commentary on Matthew's story level by affirming Jesus' pattern of withdrawing from rather than embracing controversy (Matt. 12:15; also 14:13; 15:21). In Isaiah's language, the servant "will not quarrel" (Matt. 12:19a; cf. Isa. 42:2a). The part of the plot that includes Jesus' warning against spreading news about him finds a parallel in the Isaiah quotation, where we hear that "no one will hear his voice in the streets" (Matt. 12:19b; cf. Isa. 42:2b).

On the discourse level of his narrative, Matthew also appears to draw on the Isaiah quotation to reaffirm a number of themes he has been highlighting for the reader, the foremost being the identification of Jesus as the servant of the Lord. Matthew frequently uses texts from Isaiah's Servant Songs (spread across Isa. 42–53) to make this identification.[17] By doing so,

15. Richard Beaton, *Isaiah's Christ in Matthew's Gospel*, SNTSMS 123 (Cambridge: Cambridge University Press, 2002), 30–34.

16. See chap. 1, figs. 1.1 and 1.2; also Brown, *Scripture as Communication*, 157.

17. Citations from these "songs" occur at Matt. 8:17; 12:18–21, along with allusions at 3:17; 17:5; 20:28; 26:28. For more on these texts from Isaiah 42–53 and how Matthew uses them, see

Matthew signals that Jesus is the servant of the Lord who brings about restoration for Israel and, as Israel's representative, offers salvation to the nations. In this way, Matthew ties other important themes accented in this Isaiah citation to Jesus' Galilean ministry and beyond: justice,[18] mercy,[19] and the inclusion of the gentiles ("the nations") in God's redemptive work for Israel.[20]

Stories Evoking Stories

In my own research I have proposed a storied way of understanding how New Testament writers draw upon their Scriptures.[21] It is often the case that a few carefully chosen words or images from an Old Testament text evoke the larger story projected by that text and potentially part of the Old Testament metanarrative.

For example, in Luke 22:20 Jesus offers these words to the apostles as they together celebrate Passover on the night before his death: "This cup is the new covenant in my blood." For Luke's readers conversant in the Old Testament, the phrase "new covenant" (*kainēn diathēkēn*) would have readily brought to mind the Lord's promise in Jeremiah to "covenant a new covenant" (*diathēsomai . . . diathēkēn kainēn*; Jer. 31:31 AT; 38:31 LXX) with the people, especially as this language of "new covenant" occurs in the Greek Old Testament only here in Jeremiah (and in the Gospels only in Luke 22:20).[22] Luke's audience is being invited to consider God's future story for Israel from Jeremiah, though that is not the only story in view. The backstory of the Lord's covenant (*diathēkē*) with Israel as they were redeemed from Egypt (Exod. 6:4–5; 19:5; cf. Gen. 17:7) would also come to mind. The new covenant is a renewal of that original covenant, a renewal both like and unlike that first covenant

---

Jeannine K. Brown, "Matthew's Christology and Isaiah's Servant: A Fresh Look at a Perennial Issue," in *Treasures New and Old: Essays in Honor of Donald Hagner*, ed. Carl S. Sweatman and Clifford B. Kvidahl (Wilmore, KY: GlossaHouse, 2017), 93–106.

18. See, e.g., Matt. 5:6, 10; 8–9; 23:23; 25:31–46.

19. See, e.g., Matt. 8:3; 9:13, 36; 12:7; 14:14; 15:32.

20. See, e.g., Matt. 1:3, 5, 6; 2:1; 4:15; 8:5–13; 15:21–28; 21:43; 24:14; 28:19.

21. Brown, "Metalepsis"; and Jeannine K. Brown, "Genesis in Matthew's Gospel," in *Genesis in the New Testament*, ed. Maarten J. J. Menken and Steve Moyise (New York: T&T Clark, 2012), 42–59.

22. The reference in the Hebrew Old Testament and English versions is Jer. 31:31. The Septuagint text of Jeremiah differs at various points from the Hebrew in both length and ordering, and so in chapter and verse numbering.

(Jer. 31:32–34). Even the use of a small part of a familiar text could evoke these larger stories. "Given the conviction of the writers of the New Testament that Jesus the Messiah completes the story of the Old Testament, their liberal and evocative use of not only Scriptural texts but also the Scriptural stories surrounding those texts should come as no surprise."[23]

Narrative Patterns and People from the Old Testament to the New

In line with a storied approach to intertextuality, scholars have also suggested narrative ways that New Testament authors echo the Old Testament, without necessarily drawing on the wording of an Old Testament text. Peter Mallen identifies "narrative patterns" in the Gospels (and Luke-Acts, in particular) in addition to Old Testament citations and allusions. He defines a narrative pattern as "a series of events or interactions between characters whose similarity to those in an earlier text is apparent although the specific details and the language of expression may vary."[24] These patterns between Old and New Testaments might focus on a shared setting or a similarity of event(s).

For an example of a shared setting, we can return to John 4 and the conversation between Jesus and the Samaritan woman, who meet at a well. John's story setting seems to evoke similar scenes from Genesis of a man and a woman meeting at a well (see Gen. 24:15–27; 29:1–14).[25] Precisely what the Johannine author is doing with this "type scene" is a point of debate, but it seems likely that Mallen's concept of narrative pattern is at play in this part of John.[26]

We've already noted a correspondence of events between the Old Testament and the Gospels in our exploration of Luke's reliance on Exodus. Luke's plot echoes the story line of Exodus in Jesus' protection of his followers from danger on the waters (8:22–25) and his miraculous provision of food for large crowds (Luke 9:10–17). Through these events, Luke

23. Brown, "Metalepsis," 40.

24. Peter Mallen, *The Reading and Transformation of Isaiah in Luke-Acts* (New York: T&T Clark, 2008), 24.

25. This is the case despite a lack of linguistic ties between John 4 and the Septuagint of Genesis.

26. See discussion in chap. 4 of this type scene and its relevance for the characterization of the Samaritan woman.

very likely evokes Israel's foundational events in their exodus from Egypt through the waters (Exod. 14) and their wilderness experience of manna (e.g., Exod. 16–17). Just as these events in Exodus demonstrate God's protection and provision, the similar events in Luke show that God through Jesus protects and provides.

Besides narrative patterns of setting or event linking Old Testament and New Testament passages, we also see the evangelists referring to Old Testament persons for a variety of purposes. In John, for instance, we hear Moses mentioned twelve times. Sometimes the evangelist references Moses to tap into his role as lawgiver (e.g., John 1:17, 45; 7:19, 22; 9:29; cf. 8:5). Other times John draws a comparison between the redemption provided through Moses and the even greater salvation that Jesus brings (3:14; 6:32). Interestingly, John offers Moses as a **christological figure** (anticipating Jesus as Messiah) without even using Moses' name. He does so by referencing "the Prophet" (John 1:21, 25; 6:14; 7:40),[27] an allusion to Deuteronomy 18:15, which reads, "The LORD your God will raise up for you a prophet like me from among you, from your fellow Israelites. You must listen to him."

These words, attributed to Moses in Deuteronomy, point to a future prophet like Moses. Later Jewish writers would reference this future figure for their own theological purposes. For example, Philo, referring to future prophecy, writes, "A prophet possessed by God will suddenly appear and give prophetic oracles."[28] John draws on this "prophet like Moses" tradition in two distinct ways for christological purposes. First, we hear John the Baptist affirming that he is *not* "the Prophet" (John 1:21, 25). In this way, the evangelist introduces the category and invites the reader to consider who (besides John the Baptist) might fill this role in his narrative. Second, those who see Jesus feeding the crowds in miraculous ways and hear him offering living water at the Festival of Tabernacles conclude that he must be "the Prophet" (6:14; 7:40). Through this affirmation by the people, John suggests to his reader that Jesus is the Prophet who is like Moses (and who is greater than Moses). This is just one of quite a number of christological affirmations John draws from the Old Testament.

27. In each case, John uses the definite article with "prophet," which sets him apart from the other Gospel writers in this usage (e.g., Luke 24:19).

28. Philo, *On the Special Laws* 1.65, in *On the Special Laws*, trans. F. H. Colson, Loeb Classical Library 320 (Cambridge, MA: Harvard University Press, 2014).

A significant number of Old Testament persons show up at the very beginning of Matthew's Gospel, in his opening genealogy. The genealogy of Jesus begins with Abraham and concludes with Joseph, Jesus' father (Matt. 1:2–16). A unique feature of this genealogy is the inclusion of four women early in the genealogy: Tamar (1:3), Rahab (1:5), Ruth (1:5), and "Uriah's wife" (1:6). Since ancient genealogies did not typically include mothers, their presence is marked—their inclusion would be immediately noticed and explored for meaning. In seeking what these four have in common, their non-Jewish identities stand out. Tamar is a Canaanite (Gen. 38:2), as is Rahab (from Jericho in Canaan; Josh. 2:1), and Ruth is a Moabite (Ruth 1:4). And, while Bathsheba's origins are not clearly spelled out in the Old Testament (see 2 Sam. 11:3), Matthew's designation of her as "Uriah's wife" accents her gentile association by marriage ("Uriah the Hittite"; e.g., 2 Sam. 11:3, 6, 17, 21, 24).

If Matthew's purpose for including Tamar, Rahab, Ruth, and "Uriah's wife" is to highlight the presence of gentiles within the line of the Messiah, this fits nicely with his broader theme of gentile inclusion. This motif, beginning with these four women, continues across Matthew, concluding with the commission for Jesus' disciples to disciple all the nations (see fig. 6.1).

Figure 6.1
Matthew's Gentile Inclusion Theme

Reference	Person(s) or Text	Action or Reference
2:1–12	Magi	Worship Jesus
4:12–16	Old Testament citation from Isaiah	"Galilee of the Gentiles"
8:5–13	(Roman) centurion	Great faith
12:18–21	Old Testament citation from Isaiah	"Justice to the nations"
15:21–28	Canaanite woman	Great faith
27:19	Wife of Pilate	Calls Jesus "innocent"
27:54	(Roman) centurion	Affirms Jesus as "Son of God"
28:19–20	Disciples commissioned by Jesus	"Make disciples of all nations"

How the Gospel Writers Use the Old Testament

In our review of how scholars have understood and navigated intertextuality, I've introduced a number of terms, including *citations*, *allusions*, and *echoes* (see fig. 6.2). Let's take a closer look at each of these as we think about *how* the Gospel writers use the Old Testament.

Figure 6.2
Intertextual Definitions

Citation: An Old Testament reference involving significant verbal repetition, often involving one or more verses of an Old Testament text
Allusion: An Old Testament reference of a few words (e.g., two to four words), often with a thematic connection included that helps with recognition
Echo: An implicit evocation of an Old Testament text, with some verbal and/or conceptual connections in view (recognized as they accumulate)

Citations of the Old Testament

A citation is an Old Testament reference that involves significant verbal repetition, often including one or more verses from an Old Testament text.[29] In cases of citation, there is no question that the New Testament writer is drawing on an Old Testament text. For example, in Luke Jesus begins his public ministry in his hometown of Nazareth. While he is in the synagogue on the Sabbath, he reads from the scroll of Isaiah (Luke 4:16–17)—specifically Isaiah 61:1–2. Luke uses this multi-verse citation to frame Jesus' entire ministry; it speaks to Jesus' mission of good news, healing, and freedom for those who are destitute, hurting, and captive (Luke 4:18–19).

Given a length that exceeds more than a few words, it is possible for any particular citation to explore the question of the specific source text used. The **source text** (or what's often called the "text form") is the particular version of the Old Testament verse(s) that a New Testament author seems to be using. The Old Testament was originally written in Hebrew.[30] By the first century, when the New Testament was written, the Old Testament had been translated into Greek, the trade language of the Mediterranean world at that time, with the Septuagint being one important Greek version. Most early Christians would have accessed the Old Testament in Greek—a language most knew—rather than in Hebrew. The quotations across the New Testament indicate that the New Testament writers defaulted to the Septuagint, although some show signs in their Old Testament quotations that

29. The definitions offered in this section are based on Jeannine K. Brown, *Matthew*, Teach the Text New Testament Commentary (Grand Rapids: Baker Books, 2015), 19.
30. With a few parts composed in Aramaic: Ezra 4:8–6:18; 7:12–26; Dan. 2:4b–7:28.

they knew and used Hebrew.[31] Determining what source text might have been used in any particular citation is a question that scholars explore.

Let's look at an example. In Matthew 8 the evangelist cites Isaiah 53:4: "He is the one who took our illnesses and carried away our diseases" (Matt. 8:17 CEB). To consider the question of what source text Matthew uses, we can compare an English translation of the Hebrew of Isaiah 53:4 (here, the CEB) and an English translation of the Septuagint (the NETS—an English translation of the Greek Septuagint):

Hebrew (CEB English translation)	Septuagint (NETS English translation)
Isaiah 53:4	Isaiah 53:4
It was certainly our *sickness* that he carried, and our *sufferings* that he bore.	This one bears our *sins* and *suffers pain* for us.

By comparing the nouns of the Hebrew and the Greek Septuagint (in translation), we can surmise the source text.[32] While the Hebrew carries the emphasis of sickness (and potentially suffering arising from it), the Greek has a focus on sin (and potentially pain arising from it). Turning to Matthew, we can see that the evangelist uses a text that focuses on sickness rather than sin: "He is the one who took our *illnesses* and carried away our *diseases*" (Matt. 8:17 CEB). This suggests that Matthew draws his Isaiah citation from the Hebrew rather than the Greek. If we compare the Greek terms, we can see that the two Greek words Matthew uses are different ones than in the Greek of the Septuagint:

- Matthew: *astheneia* ("illness") and *nosos* ("disease")
- Septuagint: *hamartia* ("sin") and *odunaō* (a verb: "to suffer pain")

What does this kind of textual comparison offer for better understanding Matthew's use of Isaiah? By noticing that Matthew seems to

31. Or potentially a Greek translation that was more like the Hebrew than the Septuagint. Sometime prior to the first century, some Greek versions of the Old Testament began to be revised to align more closely with Hebrew versions. For example, Greek versions by Aquila (mid-second century CE) and Theodotion (late second century CE) show signs of this alignment. Karen H. Jobes and Moisés Silva, *Invitation to the Septuagint*, 2nd ed. (Grand Rapids: Baker Academic, 2015), 24–29.

32. The second noun in the NETS is actually a verb in the Greek Septuagint, meaning "to suffer pain."

be carefully aligning this Isaiah citation with the focus from the Hebrew text on sickness and disease, we might more easily pick up a key emphasis in Matthew: Jesus as healer. This motif begins already in Matthew 4, where one of the three kingdom summary activities is healing: "Jesus went throughout Galilee . . . healing every disease [*nosos*] and sickness among the people" (4:23; cf. 9:35). Jesus as healer is on full display in Matthew 8–9. Just prior to the evangelist's citation of Isaiah 53:4, he has narrated three of Jesus' healings (Matt. 8:1–15) and a summary of many more (8:16). Jesus is a Messiah with power and compassion to heal.

Allusions to the Old Testament

An allusion is an Old Testament reference that consists of just a few (e.g., two to four) words and often includes a thematic tie from the original context to the Gospel's new setting that increases the recognition factor of the allusion.[33] One example of a brief but clear allusion comes in Mark 11:17, as Jesus has cleared out the temple courts where animals have been sold for sacrifice. He accuses the Jewish leadership in charge of the temple of making it "a den of robbers."

This brief phrase alludes to Jeremiah 7:11, which is part of a divine message Jeremiah is to deliver for the reforming of God's people (7:1–3). It warns against a false hope in the safety and indestructability of the temple (7:4, 10). If God's people are living unjustly and oppressing "the foreigner, the fatherless or the widow," they are deceived to trust in the safety of the temple (7:4–8). If they "steal and murder" and commit idolatry and other sins and then think going to the temple will protect them, they will be proven wrong because God sees all (7:9–11). In this climactic point in the divine oracle, God's words ring out: "Has this house, which bears my Name, become a den of robbers to you?" The oracle then goes on to foreshadow the temple's destruction (which occurred in 586 BCE) because of the people's unfaithfulness (7:12–15).

From this oracle, Mark draws out the short phrase "a den of robbers" in his account of Jesus' clearing the temple courts. In its new context,

---

33. It is also the case that citations often involve a thematic connection between Old Testament and New Testament contexts, but with an allusion's fewer words the thematic connection is all the more helpful for recognizing the allusion.

the phrase is an indictment of practices of buying and selling animals for sacrifice that would have been a significant disruption in the court of the gentiles, where such commerce would have largely happened.[34] Though brief (just two words in both Hebrew and Greek),[35] the particularity of the phrase and striking nature of the image clearly signal the allusion. And Mark's Jesus uses this phrase as a warning that the present temple will not escape judgment if its leaders, like the people Jeremiah indicted, do not return to God in covenant faithfulness (see Mark 12:38–40; 13:1–2).

Echoes of the Old Testament

An echo is an implicit evocation of an Old Testament text that usually has limited verbal connections but does offer important conceptual or storied ties between the Old Testament and the New Testament passage in view. As we have explored above, echoes may come in the form of narrative patterns from Old Testament to New or by reference to specific characters. Given the minimalism of textual clues for an echo, they are often recognized only in their accumulation. That is, an argument that a Gospel writer is intentionally echoing a part of the Old Testament or its story grows stronger as additional (potential) echoes are identified in the narrative.[36]

Take, for example, the word picture in John 15 of Jesus as a vine and his followers as branches (15:1, 5). This image may echo one or more Old Testament texts where Israel is pictured as a vine tended by God though often unfruitful (e.g., Isa. 27:2–6; Jer. 2:21; Ezek. 17:1–10).[37] An additional clue that Israel as a vine provides the background for John 15 is the repeated reference to an unproductive vine withering and being burned (John 15:6; cf. Ezek. 17:9; 19:12–14).

What does John mean by these combined echoes? Just this: Jesus as "the true vine" is identified as faithful Israel (John 15:1), and he comes

---

34. A citation from Isa. 56:7 begins the indictment, since the temple was to be "a house of prayer for all nations" (Isa. 56:7; Mark 11:17a).

35. The Greek, *spēlaion lēstōn*, occurs in the Septuagint of both Jer. 7:11 and Mark 11:17. While this likely indicates that Mark is drawing on the Septuagint for this citation, the Greek renders quite closely the Hebrew phrase *ham'arat paritsim*.

36. This is the criterion of repeated use mentioned above.

37. See Hays' discussion of these and other intertexts for John's imagery in Richard B. Hays, *Echoes of Scripture in the Gospels* (Waco: Baylor University Press, 2016), 336–37.

to complete the mission intended for God's people. Hays also suggests that John may be echoing Psalm 80 to connect Jesus with "the son of man" referenced there—imagery for Israel's king who comes to save (Ps. 80:17–18).[38]

It is helpful to note that these particular echoes in John are not necessarily tied to one specific Old Testament text. Instead, they draw on a common Old Testament image for Israel. We might even say these echoes evoke a story line. They tap into the story, drawn from a number of Old Testament passages, of Israel as a vine and God as the one who plants—the gardener (John 15:1). The story line would include God's tender care for them (Ezek. 17:5–6), Israel's lack of fruit (Jer. 2:21), and the promise of their restored fruitfulness (Isa. 27).[39] John marshals this part of the Old Testament story to indicate that Jesus (and those who abide in him) fulfills Israel's calling to be God's fruitful vine (and branches).

Why the Gospel Writers Use the Old Testament

To conclude our review of intertextuality, we consider why the Gospel writers use the Old Testament in the stories they tell about Jesus. We will focus attention especially on some of the evangelists' theological purposes for using the Old Testament—whether by citation, allusion, or echo—as well as the rhetorical impact this use has on their audiences.

God at Work—As Then, So Now

An important way that the Gospel writers draw upon the Old Testament is for what we might call *theological analogy*. The evangelists generally see significant continuity between what God has done in humanity's (often specifically Israel's) history and what God is doing now, in climactic ways, in the life and ministry of Jesus. To emphasize such similarities, Old Testament texts or stories are cited or evoked to clarify the activity of God in Jesus—to express the *theological meaning of Jesus*.

38. Hays, *Echoes of Scripture in the Gospels*, 337.
39. As noted above, this kind of evocation of context beyond the specific echo is called metalepsis, a literary feature that may also accompany citations and allusions. As we've been assuming across this chapter, whole Old Testament contexts and stories may be evoked by the use of a verse, phrase, or even an echo from the Old Testament.

An interesting example—interesting because it is sometimes used to demonstrate a strong *discontinuity* between the Old and New Testaments— comes in John's prologue. In John 1:17, a contrast between Old Testament law and New Testament grace is often suggested: "For the law was given through Moses; grace and truth came through Jesus Christ."

Yet if we back up and look at the intertextual clues to Exodus in the wider context (John 1:14–18), we see indications of continuity between God's revelatory work in the law and in Jesus, even though John will, not surprisingly, highlight how Jesus is the climax of God's revelation.

> The Word became flesh and *made his dwelling* [*skēnaō*] among us. We have seen his *glory* [*doxa*], the glory [*doxa*] of the one and only Son, who came from the Father, full of *grace and truth*. . . . Out of his fullness we have all received grace in place of grace already given. For *the law* was given through *Moses*; *grace and truth* came through Jesus Christ. *No one has ever seen God*, but the one and only Son, who is himself God and is in closest relationship with the Father, has made him known. (John 1:14, 16–18, emphasis added)

The italicized words above are potential echoes from across Exodus, with the Septuagint of Exodus using the term *skēnē* for the tabernacle, the place where God chooses to dwell among the people of Israel (e.g., Exod. 25:9; 40:2, 28).[40] John uses the related verb *skēnaō* to indicate the "tabernacling" of God with humanity in Jesus, the Word become flesh. This term coupled with "glory" (*doxa* in the Greek) provides a strong case that John here evokes Exodus and specifically its final moments, when the glory (*doxa*) of the Lord fills the tabernacle (*skēnē*; Exod. 40:34–35). John's language of "grace and truth" (using *charis* and *alētheia*) also echoes, though not in precise language, a revelatory high point in Exodus, when God gives the law to Israel and is revealed as "the compassionate and gracious God, slow to anger, abounding in *love* and *faithfulness*" (Exod. 34:6, emphasis added).[41] Finally, John seems to be evoking the vignette of Moses seeing God's glory though not his face (Exod. 33:18–23) when he declares that "no one has ever seen God" (John 1:18).

40. The term itself occurs close to one hundred times in Exod. 25–40, the section of the book devoted to instructions for and building of the tabernacle.

41. Anthony Hanson provides a review of scholars on the question of this allusion and the linguistic argument for it. Hanson, "John 1:14–18 and Exodus 34," *NTS* 23 (1976): 90–101.

These numerous connections to Exodus suggest that John's readers are to have these associations and stories from Exodus in mind as they think about how Jesus reveals the one true God. Rather than dichotomizing law and grace, the reader should hear how grace and truth were already revealed as part of the divine character at the giving of the law through Moses (Exod. 34:4–7). As John puts it, "The law *was given* through Moses; grace and truth *were embodied* in Jesus Christ" (John 1:17 AT). John seems to land on the contrast of the verbs more than the nouns (the names). And while this comparison clearly shows Jesus to be the climax of the covenant and the full revelation of God (1:18), there is no disparagement of the law here. Instead, John highlights Jesus as the full revelation of the God who has now come in the flesh.

Christology: Showing Who Jesus Is

In addition to illustrating a theological analogy, this example from John is one of many in which the Gospel writers draw on the Old Testament for their Christologies (their portraits of Jesus), with each Gospel having a distinctive Christology (see fig. 4.1).

At first blush we might think of the use of the Old Testament for Christology as primarily or even exclusively a matter of prediction. And it is the case that the evangelists may tie the Old Testament to their Christology by referencing a messianic prophecy. Messianic predictions often revolve around foretelling the coming of a king like David, who is projected as the ideal king in the Old Testament prophets. Passages like Micah 5—a text that celebrates Bethlehem, David's birthplace, as the origins of a future king who will shepherd God's people (Mic. 5:2–4; cf. John 7:42)—come to mind. Matthew cites this prophecy and signals Jesus as that king (Matt. 2:1–6). Later in the same chapter, Matthew plays on the word "Nazarene" (2:23), probably evoking the Hebrew *netser* (meaning "branch") from Isaiah 11:1, which itself has messianic connotations: "A shoot will come up from the stump of Jesse; from his roots a Branch [*netser*] will bear fruit."[42]

Many of the Old Testament references in the Gospels, however, do not focus on prediction. As we've seen in John, the use of analogy (sometimes called "typology") is often at the forefront of an evangelist's use of the

---

42. This messianic connotation for *netser* is attested in the Dead Sea Scrolls (1QHᵃ 15:19).

Old Testament. God's work through Jesus is understood in significant continuity with God's work in Israel's history, even as Jesus' life and mission are affirmed as the climactic completion of the story of the Old Testament. One way this kind of analogy works christologically is when an evangelist employs a representative role from the Old Testament to illuminate Jesus' identity and work. Through analogy Jesus is portrayed, for example, as prophet, king, faithful Israel, or priest, and, in each case, as the idealization of that role.[43]

Impacting the Reader

In addition to having theological and christological purposes, the use of the Old Testament in the Gospels is also meant to impact readers in specific ways. Sometimes an Old Testament reference functions as a guide toward godly behavior, as when Matthew's Jesus commends lavish forgiveness ("seventy-seven times"; Matt. 18:22) in contrast to escalating revenge in the parallel "seventy-seven times" in Genesis 4:24.[44] An Old Testament echo might also function within a warning—as in "the days of Noah" and "the days of Lot" (Luke 17:26, 28), warning believers to be prepared for "the day the Son of Man is revealed" (17:30).

We could also note the more general effects of a Gospel writer using the Old Testament. These references, generally speaking, provide a kind of authorization of what they are claiming about Jesus. This is especially the case given that when the Gospels are written there is no New Testament, only Israel's Scriptures. It might also be helpful to consider other readerly responses to the use of the Old Testament in the Gospels. The experience of recognition itself (of a familiar and authoritative text) would tend to evoke positive associations. And the evangelists' frequent evocation of the storied context of the Old Testament suggests that they are locating themselves and their readers in that broad and wide story of God's work in redemptive history. In this way, the Gospel writers draw readers into that larger story and invite them to follow Jesus, who brings that story to its culmination.

---

43. On the latter category, see Nicholas Perrin, *Jesus the Priest* (Grand Rapids: Baker Academic, 2019).

44. For a discussion of this allusion, see Brown, "Metalepsis," 37–40.

Conclusion

In this chapter, we have explored how the Gospel writers draw deeply from the reservoir of Israel's Scriptures to communicate who Jesus is and how his identity and mission are integrally connected to the divine mission for Israel and the world. I've suggested that it is beneficial to bring a storied lens to the issue and task of intertextuality, since foundational texts are themselves embedded in the larger stories of their communities. In the next chapter, we examine two motifs from John's Gospel that have their backstory in the Old Testament: Jesus as the Passover lamb and the renewal of creation that begins in Jesus' ministry and especially at his resurrection.

7

Intertextuality in John

Passover Lamb and Creation's Renewal

John's Gospel has fewer explicit Old Testament citations than the other Gospels do, and yet his use of the Old Testament is not at all limited to these (longer) quotations. John is quite liberal in his use of the Old Testament through allusions and echoes. For example, John paints Jesus as "the good shepherd" (10:11), in contrast to a "hired hand" (10:12–13) or a "thief" (10:1, 10). Ezekiel 34 very likely provides the Old Testament backdrop for this christological portrait, even though there are no citations from that chapter of Ezekiel in John 10. In Ezekiel 34 the Lord indicts Israel's leaders—their shepherds—for neglecting their role in guiding and guarding Israel. Israel is like a flock that has become prey for wild animals (34:5) because their shepherds have taken care of themselves instead of the flock (34:2). In John's context, Jesus has been indicting Pharisees for their blindness as leaders (9:35–41). John draws on potent images from the Old Testament to accent Jesus as the good shepherd in contrast to these Pharisees, who act at best like hired hands.

In this chapter, we take a closer look at two motifs that arise out of John's reliance on the Old Testament, one christological and one theological. We begin with the identification of Jesus as the incomparable Passover lamb, which John intimates early on in his Gospel and confirms through a citation from Exodus at the time of Jesus' death. The chapter concludes with an exploration of the motif of creation's renewal or "re-creation" in John. This theological theme finds its foundations in Genesis 1–2 and is signaled early on in John—in the very first words of the Gospel. It finds its conclusion in a brief but clear allusion to the breath of life from Genesis 2 given to the disciples after Jesus' resurrection.

Jesus as the Passover Lamb

Paul, in 1 Corinthians, calls Jesus "our Passover lamb" (5:7; Greek *pascha*). While this phrase is not attached explicitly to Jesus in the Gospels, John implicitly identifies Jesus as the Passover lamb through a number of Old Testament echoes, one citation, and other narrative markers. These references build across the Gospel to provide a compelling portrait of Jesus as the Passover lamb whose death brings freedom from sin and death. In the first part of this chapter, we explore these echoes and markers sequentially as they occur in John.

The Baptist's Affirmation: "Look, the Lamb of God!"

The first hint of this motif comes in the earliest part of John's story line (1:19–42). John the Baptist has clarified that he is not the Messiah but has the role of preparing the way for one who is greater (1:19–28). In the next scene the Baptist sees Jesus and proclaims, "Look, the Lamb of God, who takes away the sin of the world!" (1:29). This identification of Jesus by John the Baptist is significant. Not only is the Baptist the first character in John's story to testify to the identity of Jesus, but he is also affirmed for his role as witness (one who testifies) in John's prologue (1:6–8, 15). John the Baptist repeats this same description a day later: "Look, the Lamb of God!" (1:36).

What does "Lamb of God" (who takes away sin) signal for John's readers? The Old Testament provides more than one potential point of reference for this image. The most likely of these echoes are (1) a sacrificial lamb that addresses the "penalty for . . . sin" (e.g., Lev. 5:6); (2) the lamb symbolizing Isaiah's servant, who takes Israel's iniquity (Isa. 53:6–7); and (3) the Passover lamb, whose sacrifice protected Israel's firstborn from death (Exod. 12:1–12).[1] While these are not necessarily mutually

---

1. Craig S. Keener, *Gospel of John* (Grand Rapids: Baker Academic, 2010), 452–54. Keener also adds the category of apocalyptic or eschatological lambs of the messianic era arising from 1 Enoch (452), though not from the Old Testament.

exclusive (i.e., there could be more than one intertextual horizon), John's subsequent clues will lead the reader most clearly toward the final category of the Passover lamb. Although the Passover lamb of Exodus 12 offers the weakest connection to sin's removal (of the three possibilities in their Old Testament context), "early Judaism attached the nuances of sacrifice to Passover."[2] Through this affirmation from John the Baptist within the story line, the evangelist introduces Jesus as the preeminent Passover lamb.

Passover in John

Another indication that John means to identify Jesus as the Passover lamb comes in his emphasis on the Festival of Passover in his story line. While the Synoptics each record a single Passover (e.g., Mark 14:1, 12), John explicitly references three discrete Passovers (see John 2:13; 6:4; 13:1).[3] The account of the clearing of the temple during the first Passover occurs early in the Fourth Gospel (2:13–25; cf. 4:45). This early placement, along with the Passover's prominence at Jesus' death—the apex of the story—has the effect of "framing [Jesus'] whole ministry with the shadow of the passion week and its Johannine association with Passover."[4]

The Jewish Passover was integrally tied to the Israelites' exodus from Egypt, memorializing God's "passing over" of households that had the blood of a lamb on their doorframes (Exod. 12). The firstborn, both people and animals, in these houses were spared from death—the final plague visited upon Egypt (Exod. 11). The key symbols or elements of the Passover Festival were the lamb and unleavened bread (bread without yeast, to recall the hasty departure from Egypt; see Exod. 12:39; 13:3, 6–8). The festival was celebrated during the month of Nisan in the Jewish calendar,

2. Keener, *Gospel of John*, 454. For instance, Josephus speaks of the Jewish people offering "the sacrifice" during the Passover celebration, connecting the Passover lamb with sacrifice (*Antiquities* 2.312).

3. Some think that the unnamed festival of 5:1 may be another Passover. In 13:1 and across chaps. 11–19, John references the final Passover numerous times.

4. Keener, *Gospel of John*, 452. In comparison with the Synoptics' abbreviated time frame, John provides at least two and a half years of story time built around these three Passovers. Yet "it may be that John is less interested in *three* Passovers (years) than in three *Passovers*, the feast he most carefully emphasizes." Jeannine K. Brown, "Chronology and the NT," in *Dictionary for Theological Interpretation of the Bible*, ed. Kevin Vanhoozer (Grand Rapids: Baker Academic, 2005), 112–14, here 113.

which spans parts of March and April in our contemporary calendar.[5] It began on the fourteenth day of Nisan and lasted for a week (Exod. 12:18; Lev. 23:4–8). Passover commenced at sundown, in line with the Jewish reckoning of the start of a day. "The LORD's Passover begins at twilight on the fourteenth day of the first month" (Lev. 23:5).

John capitalizes on both Passover symbols—the bread and the lamb—for his Christology. Bread is emphasized in John's second Passover (6:4), which provides the setting for Jesus' miracles (or "signs")[6] of the feeding of the five thousand (6:1–15) and of walking on water (6:16–24).[7] As John 6 continues, Passover provides an ideal backdrop for Jesus' discourse on bread and sustenance and for the revelation that he is "the bread of life" (6:35, 48).

The third and final Passover (this time in Jerusalem) provides the setting for Jesus' death (18:28, 39; 19:14). This Passover is the extended setting for the last half of John's Gospel, with frequent references anticipating its arrival:

- 11:55: "When it was almost time for the *Jewish Passover*, many went up from the country to Jerusalem for their ceremonial cleansing *before Passover*."
- 12:1: "Six days before *the Passover*, Jesus came to Bethany" (sets the stage for Mary's anointing of Jesus).
- 12:12: "The next day the great crowd that had come for *the festival*" (introduces crowd's acclamation of Jesus as he enters Jerusalem).
- 12:20: "Now there were some Greeks among those who went up to worship at *the festival*."
- 13:1: "It was just before the *Passover Festival*" (sets the stage for Jesus washing the disciples' feet; in the same scene, see 13:29).

These repeated references to Passover form a string of echoes to the Old Testament, whether Exodus or Leviticus (or presumably elsewhere where Passover is mentioned). Yet it is less important to identify precisely

5. Nisan (e.g., Esther 3:7) was earlier referred to as Aviv (Exod. 13:4) and was identified as the first month of the Jewish year (Exod. 12:2; Lev. 23:5).
6. See the role of the Johannine "signs" in our discussion on the renewal of creation below.
7. The geographical setting for this second Passover is Galilee (John 6:1, 16–17, 25, 59) rather than Jerusalem (2:13).

a textual location for the echo than to recognize that such proper nouns may evoke any part of the history of the Passover, including its origins.

The Time of Jesus' Death in John

As we come to the part of story dedicated to Jesus' death, John signals narratively (and so implicitly) that Jesus is the Passover lamb. He does this by highlighting the timing of Jesus' crucifixion on "the day of Preparation" (John 19:14–16), when the Passover lambs were slaughtered in the area of the Jerusalem temple (i.e., on Nisan 14).

A large number of lambs had to be killed in Jerusalem for the Passover meal, especially as pilgrims to the festival would have swelled the city's population to much larger than its usual size. In preparation for the meal, which would have been eaten after sundown on the first day of Passover (Nisan 15), it is likely that the slaughter of lambs would have extended across the afternoon of Nisan 14, between about noon and sundown.[8]

John expressly notes that, when Jewish leaders bring Jesus to the palace of the Roman governor Pilate in the early morning, they intentionally avoid entering the palace so as not to become ceremonially unclean (18:28). Presumably they were already ritually clean, having pursued ceremonial cleansing in preparation for the Passover (see 11:55). John gives the reason for their scrupulous attention to purity—so they might "eat the Passover" (18:28). This locates Jesus' trial before Pilate on the morning of Nisan 14, just prior to the beginning of the first day of Passover when evening arrived (for the chronology involved, see fig. 7.1).[9]

John includes the time of day in the temporal setting for Jesus' crucifixion: "It was the day of Preparation of the Passover; it was about noon" (19:14). Craig Koester summarizes the significance of this time stamp: "Jesus was taken to be crucified on the Day of Preparation of the Passover at noon or 'the sixth hour,' which was the time the sacrificing [of lambs]

---

8. Craig R. Koester, *Symbolism in the Fourth Gospel: Meaning, Mystery, Community*, 2nd ed. (Minneapolis: Fortress, 2003), 220 (cf. *m. Pesahim* 5:1–10). As noted above, in Jewish reckoning, a day began at sundown and would continue until the inception of the following evening.

9. It is telling that John clearly avoids shaping Jesus' final meal with his disciples as a Passover meal (13:2). It occurs "just before the Passover Festival" (13:1) and not during it. There are no references to a cup (wine) or to the institution of the Lord's Supper more generally. For hints in Matthew that the Passover meal that Jesus celebrates with his disciples occurs a day early (and so is similar to John's chronology), see Jeannine K. Brown and Kyle Roberts, *Matthew*, THNTC (Grand Rapids: Eerdmans, 2018), 236–37.

began, and Jesus' sacrifice was completed before evening came (19:14, 31)."[10] In this way, John reaffirms Jesus as the Passover lamb.

Figure 7.1
The Timing of Jesus' Crucifixion in John

Nisan 14: The day of Preparation for Passover (Friday)	Nisan 15: First day of the Passover Festival (Saturday—Sabbath)
Evening: <ul><li>Upper Room Discourse (John 13–17): "It was just before the Passover Festival" (13:1)</li><li>Jesus' arrest and Jewish trial (18:1–27)</li></ul>	*Evening:* <ul><li>Jews would have eaten the Passover meal (after sundown)</li></ul>
Early in the Morning: <ul><li>(Early) Jewish leaders avoid governor's palace so they can "eat the Passover" (18:28)</li><li>Roman trial (18:29–19:13)</li></ul>	*Whole day—from sundown to sundown:*
Afternoon (during which time the Passover lambs would have been killed): <ul><li>Pilate delivers Jesus to be crucified (19:14–16a); "it was about noon" (19:14)</li><li>Jesus is crucified (19:16b–29)</li><li>Jesus dies (19:30)</li><li>Request for legs of those crucified to be broken before Sabbath arrives (at sundown; 19:31)</li><li>Jesus laid in nearby tomb (19:42)</li></ul>	<ul><li>Rest/no work, as it was the Sabbath (in fact, it was a "special Sabbath" [19:31], since it was both Sabbath and the first day of Passover in that year)</li></ul>

Exodus Echo and Citation

Final confirmation of John's portrait of Jesus as the Passover lamb comes in an echo and in a citation from Exodus, both drawn from the discussion of Passover in Exodus 12.

The echo appears in the crucifixion scene, right before Jesus' death (John 19:28–30). "Later, knowing that everything had now been finished, and so that Scripture would be fulfilled, Jesus said, 'I am thirsty.' A jar of wine vinegar was there, so they soaked a sponge in it, put the sponge on a stalk of the hyssop plant [*hyssōpos*], and lifted it to Jesus' lips. When he had received the drink, Jesus said, 'It is finished.' With that, he bowed his head and gave up his spirit."

---

10. Koester, *Symbolism in the Fourth Gospel*, 220.

John may be making note of the hyssop to evoke Exodus 12:22, where this plant (*hyssōpos* in the Septuagint) was to be the means of applying the blood of the Passover lamb to the doorframe of the house.[11] The likelihood is all the greater given John's affirmation that Jesus speaks of his thirst *in order to fulfill Scripture*. Hyssop provides the scriptural tie. And the connection hints again at Jesus' role as the Passover lamb, whose blood (i.e., death) is the means of deliverance and freedom.

Following Jesus' death, John narrates the breaking of the legs of those who had been crucified to avoid having their bodies left on the crosses over the Sabbath (19:31b–32). Given that Jesus is already dead, the soldiers don't break his legs (19:33). John concludes this narrative thread with a citation from Exodus 12, introduced by a fulfillment formula: "These things happened so that the scripture would be fulfilled: 'Not one of his bones will be broken'" (19:36). Here, John has one (or more) of three Old Testament texts in view: Exodus 12:46; Numbers 9:12; and Psalm 34:20 (compared here in Greek).

Figure 7.2
John 19:36 Allusion

John 19:36	*ostoun ou syntribēsetai autou*
	bone—not—will be broken—his [or its]
Exodus 12:46	*ostoun ou syntripsete ap' autou*
	bone—not—you will break—from it
Numbers 9:12	*ostoun ou syntripsousin ap' autou*
	bone—not—they will break—from it
Psalm 34:20 (33:21 LXX)*	The Lord guards all their bones [*osta*]†
	hen ex autōn ou syntribēsetai
	one—of—them—not—will be broken

* The chapter and verse numberings of the psalm differ among the Hebrew and its ancient and modern translations. Psalm 34:20 in English translations is 34:21 in Hebrew and 33:21 in the Septuagint (LXX).
† The pronoun "their" refers back to "the righteous ones" of the previous verse.

Both Exodus and Numbers refer to the Passover lamb (with Numbers clearly alluding back to Exodus). Both texts share with John the

---

11. Each of the Gospels references the wine vinegar in the parallel passage (Matt. 27:48; Mark 15:36; Luke 23:36). Only John refers to the hyssop (Matthew and Mark use a more generic term, translated "staff"). This specificity increases the likelihood that John intends to echo the Passover regulations of Exodus.

singular "bone" (*ostoun*) belonging to the singular person (or lamb; *autou*). Both also share the same verb with John (*syntribō*, "to break") but use the active form rather than the passive form of John ("you/they will break" vs. "will be broken"). The psalm, on the other hand, shares the passive form with John but differs by the inclusion of the plural for both the referent of the phrase ("the righteous"; Ps. 33:20 LXX) and for the word "bones" (*osta*) before isolating a single bone ("not one of them"; *hen ex auton*).[12]

While we can't be certain, it seems likely that John draws his citation from Exodus (since Numbers derives from Exodus). Maarten Menken suggests that both the psalm and Exodus are in view in John, given that the Johannine citation shares commonalities with both.[13] And the Jewish writing Jubilees (ca. 100 BCE) already brings together Psalm 34 and Exodus 12, increasing the possibility of their intentional combination by John as well: "And they shall not cook it with water, nor shall they eat it raw, but roast on the fire: they shall eat it with diligence, its head with the inwards thereof and its feet they shall roast with fire, and *not break any bone thereof;* for *of the children of Israel no bone shall be crushed*" (Jub. 49:13, emphasis added).[14]

Our discussion of the citation at John 19:36 illustrates the complexities of intertextual analysis when there is more than one possible Old Testament **intertext**. These complexities involve comparison in the Bible's original languages and are heightened by issues of the source texts of any particular New Testament citation (e.g., Does the Old Testament citation derive from Greek or Hebrew?). Our discussion has suggested that John is drawing on Exodus 12 (at least) to explain the significance of Jesus' bones remaining intact, when the others who are crucified with him have their legs broken (John 19:18, 32). Jesus, as the preeminent Passover lamb,

---

12. In Hebrew a single righteous person is in view, so it is possible John is using the Hebrew (Ps. 34:21) as the source text for this quotation.

13. Maarten J. J. Menken, *Old Testament Quotations in the Fourth Gospel: Studies in Textual Form* (Kampen, Netherlands: Kok Pharos, 1996), 152. If both texts are in view, John is highlighting Jesus as the Passover lamb (Exod. 12) *and* as the righteous sufferer whom God will vindicate (Ps. 34): "It seems that the evangelist consciously presents Jesus in two different roles at the same time" (166).

14. Charles, R. H. *The Apocrypha and Pseudepigrapha of the Old Testament* (Oxford: Clarendon, 1913). The reference to "the children of Israel" in Jubilees seems to be an interpretation of "the righteous" (plural) from the psalms (LXX; Ps. 33:20)—a common association made in the Psalter.

fulfills the Exodus regulation for the Passover lambs: "Not one of his bones will be broken."

We have explored the motif of Jesus as the Passover lamb, from John the Baptist's initial identification ("Look, the Lamb of God!") to John's intensive focus on Passover across his narrative, to the timing of Jesus' death in conjunction with the slaughter of the Passover lambs. We have concluded our exploration of this theme where John does—with the hyssop echo and the fuller citation from Exodus 12.

What do we gain from following this Johannine trail of clues toward the image of Jesus as the Passover lamb? Just this: if Jesus is the Passover lamb, then John's readers can be assured that, as they trust in Jesus, his death brings about their redemption and freedom from sin and death.[15] As the Passover lamb was given in place of Israel's firstborn for their preservation, so Jesus dies in order that his people and, indeed, "the whole world" (John 12:19; cf. 3:16) might be preserved from death.

The Renewal of Creation

Another of John's themes that emerges from his use of the Old Testament is the renewal of creation that comes through Jesus' incarnation, death, and resurrection.[16] While humanity's redemption is central to John's vision (e.g., John 3:16), the evangelist communicates that God's work in Jesus has profound effects that impact an even wider canvas. It is nothing less than the re-creation of the cosmos that is inaugurated in Jesus the Messiah. John's use of Genesis 1–2 leads the way in the development of this theme. In this section, we explore Genesis as it shows up in John's prologue (John 1:1–18) and later in the passion narrative (John 18–19) and in the resurrection accounts (John 20).

John's Prologue: A New Beginning

The very first words of John mimic the first two words of the Greek Old Testament: *en archē*—"In the beginning" (Gen. 1:1 LXX; John 1:1). The evangelist intends for his readers and hearers to catch the connection

---

15. Note sin's connection to death and slavery at John 8:34, 46.
16. Much of this material is based on my article on the topic: Jeannine K. Brown, "Creation's Renewal in the Gospel of John," *CBQ* 72 (2010): 275–90. Used with permission.

and register the new beginning that will be narrated in his own Gospel. The prologue also introduces the motifs of "life" and "light" (John 1:4–5), which will be key themes across John's story line. These are clearly drawn from Genesis 1, as God creates light as well as a host of plant life and living creatures (see Gen. 1:3, 14, 20, 24).

The key point of reference in John's prologue is the "Word" (*logos*; John 1:1, 14), who is defined as light and life, the Son and the Messiah ("Christ"). John indicates that the Word was active in creation: "Through [the Word] all things were made; without [the Word] nothing was made that has been made" (1:3). The Word (*logos*) has its origins in God's effective speech in Genesis 1: "God said . . . and it was so" reverberates across the chapter as God's speaking (*legō*; the verb related to the noun *logos*) results in created life.[17] By developing these connections between Genesis 1 and John 1, John is signaling "the centrality of creation as the context from which he will tell his story of Jesus."[18]

Echoes of Genesis in the Passion Narrative

The first clue that John returns to Genesis 1–2 as he narrates Jesus' passion comes immediately after Jesus' concluding words to his disciples, traditionally called the Upper Room Discourse (John 13–17). The passion narrative begins in John 18 with the identification of the location of Jesus' arrest: "On the other side [of the Kidron Valley] there was a garden, and he and his disciples went to it" (18:1; see 18:3, 26). John is the only Gospel writer who mentions this setting, which recurs as the setting for Jesus' crucifixion and resurrection: "At the place where Jesus was crucified, there was a garden, and in the garden a new tomb, in which no one had ever been laid" (19:41).

Might John repeat this garden setting across his passion and resurrection narratives to encourage a "comparison with another garden"?[19] The setting of the creation account of Genesis 2 is a garden (Hebrew *gan*), a repeated note across the chapter (Gen. 2:8, 9, 10, 15, 16; also in Gen. 3). In Genesis 2:8 we read, "Now the LORD God had planted a garden in the

---

17. With a kind of call and response—"God said" (Gen. 1:6, 9, 14, 20, 24, 26, 28), followed by "and it was so" (1:7, 9, 11, 15, 24, 30).

18. Brown, "Creation's Renewal," 277.

19. Nicolas Wyatt, "'Supposing Him to Be the Gardener' (John 20,15): A Study of the Paradise Motif in John," ZNW 81 (1990): 21–38, here 24.

east, in Eden; and there he put the man he had formed." While John has a different Greek term for garden (*kēpos*) than Genesis does (*paradeisos*), *kēpos* is used in other Greek translations of Genesis 2–3.[20] If John is intentionally highlighting a garden setting for the passion and resurrection narratives, he may do so to communicate that Jesus' death and resurrection inaugurate the time of new creation.

Another intimation of Genesis 2 in the passion narrative comes in the words of Pilate at John 19:5, in his presentation of Jesus to the crowd outside his palace. After his soldiers flog Jesus and mockingly dress him in a purple robe and a crown of thorns, Pilate displays him to the crowd, exclaiming, "Here is the man!" (*idou ho anthrōpos*). It is possible that John, quite apart from Pilate's motives, uses these words to echo Genesis 2 with its ongoing references to "the man" God places in the garden to care for it (Gen. 2:5, 7, 8, 15, 16). The word "man" translates the Hebrew *adam*, which in the Greek Septuagint is rendered *anthrōpos*.[21] So while Pilate is clueless about the identity of the one he interrogates,[22] John may be affirming through this brief evocation that Jesus is the new Adam, the locus of a new humanity who will tend the renewed creation.[23]

Echoes of Genesis in the Resurrection Narratives

As we reach the resurrection episodes of John 20, we again hear echoes and allusions to the early chapters of Genesis. John 20 begins by indicating the temporal setting of Jesus' resurrection: "*Early on the first day of the week*, while it was still dark, Mary Magdalene went to the tomb" (20:1, emphasis added). Each of the Gospels attests this setting feature (Matt. 28:1; Mark 16:2; Luke 24:1), but only John repeats it to introduce Jesus'

---

20. The term *kēpos* is used in the translations of Aquila (at Gen. 2:8; 3:2) and of Theodotion (at Gen. 3:2). John Suggit suggests that the evangelist uses *kēpos* instead of *paradeisos* because in the New Testament the latter refers to the final state ("paradise"; e.g., Rev. 2:7) and so would not have been appropriate to describe the garden setting of Jesus' death and resurrection. Suggit, "Jesus the Gardener: The Atonement in the Fourth Gospel as Re-Creation," *Neot* 33 (1999): 161–68, here 166.

21. E.g., at Gen. 2:5, 7, 8, 15, 16.

22. A few of John's characters *speak more than they know*; see also Caiaphas at John 11:49–53 and Mary at 20:15.

23. This example highlights the distinction between the two levels of a narrative: its story and discourse levels (see chap. 1). On the story level, Pilate speaks these words without knowing Jesus' true identity. On the discourse level, John employs Pilate's words to make a theological point.

appearance to his disciples: "On the evening of that *first day of the week*" (John 20:19, emphasis added).

This temporal marker within John's story appears to contribute to his theology. At the resurrection, a new week in human history has begun. We read in Genesis 2:2–3 that God rested on the seventh day of creation (the final day of the week). For John, a new "week" has begun: "John turns the clock ahead in his dual reference to ["the first day of the week"], thereby signaling that re-creation begins at the resurrection of Jesus Christ."[24]

Jesus' resurrection appearance to Mary Magdalene also includes another potential Genesis echo. When Mary sees the resurrected Jesus, she doesn't recognize him. Instead, she mistakes him for the gardener (*kēpouros*; John 20:15). (Recall from 19:41–42 that Jesus has been placed in a new tomb in a garden [*kēpos*].) Much like the scene with Pilate, John capitalizes on Mary's mistaken identification for his own christological purposes. As Edwyn Hoskyns incisively queries, "Mary thinks that Jesus is the gardener. The real question is, is she right or wrong?"[25] It may be that John wants his reader to hear *what is right* about this misidentification: Jesus is analogous to that first gardener, Adam. He is the new Adam of the new creation.[26] As N. T. Wright concludes, "Mary's intuitive guess, that he must be the gardener, was wrong at one level and right, deeply right, at another. This is the new creation. Jesus is the beginning of it. . . . Here he is: the new Adam, the gardener, charged with bringing the chaos of God's creation into new order, into flower, into fruitfulness."[27]

A final intimation of Genesis 2 and so creation's renewal comes in the scene where Jesus appears to his disciples (John 20:19–23) and commissions them—*breathing on them* the gift of the Holy Spirit (20:22). This action evokes "the breath of life" that God breathes into *adam* in Genesis 2:7, making him "a living being." The verb in the Septuagint for this act of God is *emphysaō*, a fairly unusual word in the Septuagint and the New Testament,[28] increasing the likelihood of its use as an echo of Genesis in

---

24. Brown, "Creation's Renewal," 283.

25. Edwyn C. Hoskyns, "Genesis 1–3 and St. John's Gospel," *JTS* 21 (1920): 210–18, here 214.

26. Some interpreters understand the identification of Jesus as gardener to align with God as gardener (creator) in Gen. 2.

27. N. T. Wright, *John for Everyone* (Louisville: Westminster John Knox, 2004), 2:146.

28. In the New Testament, *emphysaō* occurs only in John 20:22. It occurs in the Septuagint only eleven times, e.g., Gen. 2:7; 1 Kings 17:21; Job 4:21; Ezek. 21:31; 22:20; 37:9. In a close parallel to John 20, the word is used in Ezek. 37:9 for the breath of Yahweh re-creating God's people (Suggit, "Jesus the Gardener," 163).

John 20.[29] Jesus breathes upon his followers the Holy Spirit—who grants eternal life. This is John's moment of re-creation. "The climax of the Fourth Gospel presents Jesus as 'breathing' upon the apostles after the pattern of the creating God who breathed upon the Edenic couple; now they receive the Spirit, and not simply the gift of life."[30]

We've explored a number of potential echoes and allusions of Genesis 2 in John 18–20:

- Garden setting (John 18:1, 3, 26; 19:41)
- Pilate's words, "Here is the man" (19:5)
- "First day of the week" setting (20:1, 19)
- Mary's identification of Jesus as the "gardener" (20:15)
- Jesus "breathing" the Holy Spirit on his disciples (20:22)

While any individual evocation may not be compelling on its own, its probability increases through the sheer number of the additional potential Genesis echoes. As we noted in chapter 6, one benchmark for recognizing echoes is the repeated use of an Old Testament text in a New Testament book. Given the clear signals to Genesis 1 in John 1, the echoes of Genesis 2 in John's final chapters become all the more likely.[31]

Creational Themes in John's Gospel

John's narrative frame of Genesis allusions and echoes (John 1; 18–20) is reinforced by the creational themes he weaves across his narrative. These themes include the completion of the work of God, the seven Johannine signs, and the pronounced motif of life in John.

THE COMPLETION OF GOD'S WORK

In John 4–5 the evangelist conveys that Jesus has been sent to complete the work(s) of God (cf. also 5:17).

---

29. Commentators on John routinely identify this as an allusion to Gen. 2:7.

30. Edith M. Humphrey, "New Creation," in *Dictionary for Theological Interpretation of the Bible*, ed. Kevin J. Vanhoozer (Grand Rapids: Baker Academic, 2005), 536–37, here 536.

31. Another benchmark—thematic coherence with the New Testament author's own emphases—provides additional confirmation of these Genesis echoes in John 18–20, since John weaves creational themes, such as "life" and "work," into his Gospel.

"'My food,' said Jesus, 'is to do the will of him who sent me and *to finish* his work'" (4:34, emphasis added).

"The works that the Father has given me *to finish*—the very works that I am doing—testify that the Father has sent me" (5:36, emphasis added).[32]

This repeated language of finishing (*teleioō*) God's works (*erga*) likely alludes to Genesis 2:1–3.

"Thus the heavens and the earth were completed [LXX: *synteleō*][33] in all their vast array. By the seventh day God had finished [LXX: *synteleō*] the work [LXX: *erga*][34] he had been doing; so on the seventh day he rested from all his work [LXX: *erga*]. Then God blessed the seventh day and made it holy, because on it he rested from all the work [LXX: *erga*] of creating that he had done." (NIV)

In his use of these allusions, John suggests that God has given Jesus the task of finishing the *divine creative work*. In Genesis, after the work of the initial creation is completed, God rests on the seventh day (the "Sabbath"; e.g., Exod. 20:8). Completion of work and Sabbath are also paired in John, when Jesus dies for humanity (John 19:30–31). After a narrative comment that Jesus knew "that everything had now been finished [*teleō*]," John writes, "Jesus said, 'It is finished' [*teleō*]. With that, he bowed his head and gave up his spirit. Now it was the day of Preparation, and the next day was to be a special Sabbath" (19:30–31a).

John, drawing on Genesis, uses the storied setting of Sabbath to make a theological point: "Jesus' work, which culminates at the cross (19:30), completes the Father's work, ushering in the Sabbath of God's full rest."[35]

---

32. The timing of Jesus speaking about doing divine work is significant: he speaks these words on the Sabbath (John 5:9–10, 16). While the Sabbath was a day to cease from work, Jesus implies his authority over the Sabbath by claiming, "My Father is always at his work to this very day, and I too am working" (5:17). For the rabbinic notion that God has continuing work to do, even on the Sabbath, see Brown, "Creation's Renewal," 285–86.

33. Related to *teleioō* and having to do with completion.

34. In the Septuagint the word is in the plural ("works") in each occurrence in Gen. 2:1–3, as at John 5:36.

35. Brown, "Creation's Renewal," 285. Completion and Sabbath lead into 20:1, where "the first day of the week" (the day following the Sabbath) is the temporal setting of Jesus'

THE JOHANNINE SIGNS

John structures the first half of his Gospel around seven "signs"—his language for the miracles of Jesus he narrates. John explicitly notes the first two "signs" at 2:11 and 4:54. After that, as Wright suggests, "he leaves us to count up the 'signs.'"[36] The seven, as they are typically identified and counted, are shown in figure 7.3.

Figure 7.3
The Seven Signs in John (Chaps. 1–12)

"The first of the signs" (2:11)	2:1–11	Jesus turns water into wine
"The second sign" (4:54)	4:46–54	Jesus heals a royal official's son
Third sign	5:1–9	Jesus heals a man who is disabled
Fourth sign	6:1–15	Jesus feeds the five thousand
Fifth sign	6:16–21	Jesus walks on water
Sixth sign	9:1–7	Jesus heals a man born blind
Seventh sign	11:1–44	Jesus raises Lazarus from the dead

What is the significance of the number seven attached to these miracles? In addition to seven being a number that signals completion, some have also suggested a connection to creation's renewal. John Painter describes the seven signs as "new acts of creation."[37] If this is the case, then what John might offer us at the end of his Gospel is a final, culminating *eighth sign*. "The seven Johannine signs point ahead in the narrative toward that final and greatest of signs, the resurrection of the Messiah—the first moment of re-creation."[38]

John hints that Jesus' resurrection is the climactic eighth sign early in his Gospel, directly after he has introduced the language of "signs" at 2:11. Jesus, in Jerusalem for the Passover, drives out from the temple money changers and people who are selling animals (2:13–17). When he is asked, "What sign can you show us to prove your authority to do all this?"

---

resurrection. "The arrival of the first day of the week caps the various allusions to the work of God (in creation) that has now come to completion in Jesus' death, ushering in Sabbath rest and re-creation" (286).

36. Wright, *John for Everyone*, 2:131.

37. John Painter, "Earth Made Whole: John's Rereading of Genesis," in *Word, Theology, and Community in John*, ed. John Painter, R. Alan Culpepper, and Fernando F. Segovia (St. Louis: Chalice, 2002), 65–84, here 77.

38. Brown, "Creation's Renewal," 287.

(2:18), Jesus answers with a riddle: "Destroy this temple, and I will raise it again in three days" (2:19). Jesus, in riddle form, gives the future sign of his resurrected body: Though he will be killed, resurrection will follow (2:21–22). As R. H. Lightfoot claims, "The Lord, in ambiguous language [2:19–21], offers the supreme sign of the Gospel, namely, His resurrection, in other words, Himself and His work, since He is the resurrection."[39] The rest of the signs point toward and foreshadow that final (eighth) "supreme sign" of Jesus' resurrection.[40]

THE THEME OF LIFE ACROSS THE GOSPEL

Finally, and quite explicitly, John liberally weaves the motif of life across his Gospel. We have already noted this theme in John's prologue, where the preexistent Word is the bearer of "life" (Greek *zōē*; see John 1:4). The word itself—*zōē*—occurs almost fifty times across the Gospel. Additionally, the language from John 3 about the need to be "born from above / born again" (3:3, 7) and "born of the Spirit" (3:5–8) anticipates Jesus' gifting of the Holy Spirit to his followers in evocation of Genesis 2 (John 20:22). Rebirth signals re-creation.

The theme of life is also emphasized in three of John's seven "I am" statements. Jesus offers the following claims about himself as the source of life:

"I am the bread of life" (6:35, 48; "living bread," 6:51).

"I am the resurrection and the life" (11:25).

"I am the way and the truth and the life" (14:6).

Finally, John concludes with a clear purpose statement for his Gospel that thematizes life (20:30–31, emphasis added): "Jesus performed many other signs in the presence of his disciples, which are not recorded in this book. But these are written that you may believe that Jesus is the Messiah, the Son of God, and that by believing *you may have life* in his name."

As much as faith or believing is important for John's theology, faith functions as the path to receiving life from Jesus. Life—eternal life—is the

---

39. R. H. Lightfoot, *St. John's Gospel* (Oxford: Clarendon Press, 1956), 113.

40. The raising of Lazarus particularly foreshadows Jesus' resurrection, both in some of its specific language (John 11:38, 44; cf. 20:1, 6–7) as well as in its victory over death (11:25–26).

ultimate goal of Jesus' messianic work. For John eternal life begins with the arrival of the Word come in the flesh (1:1–14) and is precisely the life that anticipates new creation. "Eternal life has already begun, according to John, within the person (and then the community) of Jesus at his resurrection, in anticipation of the final resurrection."[41]

41. Brown, "Creation's Renewal," 278.

Part Five
Narrative Theology

If a story is not about the hearer he [or she] will not listen. . . .
A great lasting story is about everyone or it will not last. The
strange and foreign is not interesting—only the deeply personal
and familiar.

John Steinbeck, *East of Eden*

8

How a Story Theologizes

Long before the Gospels were written, a set of fables developed that were attributed to Aesop, a slave in ancient Greece (sixth century BCE). Over the years these famous fables have been used for instruction and have passed through various adaptations. The fables have often been boiled down to a simple moral lesson that provides the conclusion for each. "The Ant and the Grasshopper" is one example.

The Ant and the Grasshopper

In a field one summer's day a Grasshopper was hopping about, chirping and singing to its heart's content. An Ant passed by, bearing along with great toil an ear of corn he was taking to the nest.

"Why not come and chat with me," said the Grasshopper, "instead of toiling and moiling in that way?"

"I am helping to lay up food for the winter," said the Ant, "and recommend you to do the same."

"Why bother about winter?" said the Grasshopper; "we have got plenty of food at present." But the Ant went on its way and continued its toil. When the winter came the Grasshopper had no food, and found itself dying of hunger, while it saw the ants distributing every day corn and grain from the stores they had collected in the summer. Then the Grasshopper knew:

"IT IS BEST TO PREPARE FOR THE DAYS OF NECESSITY."

This fable concludes with and is well summed up by the pithy proverb, "It is best to prepare for the days of necessity."[1] On this front, the Gospels are quite *unlike* Aesop's fables. It is not possible to distill a Gospel to a simple proverb, principle, or even set of principles without doing damage to its narrative complexities and storied theology. Yet it has proved tempting across the history of interpretation to experiment with such distillation. As we noted in chapter 1, there has often been a tendency to atomize a Gospel. By reducing a Gospel to its smallest passages (called pericopes), we might attempt to derive a lesson from each story or teaching of Jesus. But to grasp the whole of a Gospel, we are pressed beyond simple lessons and moral proverbs. We will need to grapple with the inherent narrativity of a Gospel if we are going to understand its theology.

As we consider the theology of any of the Gospels, a caveat is in order. In much of the book, I have isolated various strands of a Gospel narrative in order to think reflectively about the question of how to read a story well. We've focused discretely on plotting, on characterization, and on intertextuality, with less attention to the complexity of a narrative as it weaves together plot and theme, character and setting, and citations and allusions from Israel's Scriptures. In this chapter and the next, we focus a theological lens on the Gospels. This theological focus will necessarily involve bringing together all these facets of narrative for considering *how a story theologizes.*

I suggest the language of **narrative theologizing** (along with the more usual **narrative theology**), because it highlights that each evangelist is reflecting intentionally and theologically on the Jesus story. Yes, Luke has a theology, but, more to the point in this chapter, he theologizes as he narrates. His theology is not separate from or incidental to his narrative; instead, it is borne along by his story of Jesus.[2]

Narrative's Capacity to Maintain Tensions

As we think about the Gospels as stories, it can be helpful to take a step back and consider how story is a fundamental human category. Human

---

1. Aesop, *Fables*, retold by Joseph Jacobs, in *The Harvard Classics* (New York: Collier, 1909–1914), https://www.bartleby.com/17/1/36.html.
2. C. Kavin Rowe argues for "narrative itself as the bearer of theological meaning." Rowe, *Early Narrative Christology: The Lord in the Gospel of Luke* (Grand Rapids: Baker Academic, 2009), 12.

beings experience life as "narratively plotted."[3] This makes sense of the human predisposition to tell about our lives in story form. As Peter Brooks suggests, "Narrative is one of the ways in which we speak, one of the large categories in which we think."[4] Stories not only represent our reality, but they also help us to understand and speak of our lived experience coherently.[5]

What does this mean for conceiving of the theology of a Gospel? It indicates that the narrative shape of a Gospel is not merely a formal characteristic. Instead, it is an evangelist's chosen mode for doing theology—for *theologizing*. A Gospel "is theological *because* of its narrative shape and not *in spite of it*."[6] And narrative allows for greater levels of tension without sacrificing coherence. As John Goldingay notes, "Part of narrative's genius is its capacity to embrace ambiguity, to discuss complexity, to embrace mystery."[7] In her work on the narrative theology of Acts, Beverly Gaventa follows the themes of the triumph of God in the gospel *and* the gospel's rejection, suggesting that Acts in its narrative development is able to hold both of these motifs in a productive tension. Attending to the shape of the story line for theology honors the complexities and the "rich texture" of narrative.[8]

This is an important insight and one that warrants an extended illustration. Let's take as an example the tension between divine revelation and human reception in Matthew's Gospel. First, we should note how Christian theology has addressed this tension more generally (not just in

3. Steven J. Sandage and Jeannine K. Brown, *Relational Integration of Psychology and Christian Theology: Theory, Research, and Practice* (New York: Routledge, 2018), 151. N. T. Wright speaks of "the storied and relational nature of human consciousness." Wright, *New Testament and the People of God* (Minneapolis: Fortress, 1992), 61.

4. Peter Brooks, *Reading for the Plot: Design and Intention in Narrative* (New York: Knopf, 1984), 323.

5. Jeannine K. Brown, *Scripture as Communication: Introducing Biblical Hermeneutics* (Grand Rapids: Baker Academic, 2007), 44.

6. Jeannine K. Brown and Kyle Roberts, *Matthew*, THNTC (Grand Rapids: Eerdmans, 2018), 269 (emphasis original).

7. John Goldingay, "Biblical Narrative and Systematic Theology," in *Between Two Horizons: Spanning New Testament Studies and Systematic Theology*, ed. Joel B. Green and Max Turner (Grand Rapids: Eerdmans, 2000), 123–42, here 135. Rowe argues that "narrative has the inherent structural ability to exhibit considerable diversity and discontinuity within the unity and continuity of one story." C. Kavin Rowe, "New Testament Theology: The Revival of a Discipline," *JBL* 125 (2006): 393–419, here 409.

8. Beverly Roberts Gaventa, "Toward a Theology of Acts: Reading and Rereading," *Int* 42 (1988): 146–57, here 157.

Matthew), often using the language of divine will and human (free) will. Given the tendency to express doctrine in propositions (see below), what usually has happened is that one side of this tension has been subordinated to the other in the seeking of theological coherence.[9] Yet Matthew, through his use of narrative, maintains the tension in a rather delicate balance.

In Matthew's narrative sequence, a complex interplay occurs between these motifs of divine revelation and human reception (e.g., faith, understanding). Jesus' public ministry begins with a summary call to repent in light of the arriving kingdom (Matt. 4:17). When Jesus calls disciples or when would-be disciples approach him, some follow him and some find the cost too great (cf. 4:18–22; 8:18–22; 9:9).[10] Numbers of people come to Jesus trusting that he is able to heal them or those they bring to him, and Jesus commends their faith (8:2, 10; 9:2, 22, 29). These various episodes imply human choice in responding to Jesus and the kingdom he brings.

When Matthew introduces a significant connection between Jesus and Wisdom in 11:2–30, the themes of revelation and hiddenness emerge, as we would expect in relation to the notion of wisdom (cf. Dan. 2:19–23). We hear that God through the Son reveals truth to those least expected to have such knowledge—to "little children" (Matt. 11:25), a group that represents metaphorically (at least in part) Jesus' followers. Revelation, ironically, does not come to "the wise and learned" (11:25). The Son chooses those to whom he will reveal divine knowledge (11:27). Yet these words about what would seem to be selective revelation are immediately followed by Jesus taking on the voice and demeanor of Wisdom, as he invites "*all* you who are weary and burdened" to come to him (11:28, emphasis added). Whatever the revelation referred to in 11:25–27, it is not esoteric knowledge accessed only by a few. It is accessible to all who are in need and are willing to take up Jesus' yoke (his teachings) and learn from him (11:29).

---

9. For example, Calvin in his *Institutes* (which intentionally provides doctrinal statements) subsumes human agency to divine will: "Predestination we call the eternal decree of God, by which He hath determined in Himself what He would have to become of every individual of mankind. For they are not all created with a similar destiny; but eternal life is foreordained for some, and eternal damnation for others" (*Institutes* 3.21, in *Institutes of the Christian Religion: A New Translation*, trans. Henry Beveridge (Edinburgh: Calvin Translation Society, 1845).

10. Commentators debate whether or which of the two potential disciples of Matt. 8:18–22 become true followers. See Jeannine K. Brown, *The Disciples in Narrative Perspective: The Portrayal and Function of the Matthean Disciples*, SBLAB 9 (Atlanta: Society of Biblical Literature, 2002), 40n5.

In the Parables Discourse (Matt. 13:1–52), divine revelation receives particular emphasis. Jesus affirms that "the knowledge of the secrets of the kingdom of heaven has been given" to his disciples and not to the crowds who listen to him teach in parables (13:11). This distinction is only heightened by a citation from Isaiah 6:9–10 about the lack of understanding of Israel in Isaiah's day, now recapitulated in Jesus' ministry (Matt. 13:13–15). The distinction is also emphasized as Jesus' disciples are privy to additional interpretations of the parables that the crowds are not given (13:36–50). In this chapter it seems clear that revelation is given to some and not to others.

Yet revelation apparently does not guarantee human understanding. Although the disciples claim to have understood Jesus' teachings in parables (Matt. 13:51), they consistently misunderstand his teachings (including parables!) as the story continues (15:15–16; 16:8–11).[11] And though Peter confesses Jesus as Messiah by divine revelation (16:16–17), he almost immediately shows his lack of understanding about the nature of Jesus' messianic ministry and his resistance to the suffering it will entail (16:21–23). It is also the case that Matthew portrays the Galilean crowds—those referenced in Matthew 13 as not privy to "the secrets of the kingdom"—correctly proclaiming Jesus "Son of David" (i.e., Messiah) and rightly identifying him as "the prophet from Nazareth in Galilee" (21:9, 11) as he enters Jerusalem.

A reading of Matthew as narrative discourages us from collapsing the twin themes of divine revelation and human reception into an easy synthesis. Yet the story itself—its plot sequence and narrative logic—has a "binding function," the capacity for a kind of coherence that is not "too-coherent."[12] It moves away from a monolithic lens for what are complex theological and human realities. Richard Hays suggests the analogy of drama as productive for understanding the kind of coherence we might envision in a Gospel: "The complexity of viewpoints in a drama is not necessarily a sign of incoherence; it may be instead a sign of the drama's depth of engagement with human life."[13]

11. For an in-depth discussion of the frequent and ongoing misunderstandings of the Matthean disciples, see chap. 5.

12. The language comes from Jonathan M. Adler's work in narrative psychology: "Sitting at the Nexus of Epistemological Traditions: Narrative Psychological Perspectives on Self-Knowledge," in *Handbook of Self-Knowledge*, ed. Simine Vazire and Timothy D. Wilson (New York: Guilford Press, 2012), 327–42, here 329–30.

13. Richard B. Hays, "Can Narrative Criticism Recover the Theological Unity of Scripture?," *Journal of Theological Interpretation* 2 (2008): 193–211, here 201. In context, Hays is using this category of drama as an analogy to consider how the whole Bible might hold together coherently.

This kind of narrative-theological reading of a Gospel involves allowing the story's movement to impact its theological expression. Narrative theology avoids taking a snapshot from one part of a Gospel and assuming that this single frame adequately expresses the entirety of the evangelist's theology on any particular subject. The whole story must be allowed to speak in order for an evangelist's theology in all its complexity to emerge.

Yet a sensitivity to the Gospels as stories has not characterized much of the interpretive landscape during the modern era, especially when it came to thinking theologically about the Gospels. We can look more closely at these modernist tendencies as we press toward a more storied way of hearing the Gospels as theology.

Moving beyond Modernist Preferences for Theology as Propositions

We have inherited from modernism a preference for abstraction. And while some amount of generalization or abstraction is necessary for theological reflection, modernist ways of doing biblical theology have tended to prefer abstraction to the particularity of the relevant contexts, whether the sociohistorical contexts in which theology is done or the contexts of the biblical authors themselves.[14] The preference for abstraction has minimized the importance of story for doing theology. As J. Richard Middleton and Brian J. Walsh have noted, "Under the impact of modern ideals Christians have long ignored the narrative infrastructure of Scripture, as well as the literary narratives within the Bible, as so much extrinsic packaging for timeless theological or moral truths . . . which is [considered to be] what *really* matters."[15]

We can see this pattern worked out in biblical studies in the rationalism prominent in the last couple of hundred years. The goal as it was expressed by many was to arrive at universal truth extracted from particularities of culture, history, and context. It was a matter of removing the kernel from the husk, or what was abiding from what was

14. For an analysis and critique of this marked preference, see Jeannine K. Brown, "Is the Future of Biblical Theology Story-Shaped?," *HBT* 37 (2015): 13–31.
15. J. Richard Middleton and Brian J. Walsh, *Truth Is Stranger than It Used to Be: Biblical Faith in a Postmodern Age* (Downers Grove, IL: InterVarsity), 68 (emphasis original).

disposable. For example, Adolf Harnack, in his famous lecture "What Is Christianity?" (first published in 1900), distilled Jesus' teaching in such a way that its core—focused on his ethical teaching—was removed from the "husk" of its Jewish context and particularities (a move that revealed Harnack's own context of German anti-Semitism).[16] In these kinds of extractions, what was abiding and universal inevitably turned out to be expressed in terms of general principles or propositions (e.g., love for neighbor).

This preference for propositional theology also became a fixture of evangelicalism, especially because of its commitment to revelation as "what God says as well as what God does."[17] In the process, however, propositions have often been elevated above the biblical narratives to which they are integrally connected and from which they are derived. Yet it is always the case that "some version of a canonical story sits behind any formulation of doctrines or themes."[18] As George Lindbeck has argued, "The story is logically prior. It determines the meaning of images, concepts, doctrines, and theories . . . rather than being determined by them."[19] Much of the Bible consists of narrative, and its other genres assume particular stories and assert a story about God, humanity, life, and faith (i.e., a worldview). So given the thoroughly storied nature of the Bible, how do we do theology in the Gospels? Or to be more specific, how do we listen well to the narrative theologizing of the evangelists themselves?

Let's take another example from Matthew's Gospel. In Matthew 19–20, Jesus repeats a maxim about reversal: "Many who are first will be last, and many who are last will be first" (19:30, with the maxim inverted at 20:16). If we were to extract this maxim and isolate it as a theological proposition, we might assume Jesus is providing a path for being first in God's kingdom. Yet the narrative context of this maxim

---

16. Adolf von Harnack, *What Is Christianity?*, 2nd ed. (London: Williams and Norgate, 1902).

17. Gabriel Fackre critiques not this commitment but the loss of "the narrative quality of faith" that can occur in the process. Fackre, "Narrative Theology from an Evangelical Perspective," in *Faith and Narrative*, ed. Keith E. Yandell (New York: Oxford University Press, 2001), 188–201, here 199.

18. Brown, "Future of Biblical Theology," 17.

19. George Lindbeck, "The Story-Shaped Church: Critical Exegesis and Theological Interpretation," in *Scriptural Authority and Narrative Interpretation* (Philadelphia: Fortress, 1987), 161–78, here 165.

suggests a more nuanced way for understanding it. First, the story line from Matthew 18–20 features Jesus pressing his followers to live in a countercultural way regarding status. Greatness is subsumed to service (18:1–5; 20:25–28), and Jesus so redefines "being first" that a slave—one with no status—can be the epitome of this kind of discipleship.[20] This storied context signals that true discipleship is about avoiding presumption about status and disavowing the pursuit of higher status in the kingdom (cf. 19:27–30; 20:25). Jesus is not providing a revised pathway for gaining status.

Second, the maxim about first and last forms an *inclusio* around the parable of the first- and last-hour workers. The upshot of the parable becomes clear in the affront felt by the first-hour workers when they hear they will be paid the same amount for working twelve hours as those who worked only one hour: "You have made them equal to us who have borne the burden of the work and the heat of the day" (20:12). It is the surprising (and maddening) equality of God's kingdom that Jesus is communicating in the parable and so likely in the maxim that bookends it. This narrative truth of equal status in the community of Jesus is picked up later in the Gospel, when Jesus calls his followers to living as brothers and sisters under one God and one Messiah (23:8–10).

Paying attention to where and how theology is developed (i.e., how theologizing happens) in a narrative is important for understanding the theology of a Gospel. This attentiveness enables the interpreter to stay engaged with the narrative genre and structure of a Gospel rather than discarding the story as merely a formal characteristic. As Alan Culpepper suggests, "The biblical stories . . . cannot be reduced to a simple 'message' as though the story could be discarded once a reader had gotten the message."[21] To deal seriously with the Gospels *as stories* means pressing against the notion that a Gospel is "a theological argument somehow encased—or even imprisoned—in a narrative."[22]

---

20. Brown and Roberts, *Matthew*, 187–88.

21. R. Alan Culpepper, "Narrative Criticism as a Tool for Proclamation: 1 Samuel 13," *RevExp* 84 (1987): 33–40, here 34.

22. This is Gaventa's language in relation to the narrative of Acts in "Toward a Theology of Acts," 149. She goes on to suggest, "The assumption seems to be that Luke [in Acts] has a thesis or main point to demonstrate, and he creates his story in order to bear the thesis. . . . [Yet] Luke's theology is intricately and irreversibly bound up with the story he tells and cannot be separated from it" (150).

In a storied approach to the theology of the Gospels, it is also important to attend carefully to the set of stories that are *assumed* by the evangelists as they narrate their own stories of Jesus.[23] These assumed stories include Israel's Scriptures, easily observed in the thoroughgoing use of Old Testament citations, allusions, and echoes across the Gospels. The backstories of the Gospels also include their sociohistorical contexts, which are themselves multilayered and involve the intersecting "worlds" of Jewish, Greek, and Roman realities and influences. Taking account of the layers of stories in a particular Gospel helps us to move beyond a modernist preference for mere propositional theology to a more fully orbed, narratively sensitive theological reading.

How to Discern Theology in Narrative

So what is involved in attending to the theology of any particular narrative? Discerning theology in a story is not so much a method as it is an engagement with a set of interpretive lenses. In other words, following the theology of a Gospel doesn't lead us down a single-file path of discrete steps. Instead, it involves drawing on a number of storied lenses and embracing a set of holistic practices for interpreting a Gospel. In the end it is about following the Gospel story line where its author leads us.

Lenses and Questions for Discerning Narrative Theology

Throughout the book, I have suggested a number of lenses for reading the Gospels as stories, including plotting, characterization, and intertextuality. Discerning narrative theology involves bringing these together to envision a more holistic picture. If we think about these three narrative lenses, each potentially raises a number of interpretive questions (see fig. 8.1).

---

23. This point is regularly affirmed; e.g., Brown, *Scripture as Communication*, 46; Joel B. Green, "Practicing the Gospel in a Post-Critical World: The Promise of Theological Exegesis," *JETS* 47 (2004): 387–97, here 392–93. Goldingay writes that even "nonnarrative books such as the Psalms, the Prophets, and the Epistles abound in material that has taken the first step from narrative to discursive statement, while keeping its implicit and explicit links with the gospel, with the OT and NT story" ("Biblical Narrative," 134).

Figure 8.1
Interpretive Questions from Story to Theology

Plotting	Characterization	Intertextuality
• How does an evangelist's plotting of his story contribute to his theology? • Does attending to narrative development add nuance to this theology? • How do plot and theme interact to contribute to the Gospel's theology?	• How does an evangelist develop his characters across the story, and how does this development contribute to his theology? • How do key characters interact, and how does this interaction illuminate theology?	• How does the evangelist's use of the Old Testament provide a "backstory" or a "back-theology" for his own story and theology? • How are Old Testament categories employed to illuminate a Gospel's settings, characters, or events?

These multiple questions from multiple lenses contribute to a thoughtful reading of a Gospel, one that attempts to integrate across the lenses to bring an evangelist's theological vision into sharper focus. As Gaventa suggests (for Acts as narrative), "An adequate treatment of the theology of [a narrative] needs to attend to the elements the narrative repeats, the information omitted, the appearance and disappearance of individuals and groups of people, the rich interweaving of story lines, asking what each of these suggests about the theology of the author."[24]

It is important to include at this juncture an additional lens—this one historical. To read a narrative well, we'll need to take into consideration its historical context, what we might think of as the backstories of a Gospel. As we noted in chapter 1, narrative criticism in its more mature forms has included attention to the sociohistorical contexts of a Gospel for interpretation. In narrative theory, the implied author expects the implied reader to know linguistic and contextual information that provides a set of backstories to a Gospel.[25]

For example, the Gospels have as one relevant backstory the reality of Roman occupation, since Rome controlled Judea and Galilee during the time of Jesus' life and ministry. Yet if you were to search for the language

24. Gaventa, "Toward a Theology of Acts," 157.
25. Mark Allan Powell, "Expected and Unexpected Readings of Matthew: What the Reader Knows," *AsTJ* 48 (1993): 31–51, here 32. See also Joel Green, *Gospel of Luke*, NICNT (Grand Rapids: Eerdmans, 1997), 19. Some of these backstories come from the Old Testament, so that intertextuality will help us hear how these prior stories illuminate a Gospel.

of "Rome" or "Roman" (*Rōmē* or *Rōmaios*) in the Gospels, you'd find only one occurrence of the adjective, in John 11:48. Why so few references? The reason is that Rome is almost everywhere assumed rather than named or discussed. Rome's presence in the Gospel stories does show up in Roman authorities, like Caesar Augustus (Luke 2:1) and Pilate (Mark 15:1), as well as Herod the Great (Matt. 2:1–23), who had been installed by Rome to rule the Jewish people. Rome's presence is also signaled, more subtly, in Latin loan words (e.g., *denarius*, *legion*, and *praetorium*), in references to Roman census taking and taxation (e.g., Luke 2:1–3; 20:20–26), and in various minor characters like centurions (e.g., Luke 7:1–10) and tax collectors (Matt. 9:9–13) who are Roman or are allied with Rome. Yet the backstory of Roman influence is more potent than the sum total of these sporadic references. "Roman occupation of Palestine would mean that Roman presence and propaganda would be ubiquitous in the world in which Jesus . . . lived."[26]

Given these various interpretive lenses arising from the complexities of a narrative, as well as its storied contexts, it should come as no surprise that a Gospel has multiple themes and motifs that an evangelist offers to his audience. Even in a single area of analysis, such as an evangelist's characterization of Jesus, there are multiple themes woven across the narrative. Christology in a Gospel is multifaceted. If we were to analyze Luke's Christology—his portrait of Jesus—we'd see a complex interweaving of messianic titles, Old Testament figures and texts, and narrative actions that point to and fill out Jesus' identity (see fig. 4.1). This narrative configuration provides more than a single christological theme; it provides a rich web for understanding Jesus' messianic identity. As Joel Green summarizes this narrative identity, "Jesus is a prophet, but more than a prophet. He is the long-awaited Davidic Messiah . . . , Lord and Son of God. He fulfills his career as a regal prophet for whom death, while necessary, is not the last word. Early on Jesus is identified as Savior (Lk 2:11), a role that is subsequently expressed in his miracles of healing and exorcism, his practices of table fellowship, his readings of Scripture and his prayers, all of which broadcast the message of God's kingdom."[27]

Given the vibrant texture of narrative, we'll need to work against any tendency to think that Luke (or any of the other evangelists) has

---

26. Brown and Roberts, *Matthew*, 489. See 489–93 for more examples.
27. Joel B. Green, "Luke, Gospel of," in *DJG*, 540–52, here 547.

a single overriding concern in his Gospel, or even in his Christology.[28] Attending to a Gospel's thickly textured narrative will reap rich theological rewards.

Reading Practices for Discerning Narrative Theology

In addition to these lenses and questions, the interpreter's reading approach is important for gaining theological insight into a narrative. Reading the entirety of a Gospel, not just once but repeatedly, is an essential narrative reading practice. The practice of "reading and rereading"[29] has as its goal an understanding of a Gospel in its totality—as a narrative unity.[30] We explored in chapter 1 how recent history of Gospels scholarship and practices of the church have often converged to work against reading the Gospels as wholes. So it may take intentional rethinking of our reading values to embrace the task of hearing a Gospel's theology at the level of the whole. If we are used to studying or hearing the preaching of a passage that consists of five to fifteen verses, it might seem daunting to take on twenty-eight chapters of Matthew or even sixteen chapters of Mark. Yet if we pick up a novel or modern biography without a thought to its length and with a commitment to read for its story, we are quite able to do the same for a Gospel.

In addition to reading a Gospel in its entirety and for a sense of the whole, a narrative-theological reading will be attuned to its textual details. In other words, understanding the parts is essential for understanding the whole, since an evangelist's aims for his narrative cannot be grasped apart from its particularities.[31] Narrative readers, then, will become fairly adept at moving between the parts and the whole—between the forest and the trees—of the narrative enterprise. It's a bit like looking at a dual image, where a slight reframing of the image in your mind's eye changes significantly your perception—you now see an entirely different image. Reading a Gospel carefully and with its details in mind is a commitment

---

28. Gaventa writes about this tendency for Acts: "Students of Luke sometimes identify particular theological threads and then elevate or promote them to 'the' theology of Acts. . . . Seldom, if ever, do these attempts take into account the place of a particular theological theme alongside other themes or concerns" ("Toward a Theology of Acts," 149).

29. Gaventa's subtitle in "Toward a Theology of Acts."

30. Northrup Frye, *The Great Code: The Bible and Literature* (New York: Harcourt Brace Jovanovich, 1981), 6; Gaventa, "Toward a Theology of Acts," 151.

31. Rowe, *Early Narrative Christology*, 14.

to (what Gaventa calls) "the blessed messiness of the text,"[32] all the while keeping our eye on the whole.

Reading for Narrative Development

Another important consideration for a narrative-theological reading relates to the issue of **narrative development**. We've noted that part of the genius of narrative is its ability to hold in tension what in other genres or contexts might look to be competing themes or ideas. This feature arises from the developmental quality of narrative. Characters often develop and change as the story progresses. The plot shifts and turns, providing a sense of narrative movement and progress as we read. On the discourse level, themes emerge, deepen, and sometimes even change direction.[33] The way a story begins is not the way it ends. And this feature of narrative allows for greater nuance in its theological vision.[34]

Let's take, as an example, disciples and discipleship in Mark's Gospel. Early scenes involving Jesus' disciples offer a quite positive portrait of the twelve as they leave everything to follow Jesus and are "with him" (Mark 3:14) in his ministry (e.g., 1:16–20; 2:13–14; 3:13–19, 20; 4:34–35). Yet as the story develops, Mark's Jesus begins to identify character traits in the disciples that are quite negative: they are fearful and lack faith (4:40) and are even described as having hard hearts (by the evangelist at 6:52; by Jesus at 8:17). At Jesus' arrest, the disciples desert him and flee (14:50). At the end of the Gospel there is no reunion of Jesus with the disciples, only the promise of one after the story line concludes (16:7). The character development of the (twelve) disciples moves on a negative trajectory in Mark. While this movement has been variously interpreted,[35] it is important to follow this narrative development rather than assuming a snapshot of the disciples at any particular turn is an adequate representation of Mark's

32. Beverly Roberts Gaventa, "Reading for the Subject: The Paradox of Power in Romans 14:1–15:6," *Journal of Theological Interpretation* 5 (2011): 1–11, here 3.

33. An example is Mark's Christology that begins with Jesus Messiah acting with authority over all areas of life, yet takes an ironic turn when he announces his mission to exchange power and prerogative for service and sacrifice (8:31; 10:45).

34. For a corresponding nuance from the interpreter, see my discussion of the way narrative lends itself toward a dynamic hermeneutic in Brown, "Future of Biblical Theology," 21–24.

35. This feature of Mark's portrait of disciples is often understood as a foil for the implied reader, who is encouraged toward more faithful discipleship than the disciples exhibit.

characterization of the group. "Only when we arrive at the end can we look back to divine the whole."[36]

An Example of Narrative Theology: John's Christology around Festivals

An intriguing example of narrative theologizing at work is John's structural use of various Jewish festivals as settings for Jesus' words and actions. In John 5–10 the evangelist highlights four Jewish festivals as he narrates the healings and other miracles performed by Jesus, weaving these together with Jesus' commentary about the miracles (or "signs") and with the ensuing controversies over his words and actions (see fig. 8.2).[37]

Figure 8.2
Festival Settings in John 5–10

John 5	Sabbath (5:9)
John 6	Passover (6:4)
John 7–8 (9?)	Tabernacles or Booths (7:2)
John 10	Festival of Dedication or Hanukkah (10:22)

The Sabbath provides the setting for John 5, which begins with Jesus healing a man and then narrates the resulting controversy with Jewish leaders over this Sabbath healing.[38] Jesus' commentary on this issue highlights multiple themes, including his own authority to act in ways that only God acts as well as the motif of work—for example, "My Father is always at his work to this very day, and I too am working" (John 5:17). In this way, John artfully weaves together the setting of the Sabbath—on which Israel was not to do any work—with the motif of Jesus' work and authority corresponding to his Father's work (see 5:20, 36; cf. 4:23).[39] The effect for

36. Rowe, *Early Narrative Christology*, 14, as applied to Luke's use of "Lord" for his Christology.

37. Craig R. Koester, *Symbolism in the Fourth Gospel: Meaning, Mystery, Community*, 2nd ed. (Minneapolis: Fortress, 2003), 19–20.

38. Although we might not immediately think of Sabbath as a festival, it is implied as such in Lev. 23:1–3. In addition to or possibly as an indication of Sabbath, John refers to the setting of "one of the Jewish festivals" at 5:1.

39. For a helpful exploration of Jewish reflection on God's work on the Sabbath, see Koester, *Symbolism in the Fourth Gospel*, 91–92. For intertextual echoes of Sabbath and work in

John's characterization of Jesus is to suggest Jesus' unity of purpose and even his shared identity with God (cf. John 10:30).

The Passover forms the backdrop for John 6 and is a festival that John highlights at least two other times in his Gospel (2:13; 13:1, running until 19:42). Jesus performs two miracles during this particular Passover celebration: the feeding of the five thousand and walking on water. Both miracles have intertextual echoes to central events in Exodus: (1) God's wilderness provision of manna for Israel (Exod. 16:4; cf. John 6:31, 49, 58) and (2) the exodus itself, when Israel is brought out of Egypt through the waters of the Red Sea (Exod. 13:17–18).[40] Jesus' commentary that follows these miracles emphasizes how he gives sustenance to those who believe in him—he is the "true bread from heaven" (John 6:32). With this theme, the Passover setting in John 6 provides the first occasion for John's seven "I am" statements from Jesus: "I am the bread of life" (6:35, 48).

John 7–8 (and possibly 9) is set during the Festival of Tabernacles, when the people of Israel would set up temporary shelters to recall their time in the wilderness and God's provision for them there (Lev. 23:42–43). This festival drew on the symbols of water and light as the people celebrated God's provision of water in the desert and of light from the cloud by day and the fire by night (Exod. 13:21). During this festival, Jesus' claims to be both water and light are profoundly significant:

> "On the last and greatest day of the festival, Jesus stood and said in a loud voice, 'Let anyone who is thirsty come to me. And let anyone drink who believes in me.' As Scripture has said, 'Out of him [i.e., Jesus] . . . will flow rivers of living water'" (John 7:37–38).[41]

> "When Jesus spoke again to the people, he said, 'I am the light of the world. Whoever follows me will never walk in darkness, but will have the light of life'" (8:12; cf. 9:5).

John 5 (and 19:30) with Gen. 2:1–3, see Jeannine K. Brown, "Creation's Renewal in the Gospel of John," *CBQ* 72 (April 2010): 275–90, here 284–86.

40. Richard B. Hays, *Echoes of Scripture in the Gospels* (Waco: Baylor University Press, 2016), 301.

41. This is the footnoted reading in the NIV. See Hays, who suggests this christological reading via allusion to Ezek. 47:1–2, with Jesus now embodying what the temple signified (*Echoes of Scripture in the Gospels*, 314–16).

In John 10:22 the evangelist provides another festival setting, this time the Festival of Dedication, or Hanukkah. This festival celebrated the restoration of the temple in 165 BCE after it had been defiled by the Greek ruler Antiochus IV. Since Hanukkah, like Tabernacles, was also associated with light (see 2 Macc. 1:7–9), it is unclear where to locate precisely the shift from one festival to the other in John 9–10.[42] Hanukkah's emphasis on faithful worship of the true God accentuates Jesus' claims in John 10 that he shares in the unique identity of Israel's God (10:30, 33, 38).[43]

For each festival in John 5–10, John metaphorically places Jesus in the middle of the particular Jewish festival and then claims that Jesus is the fulfillment of that festival. Jesus is at the center of true worship (cf. 4:24), a truth John has already emphasized in his alignment of Jesus and the temple (2:19–22). As Richard Hays contends, "Just as Jesus becomes the embodiment of that which the temple had signified, so also he now embodies everything to which Israel's feast and cultic observances had pointed."[44]

This example of John's narrative theology illustrates how a Gospel writer weaves together plotting (John's festival settings and related plot elements), characterization (Jesus' words and deeds), and intertextuality (allusions and echoes to various Old Testament texts and events) to implicitly and yet clearly communicate who Jesus is. By paying attention to these literary facets, along with important historical information about these Jewish festivals, we hear more emphatically that Jesus is worthy of worship.

Conclusion

In this chapter, we have turned from the narrative shaping and literary features of the Gospels (chaps. 2–7) to their theological import. This

---

42. See Josephus, *Antiquities* 12.324–25. Although John 10:22 seems to indicate a new temporal setting, Jesus' discourse about being a shepherd to his sheep ties 10:1–21 closely with what follows (10:26–28).

43. Koester, *Symbolism in the Fourth Gospel*, 144. If John 10:1–22 is associated by the evangelist with Hanukkah, then it is intriguing that Jesus as the true shepherd of Israel affirms that he has "other sheep that are not of this sheep pen" (10:16), a likely reference to future gentile believers. While Hanukkah celebrated the cleansing of the temple from gentile impurity, Jesus will, in a surprising turn, bring gentiles into the fold of God apart from conversion to Judaism (cf. 12:20–22).

44. Hays, *Echoes of Scripture in the Gospels*, 314.

theological turn does not leave behind the storied qualities of a Gospel. Instead, we have explored what it looks like to give attention to the narrative theology of the evangelists by reading carefully and holistically the Gospels as stories. In the next chapter, we'll examine Mark's Gospel for his portrait of God, taking a narrative look at Mark's theology proper.

9

The God of Mark's Gospel

As we have explored in the previous chapter, the Gospel stories are inherently theological, and they communicate theology not apart from their narrative shaping but because of and through their stories.

It is true that, on first blush, the four Gospels provide narratives focused expressly on Jesus.

> "This is the genealogy of Jesus the Messiah . . ." (Matt. 1:1).
>
> "The beginning of the good news about Jesus the Messiah . . ." (Mark 1:1).
>
> "In my former book, Theophilus, I wrote about all that Jesus began to do and to teach . . ." (Acts 1:1, about Luke).[1]
>
> "In the beginning was the Word . . ." (John 1:1).

Yet these biographies of Jesus are also set within a wider framework that assumes and affirms that the God of Israel is at work in Jesus of Nazareth. If we take a panoramic view of a Gospel, we'll see that its "theocentric" aim is to reveal God's self and mission as expressed and enacted in Jesus.[2] This focus on God—the divine character and action—is what theologians call **theology proper**.

---

1. While Luke doesn't get around to mentioning Jesus until Luke 1:31, his second volume, Acts, makes it clear that Luke focuses his first volume, his Gospel, on Jesus.

2. Green notes that "Luke's narrative is fundamentally theocentric in its emphasis." Joel B. Green, *The Gospel of Luke*, NICNT (Grand Rapids: Eerdmans, 1997), 292.

In this chapter, we take a close look at Mark's Gospel to see how the evangelist presents God and the divine mission as central to his narrative. As Suzanne Watts Henderson suggests about Mark, "The Gospel frames its story about Jesus the Christ within the wider landscape of God's impinging rule on the earth."[3] We begin this study by defining the parameters of the task, especially given the often indirect way God appears in the Gospel and Mark's close alignment of the person and work of Jesus with the person and work of God. Then we take a sequential tour through Mark's Gospel to see how the narrative's flow and shape contribute to its theology proper.

Defining the Parameters for Studying Mark's Theology Proper

Given that a Christian perspective on Mark already assumes a trinitarian view of God, it is important to distinguish reading for *theology proper* from reading for *Christology*. Readers might assume that when we "see Jesus" in Mark we are "seeing God," and there is certainly truth in that parallel. Mark itself is a source for a divine Christology—the view that Jesus comes as the embodiment of the God of Israel.[4] Yet it is a valuable exercise to treat separately Mark's portrait of Jesus (Christology) and his portrait of God (theology proper).[5] This differentiated theological study of Mark is helpful as readers grapple with the humanity of Jesus, which Mark both assumes and consistently illuminates.

To focus our study, we'll explore Mark's perspective on God, identified as "the Father." Although Mark references "the Father" only four times in his Gospel, this descriptor or name identifies Israel's God, Yahweh, in distinction from Jesus, and yet precisely in intimate, **filial** relationship to Jesus as "the Son" (Mark 8:38; 13:32; 14:36; cf. 11:25). Jesus himself is the one who uses the language of "Father" for God, which is telling and likely has messianic reverberations of Jesus as Son and of deeper relational

---

3. Suzanne Watts Henderson, "The 'Good News' of God's Coming Reign: Occupation at a Crossroads," *Int* 70 (2016): 145–58, here 146.

4. This high Christology arises, in part, from Mark's use of Old Testament quotations about Israel's God, Yahweh ("Lord"), to refer to Jesus (as "Lord"; e.g., Mark 1:2, 3). Such examples of overlapping referents add extra weight to the use of "Lord" for Jesus at other key points in the narrative (e.g., 12:36).

5. This also applies to Mark's characterization of the Holy Spirit (his pneumatology). While the Holy Spirit is portrayed with direct agency only twice in Mark (1:10, 12), it is precisely at this juncture that the evangelist provides the reader a glimpse of trinitarian reality (1:10–11).

associations. "Jesus' address to God as Father may denote the filial relationship between the king of Israel and God (2 Sam. 7:12–14; Ps. 2) [but it]
further speaks of his trust and confidence in God's provision, mercy, care
and salvation, such as was predicated of God's fatherly ways toward Israel
in the Old Testament (Ps. 103:13–14; Jer. 3:4, 19; 31:9–11; Hosea 11:1)."[6]

By taking a discrete look at Mark's portrait of God, we will be in a
better position to understand Jesus' relationship with God and the occasions when Mark blurs the distinction between the two to show Jesus to
be the embodiment of God (e.g., Mark 2:6, 10).[7]

Looking for God in a Gospel also raises an important distinction between
direct agency and **oblique agency**. God often works through others in the
narrative, and we can refer to this as *oblique divine agency*. This would include not only human characters like John the Baptist, who, as a prophet, can
speak for God (e.g., Mark 1:7–8). It also includes Jesus, God's human agent
par excellence, who at times is characterized as doing things that only God
can do (e.g., 2:1–12, where Jesus forgives sins). Jesus' healing and exorcism
ministry is an example of oblique divine agency—God is working through
Jesus to heal people suffering from disease or from the demonic. It is also
the case that we can hear God's "speaking" in some of the Old Testament
quotations that occur in Mark's Gospel (e.g., 1:2–3). These quotations form
another layer of oblique divine agency. In fact, much of what we understand
as divine activity in the Gospels comes in oblique form.[8]

Yet Mark (and the other evangelists) also portray God working more
directly in the life and ministry of Jesus. *Direct divine agency* can be observed at moments where God "shows up" in word or action. For example,
the voice of God is narrated on two occasions in Mark (1:11; 9:7). And
Mark gives us a glimpse of God's activity through what is called the **divine passive**—the use of a passive verb that can be attributed to God even
though God is not mentioned explicitly in the story line at these points

---

6. Marianne Meye Thompson, "God," in *DJG*, 315–28, here 317.
7. As Paul L. Danove notes about Mark as a whole, "The direct or indirect insinuation of
Jesus into every aspect of God's characterization in 1:1–15 engenders an indelible bond between
God and Jesus that precludes any understanding of either character without immediate reference
to the other." Danove, *The Rhetoric of the Characterization of God, Jesus, and Jesus' Disciples
in the Gospel of Mark*, JSNTSup 290 (New York: T&T Clark, 2005), 51.
8. Geert Van Oyen, "The Paradoxical Presentation of God in the Gospel of Mark and the
Table of Silence of Constantin Brancusi," in *Let the Reader Understand: Studies in Honor of
Elizabeth Struthers Malbon*, ed. Edwin K. Broadhead, LNTS 583 (New York: Bloomsbury T&T
Clark, 2018), 265–79, here 267–68.

(e.g., 1:10; 8:31; 15:38). We will focus more closely on these occurrences of direct agency in our explorations below.

With these considerations in mind, let's take a look at who God is and what God does in Mark's Gospel.

What Does Mark's Story Tell Us about God?

As suggested in the previous chapter, we can consider the theology of a Gospel through a number of storied lenses, including an evangelist's use of plotting, intertextuality, and characterization. It is the case, however, that an evangelist weaves together these various angles across the story. So as we walk through the second Gospel sequentially, we'll note how Mark's plotting, characterization, and use of the Old Testament intersect to illuminate his understanding of God. This kind of integrated reading of a Gospel—and a Gospel in its entirety—best serves the goal of hearing narrative theology.[9] Additionally, as we move across Mark, we will highlight any narrative development that occurs in the evangelist's characterization of God.

The Primacy Effect: Where Mark Begins (Mark 1:1–15)

The sheer number of references to God and God's activity in Mark 1:1–15 "places the character God in the foreground" of the Gospel.[10] While Mark unsurprisingly begins his Gospel by focusing on Jesus, he signals at a number of early moments that "the good news about Jesus" (1:1) is set in a wider context that is carefully orchestrated by Israel's God. We can see this clearly in Mark's companion message about the gospel or "good news" at the conclusion of Mark's introduction and in his opening summary of Jesus' ministry (1:14–15). While the "good news" is "about Jesus" (1:1), it is also, more fundamentally, "the good news of God" (1:14), pointing to God as its subject (with Jesus as its object).[11] The God of Israel is the author of good news, a reality already highlighted in the Old Testament

9. Frank J. Matera, *New Testament Theology: Exploring Diversity and Unity* (Louisville: Westminster John Knox, 2007), 5.

10. Danove, *Characterization of God*, 52.

11. Both Greek constructions involve genitives. Preceded by "good news," a genitive would signal either the object ("about") or the subject of ("of" or "coming from") the good news. In context, it seems most likely that Jesus is the object (1:1) and God is the subject (1:14).

(see Isa. 40:9; 52:7; see also fig. 9.1).[12] As we saw in our discussion of plot and plotting (chap. 2), early emphasis sets the tone for the rest of a narrative, establishing a primacy effect. This "good news" *inclusio* at the front of Mark puts God right at the center of the redemptive plan for humanity. As Philip Johnson notes, "God's character serves as a central and framing element of Mark 1:1–15."[13]

This theological focus fits hand in glove with the substance of the good news according to Mark—"the kingdom of God" (1:15). If God is the author of the good news, then it comes as no surprise that a shorthand for that news is *God's kingdom*—God's benevolent reign now established in this world through the life and ministry of Jesus. Jesus' preaching is summed up by Mark like this: "The kingdom of God has come near. Repent and believe the good news!" (1:15). This constellation of "good news" and "kingdom of God" reverberates back to the time of Isaiah, who speaks of the restoration of Judah from exile with the language of God's own return to Jerusalem. For Isaiah, the "good news" is the restored presence and reign of God among the people of God.[14] Mark picks up this language and its meaning to show that God's reign is now being inaugurated in the ministry of Jesus.

Figure 9.1

The "Good News" according to Isaiah

Isaiah 40:9	Isaiah 52:7
You who *bring good news* to Zion, go up on a high mountain. You who bring good news to Jerusalem, lift up your voice with a shout, lift it up, do not be afraid; say to the towns of Judah, "Here is your God!"	How beautiful on the mountains are the feet of those who *bring good news,* who proclaim peace, who bring good tidings, who proclaim salvation, who say to Zion, "Your God reigns!"

12. Thompson points out that "to speak of God in biblical terms always requires that one articulate God's identity as the one true God, the God of Israel" ("God," 318).

13. Philip R. Johnson, "God in Mark: The Narrative Function of God as a Character in the Gospel of Mark" (PhD diss., Luther Seminary, 2000), 161. I am grateful to have been Dr. Johnson's colleague during doctoral work and present at his dissertation defense to hear his reading of God in Mark, which has made a deep impression on my own interpretation of this Gospel.

14. What is expressed by a noun in Mark (*euangelion*, "good news"; 1:14, 15) is communicated with the cognate verb in Isaiah (*euangelizō*, "bring[ing] good news"; 40:9; 52:7).

Mark also introduces his theology proper through a cluster of Old Testament citations that begins his Gospel. In 1:2–3 Mark combines Malachi 3:1 (mixed with a bit of Exod. 23:20) and Isaiah 40:3 to interpret for his readers what they are about to encounter: John the Baptist preparing for the arrival and ministry of Jesus the Messiah (Mark 1:4–11).[15] Yet this Old Testament textual cluster not only introduces the story ahead but also indirectly provides God's voice. It is "Yahweh Almighty" who speaks in Malachi 3:1, the first of Mark's citations. So Mark's use of pronouns is instructive:

> "*I* will send *my* messenger ahead of *you*,
>   who will prepare *your* way"—
> "a voice of one calling in the wilderness,
>   'Prepare the way for the Lord,
>   make straight paths for *him*.'" (1:2–3, emphasis added)

In Mark's story, as in Malachi (and Exodus), Yahweh is the "I" speaking. Yet unlike the Hebrew and the Septuagint of Malachi, which continue the first-person pronouns ("who will prepare the way before me"), the second set of pronouns comes in second person (reflecting Exod. 23:20, referring to Israel). In Mark, these correspond to Jesus, with John the Baptist filling the role of "a voice" who calls for readiness for "him" (for the Messiah). This change in pronouns signals that, for Mark, Jesus comes to fulfill the expectation of God's return to Zion—and to the people of Israel. While we've already addressed briefly this kind of blurring of boundaries between Jesus and God in Mark, here a critical observation is that the first speaker in the Gospel (apart from Mark himself) is God via the Old Testament Scriptures. And the words uttered confirm that it is God who is orchestrating John's coming and Jesus' arrival in line with the divine plan.[16]

As his narrative begins, Mark also highlights God's action and speech quite directly in the scene of Jesus' baptism. As Jesus emerges from the water, Mark narrates that Jesus "saw heaven being torn open and the Spirit descending on him like a dove" (Mark 1:10). The language "being torn"

---

15. For a discussion of the full import of this trio of Old Testament texts, see Rikki E. Watts, *The Isaianic New Exodus in Mark* (Grand Rapids: Baker, 1997), 53–90.

16. Watts argues that this configuration of Old Testament texts indicates that Isaiah's promise of a "new Exodus" is now coming to pass in Jesus (*Isaianic New Exodus*).

is a passive verb (from *schizō*), which begs the question, Torn by whom? It is clear from context that God is the one who tears apart the heavens in this weighty moment of revelation, as the Holy Spirit comes upon Jesus.[17] Mark uses the divine passive here to illuminate an act of revelation, or what Mark Strauss refers to as "a powerful theophany."[18]

God also speaks at Jesus' baptism, one of only two times in Mark where the divine voice is heard. "And a voice came from heaven: 'You are my Son, whom I love; with you I am well pleased'" (Mark 1:11; cf. 9:7). These words, echoing Psalm 2:7 and Isaiah 42:1, commend Jesus as God's beloved and faithful servant (cf. Isa. 42:1) and illuminate the deep, filial relationship between God and Jesus (cf. Ps. 2:7). This commendation sets the tone for the reader's experience of Jesus in the rest of the Gospel. Whatever the range of responses to Jesus' ministry that will emerge, both positive and negative, we know from the start that Jesus acts on behalf of God and with the divine blessing fully upon him.

In the opening chapter of Mark, we see God acting and speaking. God speaks obliquely through Old Testament texts (1:2–3), as well as directly in affirmation of Jesus' person and calling (1:11). Mark also characterizes God as acting and revealing through the divine passive of the tearing of the heavens and in the coming of the Holy Spirit upon Jesus at his baptism (1:10). Additionally, the evangelist highlights the activity and work of God implicitly as he references the "good news of God" and defines this news as the arriving reign of God in the ministry of Jesus (1:14–15). This clustering of God's speech and actions at the front of the Gospel sets the tone and expectation for what God will do in the rest of Mark's story.

God in the Ministry of Jesus

Jesus' Galilean ministry begins at Mark 1:14–15 with an opening summary and runs through 8:21. If we were to ask about the portrait of God that Mark sketches as he narrates this part of Jesus' life and ministry, we'd

---

17. The actions of the Holy Spirit coming upon Jesus and sending Jesus into the wilderness (1:10, 12) are also to be understood as divine actions that show Jesus to be the Messiah and to be empowered by the Spirit for his coming ministry. Mark L. Strauss, *Mark*, ZECNT (Grand Rapids: Zondervan, 2014), 72.

18. Strauss, *Mark*, 75. A theophany is a divine revelation or manifestation when the unseen God is made visible in some way. A parallel moment of divine "tearing" comes at the end of Mark (15:38); see the discussion below on the significance of this *inclusio*.

notice that much of what we learn about God we learn through oblique divine agency. Mark has encouraged the reader to see God's involvement in Jesus' ministry through the Spirit's empowerment (1:10). The life-giving healing Jesus offers comes from the hand of God.[19] This is confirmed as Jesus relies on God in prayer (1:35; 6:46; cf. 14:32–42) and as crowds praise God when they witness Jesus' healing power (2:12). We also learn more about God through Jesus' teachings, which prioritize God's kingdom (4:11, 26, 30) and God's will (3:34). As Johnson summarizes it, "God is at work in the actions, miracles, healings, and exorcisms of Jesus in these chapters . . . because it was God who split apart the heavens to come down and enter the world through Jesus of Nazareth."[20]

The middle section of Mark (8:22–10:52) narrates Jesus' predictions about his impending death, as well as the movement of Jesus and his disciples toward Jerusalem. In this section of the Gospel, God again has a more direct role, in both word and deed. Divine activity is implied in Jesus' first passion prediction: "[Jesus] then began to teach them that the Son of Man must suffer many things and be rejected . . . and that he must be killed and after three days rise again" (8:31). The language of "must" (or "it is necessary" for *dei* in Greek) refers to the divine necessity of Jesus' ministry that will culminate in his missional death. Implicit in this necessity is God's direction that guides Jesus in his mission. As Joel Marcus suggests, "It is vital for the Markan Jesus to stress, in this first open prophecy of his death and resurrection, that those unexpected occurrences reflect the divine will."[21]

God's action is portrayed more directly at Jesus' transfiguration (Mark 9:2–13), where the divine passive, "he was transfigured," implies God's agency in revealing and foreshadowing Jesus' glory (9:2). In this scene, we again hear the divine "voice" (as at 1:11) affirming Jesus' favored status and relationship: "This is my Son, whom I love. Listen to him!" (9:7). This relational emphasis seems to be the focus of both God's action (transfiguring Jesus) and his words. "God grants Jesus a moment

---

19. Mark encourages this alignment, for example, by his ambiguous use of "Lord" at 5:19, in Jesus' response to a man he has rid of demons: "Go home to your own people and tell them how much the Lord has done for you, and how he has had mercy on you." This reference to "Lord" could refer to God or to Jesus as the one who acts uniquely on behalf of Israel's God.

20. Johnson, "God in Mark," 250.

21. Joel Marcus, *Mark 8–16*, AB (New Haven: Yale University Press, 2009), 613.

of borrowed radiance, a sign of God's close presence with, and fatherly love for, Jesus."[22]

We also hear of God and God's work indirectly through Jesus' teachings in Mark 8:22–10:52 (e.g., 8:33; 10:6–9). For example, Jesus affirms God's power to do what is impossible for humans to accomplish (10:27). As we move to Mark's narration of Jesus in Jerusalem during the final week of his life (11:1–16:8), we continue to learn about God indirectly through Jesus' actions and teachings. Jesus enters Jerusalem, affirmed by the crowds as the one who comes "in the name of the Lord"—in the name of Israel's God (11:9). The divine orchestration of Jesus' mission is reaffirmed in a quotation from Psalm 118:22–23: "the LORD has done this" (at Mark 12:10–11), with "this" referring to Jesus' role as cornerstone in spite of rejection.[23] And in a confrontation with Sadducees, Jesus affirms foundational truths from Israel's Scriptures about their God, who is (1) the covenant God—"the God of Abraham, the God of Isaac, and the God of Jacob," identified as the God of the living (Mark 12:26–27), and (2) the one and only God (citing the Shema from Deut. 6:4–5 in Mark 12:29).

God and the Missional Death of Jesus

We have already noticed the divine imperative of Jesus' mission that will lead to his death (Mark 8:31). By the time we reach the passion narrative (14:1–15:47), we've heard Jesus predict his coming death, not just once but three times (8:31; 9:30–32; 10:32–34). We've also heard Jesus provide the purpose of his mission: "To give his life as a ransom for many" (10:45). As Johnson aptly notes, "God's 'must' is passion-shaped."[24] And, we might add, God's "must" comes so that life might be granted to "many"—to Israel and, by extension, to the nations.[25]

A Silent God at Gethsemane

As we reach the passion narrative, the reader might very well be expecting God to speak, especially since Mark's primacy effect has encouraged

22. Johnson, "God in Mark," 284.
23. Strauss highlights the use of the psalm as a confirmation of "the divine necessity . . . behind Christ's passion" (*Mark*, 520).
24. Johnson, "God in Mark," 412.
25. For this interpretation of the referent of "many" in the parallel context in Matthew, see Jeannine K. Brown and Kyle Roberts, *Matthew*, THNTC (Grand Rapids: Eerdmans, 2018), 366.

such a prospect. The divine voice, along with divine action, has already been heard at climactic moments of the Gospel (1:10–11; 9:2, 7). Yet now, in a shift of characterization, God's voice is markedly absent, especially at the two places we might most expect to hear it.

The first comes in the Gethsemane narrative, where Jesus fervently prays for God to change the direction of his mission (Mark 14:32–42). He prays, "*Abba*, Father, . . . everything is possible for you. Take this cup from me. Yet not what I will, but what you will" (14:36). Jesus has earlier accented God's supreme power when he has taught his followers that "all things are possible with God" (10:27). But this possibility, that God might change the course of Jesus' mission, is not to be. In spite of Jesus' repeated requests that God remove "this cup" (he prays three times: 14:36, 39, 41), Mark signals no response from God. And while Jesus yields himself to God's will,[26] we have no narrative indication that Jesus hears a reassuring word in response to his prayer. "Each time Jesus prays, God remains silent. There is no φωνή [voice] as in 1:11 and 9:7. There is no splitting of the heavens nor coming close in a cloud."[27]

A Silent God at Golgotha

The crucifixion scene in Mark continues the motif of divine silence. Jesus has been tried by Rome and sentenced to death by crucifixion (15:1–15). After narrating Jesus' crucifixion along with two "rebels" (15:21–32), Mark provides the first intimation of God's activity in the entire passion narrative: "Darkness came over the whole land until three in the afternoon" (15:33). If Mark expects his reader to hear this as an extraordinary, supernatural event, then he likely is signaling that God is the precipitator of the darkness.[28] Yet this divine act of removing light provides little hope for divine intervention to reverse Jesus' fate, especially given the way the Gethsemane scene has unfolded. Jesus' words that follow serve only to confirm his experience of divine silence: "My God, my God, why have you forsaken me?" (15:34).[29]

---

26. His prayer "that if possible the hour might pass from him" (14:35) turns into his acknowledgment that "the hour has come" (14:41).

27. Johnson, "God in Mark," 345.

28. Johnson, "God in Mark," 369–70. He suggests that the supernatural elements evident at 1:10 and 9:7 lead the reader to this conclusion.

29. Johnson suggests as significant a change from Gethsemane to Golgotha: Jesus no longer refers to God as father ("*Abba*, Father"; 14:36) but as "my God" (15:34). The filial language is notably absent ("God in Mark," 375).

A key question that surfaces among interpreters regarding Jesus' "cry of dereliction" is whether God is only silent or truly absent. In other words, does Jesus *experience* being forsaken by God or is he *actually* forsaken by God? While the text itself doesn't provide a definitive answer, the use of Psalm 22:1 to express Jesus' experience points to a subjective rather than an objective understanding of God's "absence." "It should not be surprising that the words that would come to expression on Jesus' lips in the final moments of his life would derive from Israel's prayer book. How often would a Jew sing or cry this or other prayers of lament in their times of deepest crisis and sorrow? In these words . . . , we hear Jesus—like the psalmist—expressing his feelings of God's absence as death approaches."[30]

This reading in no way downplays Jesus' (or the reader's) experience of God's absence, but it does better account for the activity of God that precedes and follows Jesus' cry and death (Mark 15:34–37). "As Mark presents it, God is active in, through, and near Jesus' death. This means that Jesus' cry of forsakenness from the cross is not the last word about God, even at Golgotha."[31] In paradoxical fashion, both divine revelation and divine silence occur in the story line at this singular climactic moment of the story (see fig. 9.2).

GOD'S ACTION AT GOLGOTHA: A TEARING OF THE TEMPLE CURTAIN

Immediately after Jesus dies, we hear that "the curtain of the temple was torn in two from top to bottom" (Mark 15:38). As he has done elsewhere, Mark uses a passive verb to signal God's activity. What's particularly interesting about this divine passive is that it mirrors the tearing activity of God from 1:10 (the passive form of the Greek *schizō* in both cases). These are the only two occurrences of *schizō* in Mark, forming an intentional *inclusio* that signals God's activity at the beginning of Jesus' ministry and at his death.

While Mark gives no specific details and does not interpret the rending of the temple curtain, most commentators suggest that the evangelist is referring to the inner temple curtain that separated the Most Holy

---

30. Brown and Roberts, *Matthew*, 370. This comment, though reflecting the Matthean version of Jesus' words, is equally applicable to Mark's quite similar wording and context.

31. Laura C. Sweat, *The Theological Role of Paradox in the Gospel of Mark* (New York: Bloomsbury, 2013), 133.

Place from the rest of the temple (see Exod. 26:32–34).[32] The meaning often deduced from the tearing of the inner curtain is that God joins humanity and creation in a new way at the death of Jesus. The temple no longer functions as the center point of God's dwelling with humanity (through Israel). As Johnson puts it, "God's tearing tendencies in Mark bring God close to [God's] creation."[33] And as Clifton Black frames it,

> By God's deliberate intervention, there is no longer any shield between the holy presence and the world around it. . . . Even prior to the resurrection, Jesus' death spells the defeat of any human attempt to localize divinity—whether in a religious structure, such as the temple or tabernacle . . . , or in the religious imagination that would fix God in the heavens—which, like the curtain in 15:38, have been decisively ripped asunder (*schizō*) . . . by God (1:10). The expiration of the beloved Son coincides with and is ratified by the apocalyptic release of God's living yet covert, holy presence.[34]

In the missional death of Jesus, the God of the living comes to live with humanity. Yet, as Black notes, the divine presence remains a covert presence. I would suggest that this "covertness" is expressed *literally* in a way that has an impact *theologically* on Mark's reader. On the literary level in the passion narrative, God acts but does not speak. At the two most significant points of divine characterization prior to the passion narrative, God's words and actions have been paired (1:10–11; 9:2–7; see fig. 9.2). So, given the divine actions at Jesus' death, the reader could expect to hear the divine voice. *But God is silent.*

The omission of God's voice is all the more potent given the presence of a human affirmation about Jesus just after the veil is torn (Mark 15:39). "And when the centurion, who stood there in front of Jesus, saw how he died, he said, 'Surely this man was the Son of God!'" If we recall that affirmations of divine sonship have been God's purview in Mark (1:11;

32. Daniel M. Gurtner, "The Rending of the Veil and Markan Christology: 'Unveiling' the ΥΙΟΣ ΘΕΟΥ (Mark 15:38–39)," *BibInt* 15 (2007): 292–306.

33. Johnson, "God in Mark," 416. He also notes, "God's action at Golgotha is for his world, not his son" (387).

34. C. Clifton Black, "The Face Is Familiar—I Just Can't Place It," in *The Ending of Mark and the Ends of God: Essays in Memory of Donald Harrisville Juel*, ed. Beverly Roberts Gaventa and Patrick D. Miller (Louisville: Westminster John Knox, 2005), 33–49, here 44.

9:7), the centurion's words emphasize the divine silence. Johnson laments that "this is God's line on the lips of a centurion."[35]

What impact do these literary features have on Mark's readers as they grapple with the portrayal of God in Mark's crucifixion scene?[36] The substitution of a centurion's affirmation for what have been God's words earlier in the narrative seems to place God at something of a distance. Coupled with Jesus' final words about being forsaken by God, the effect is likely that God becomes more remote to the reader (as for Jesus).[37] Though present, "God is hidden so thoroughly that not even God's son can perceive the divine presence."[38] This remoteness has an impact on the implied reader, who has been identifying and sympathizing with Jesus in the passion narrative. And this literary impact has a theological analog: God is experienced paradoxically as present through continued action and revelation and also as increasingly remote as the story progresses, given divine silence. Revelation and hiddenness are both theological realities as the reader reaches Mark 16.[39]

Figure 9.2
Hearing from God in Mark

	Mark 1:1–8:21	Mark 8:22–10:52	Mark 11:1–16:8
Divine Voice	"You are my Son, whom I love; with you I am well pleased" (1:11).	"This is my Son, whom I love. Listen to him!" (9:7).	Divine silence (15:34). (Centurion: "Surely this man was the Son of God" [15:39].)
Accompanying or Related Action(s)	"Heaven being torn" (1:10). "I will send my messenger" (1:2–3).	"[Jesus] was transfigured" (9:2). "The Son of Man must suffer" (8:31).	"The curtain of the temple was torn in two" (15:38). "Darkness came over the whole land" (15:33).

35. Johnson, "God in Mark," 388. Interpreters debate whether the centurion's statement should be read as sincere or as sarcastic (with the latter potentially suggested by the tone of other responses during Jesus' crucifixion; cf. 15:18–20, 29–32, 36).

36. As discussed in chap. 1, narrative criticism focuses on the "implied reader"—a (at least partially) textually constructed reader that is derived from clues within the Gospel.

37. Danove uses language of God's "remoteness" from Jesus to express the reader's experience at the end of Mark (*Characterization of God*, 53–55).

38. Sweat, *Theological Role of Paradox*, 140.

39. Sweat suggests that "paradox is an appropriate way to speak about a God whose presence resists definition and whose actions are often surprising" (*Theological Role of Paradox*, 133).

An Unsatisfying Ending? (Mark 16:1–8)

In Mark's passion narrative, God doesn't speak when expected and acts in ways that are less than transparent. Yet in the tearing of the temple curtain something quite profound has occurred. God is now present in a new way with humanity and creation. Nevertheless, because of the way divine action (and voicelessness) is expressed at Jesus' crucifixion, the reader may experience God as more remote (subjectively) even though God is revealed as profoundly present (objectively). This paradoxical experience continues into the resurrection account (Mark 16:1–8), especially given the abrupt ending of the Gospel. When women who had followed Jesus from Galilee (15:40–41) come to Jesus' tomb, they find the stone rolled away from its entrance (16:1–4). A young man (an angelic figure) says to the women (16:6–7), "Don't be alarmed. . . . You are looking for Jesus the Nazarene, who was crucified. He has risen! He is not here. See the place where they laid him. But go, tell his disciples and Peter, 'He is going ahead of you into Galilee. There you will see him, just as he told you.'"

The divine passive form occurs a final time at Mark 16:6—Jesus is raised from the dead by God. God acts a final time in Mark's story line. The hope of Jesus raised from the dead and able to fulfill his promise to meet his disciples (cf. 14:28) is potent here. Yet the Gospel ends without full resolution—there is no narration of the women reaching and communicating with the disciples. Instead, "trembling and bewildered, the women went out and fled from the tomb. They said nothing to anyone, because they were afraid" (16:8).[40]

Commentators have noted that this disquieting ending offers something for the reader of Mark. Donald Juel explores the effect of the Markan ending when he writes, "Mark's Gospel forbids . . . closure. There is no stone at the mouth of that tomb. Jesus is out, on the loose, on the same side of the door as the women and the readers. The story cannot contain the promises. . . . Mark's Gospel—and, we might add, the whole Christian tradition—argues that our lack of enlightenment and bondage arise from attempts to box God in or out

---

40. Even the grammar of the ending is abrupt, with the Greek word *gar* ("because") providing the last word of the entire book. For the view that this is not likely the original ending of Mark (which has been lost), see, e.g., Ben Witherington III, *The Gospel of Mark: A Socio-Rhetorical Commentary* (Grand Rapids: Eerdmans, 2001), 411.

of experience. All such attempts come to grief in the resurrection of Jesus."[41]

If theologically Mark *doesn't* allow us to "box God in," what *does* Mark give to his reader? As we have seen, Mark's Gospel portrays a God who both reveals and remains elusive.[42] Mark reveals that God is for humanity and creation in the death of Jesus—at the tearing of the temple curtain and in the raising of Jesus from the dead. Yet as the narrative progresses, God acts less frequently, especially in relation to Jesus' prayers (at Gethsemane and Golgotha), and stops speaking altogether. So, in one sense we could say that God becomes more hidden as the story moves toward its conclusion. By the end of Mark, we can affirm that God is truly revealed in Jesus' life, death, and resurrection *and* that God cannot be fully fathomed or explained.[43]

The reality of this paradox—this both/and—offers a theological vision that has a certain coherence with the discipleship questions raised by the Markan ending. If God is both revealed and not fully knowable, then there is a sense in which the reader of Mark, along with the women at the tomb, might feel bewildered, might tremble, might even be afraid (16:8).[44] At the very least, such a stance is an antidote to thinking that we have "a corner on God."[45] Mark leads his readers toward a humble stance that precludes the assumption that they now fully understand the eternal God. In this way, Mark's paradox of hiddenness and revelation might prove to be a theological gift.

---

41. Donald H. Juel, "A Disquieting Silence: The Matter of the Ending," in Gaventa and Miller, *The Ending of Mark and the Ends of God*, 11.

42. This is in line with the "mysteries about God's kingdom" (Mark 4:11 GW).

43. This coheres with the Eastern Orthodox affirmation that we can know God truly without claiming to know God fully. Van Oyen suggests, "A reading of Mark that characterizes God as a mystery is the best drug to protect people from the idolatry of thinking that one is able to know and understand God" ("Paradoxical Presentation of God," 271).

44. While these are not discipleship traits that the evangelist commends for the implied reader, they are ones with which real readers might very well identify.

45. Barbara Brown Taylor suggests the language of "dumbfoundedness" as a suitable response to Christian theology proper: "If it is true that God exceeds all our efforts to contain God, then is it too big a stretch to declare that *dumbfoundedness* is what all Christians have most in common? Or that coming together to confess all that we do not know as we reach out to one another is at least as sacred an activity as declaring what we think we do?" Taylor, "Way Beyond Belief: The Call to Behold," in *Shouts and Whispers: Twenty-One Writers Speak about Their Writing and Their Faith*, ed. J. L. Holberg (Grand Rapids: Eerdmans, 2006), 1–12, here 11.

Part Six
Conclusion

The person, be it gentleman or lady, who has not pleasure in a good novel, must be intolerably stupid.

Jane Austen, *Northanger Abbey*

It was a dark and stormy night.

Snoopy
("Peanuts," Charles Schultz)

10

The Ongoing Power
of the Gospels as Stories

The Gospels have been understood in a great variety of ways and from multiple angles. My own understanding of the Gospels has been immensely enriched by the sustained use of storied categories for their interpretation. My first real encounter with the Gospels as intentional works viewed as wholes came in my master's work when I was introduced to redaction criticism, with its focus on the writer's intentions for the shaping of his Gospel.[1] When I engaged with narrative criticism in my doctoral work, I became captivated by the Gospels *as stories*. What should have always been obvious disrupted my interpretive practices and reframed the way I engaged the Gospels. Reading the Gospels for their story line is not only organic to their form but also immensely helpful for hearing what these writers wanted to communicate about Jesus and what they wanted their audiences to experience.

By focusing on the story line of a Gospel, we give our attention to what an evangelist wanted to most highlight—his particular telling of the Jesus *story*. Nevertheless, narrative criticism has been a flexible methodology, with most of its practitioners recognizing the benefit of hearing a Gospel

---

1. The version of redaction criticism I was taught had significant affinities with composition criticism, which in general is more attentive to the entirety of a Gospel. For their distinction and relationship, see Michael J. Wilkins, *The Concept of Disciple in Matthew's Gospel*, NovTSup 59 (Leiden: Brill, 1988), 6.

within its sociohistorical context. So *history*, and not just story, has been an important part of the narrative task as we've explored it in this book. And while narrative critics haven't always moved from the literary and historical to the expressly theological, a narrative approach is well suited for hearing the *theology* of a Gospel. This trio of history, story, and theology has informed the narrative approach I have proposed in this book. Yet in each case the story is the first point of entry. Story informed by history leads us to theology and theologizing (fig. 10.1). And staying close to the story helps us to know *when* to fill in narrative gaps with historical information and *how* to hear a Gospel's theology.

Figure 10.1
Starting with the Story

The narrative method I have proposed draws on a wide variety of theorists and practitioners of narrative methodologies. Yet I have attempted to avoid unnecessary jargon as much as possible. Any new intellectual endeavor requires grappling with a new vocabulary to some extent, but I have tried to keep this new terminology manageable for my reader. I appreciate Robert Alter's own sensibility in this regard: "I am particularly suspicious of the value of elaborating taxonomies and skeptical as to whether our understanding of narrative is really advanced by the deployment of bristling neologisms like *analepsis, intradiegetic, actantial.* . . . I cling to the belief that it is possible to discuss complex literary matters in a language understandable to all educated people."[2]

In the interest of full disclosure, I do introduce and describe the first of the three narrative terms Alter mentions (see chaps. 2 and 3 for the meaning and use of *analepsis*). Yet Alter's challenge resonates with me, and those new terms I do introduce (see the glossary), I offer as an entrée

---

2. Robert Alter, preface to *The Art of Biblical Narrative*, rev. ed. (New York: Basic Books, 2011), xiv.

into a set of ideas that can be transformative for reading the Gospels as stories.

Even if readers are selective about what they take from these narrative offerings (as I have been with the theory I've engaged), taking on the challenge of reading the Gospels as stories will inevitably shape reading values and practices. I recall becoming deeply aware of one of these values when teaching a course on "Matthew for Theology" a number of years ago. In a conversation about Matthean Christology, one of the students suggested a particular christological portrait by noting something Jesus did. I responded, "Not in Matthew he doesn't."[3] A value that has taken deep root in my own reading practices is that of hearing how a particular Gospel writer shapes his narrative—the particular stories and sayings of Jesus he uses or doesn't use. Even when all four Gospels draw upon a common saying or action of Jesus, I find it immensely helpful to examine how the particular evangelist uses it for his own communicative purposes.

In the end, it matters for their story lines that Luke narrates that shepherds come to see the newborn Messiah, while Matthew tells of Magi seeking him out.[4] It matters narratively that John is the only evangelist to draw on the festival settings of Tabernacles and Hanukkah.[5] It matters for Mark's story that Jesus partially heals a man who is blind before healing him fully.[6] It even matters for their particular stories that Luke's parable of a lost sheep comes in the form of the parable of a wandering sheep in Matthew's Gospel.[7]

The quest to read and understand the Gospels as stories also counters the tendency to read a Gospel as a myriad of discrete and fairly independent

3. See Jeannine K. Brown and Kyle Roberts, *Matthew*, THNTC (Grand Rapids: Eerdmans, 2018), 8.

4. The shepherds fit Luke's motif of reversal, where those of lower status are at the center of God's restoration in the Messiah. The Magi fit Matthew's theme of gentile inclusion.

5. For John's use of festival settings for his Christology, see chap. 8.

6. As Morna Hooker suggests about the narrative placement of Mark 8:22–26, "Mark has enclosed Jesus' teaching about his own role and the meaning of discipleship between two miracles of restored sight [8:22–26 and 10:46–52]: the first blind man had difficulties in seeing even after his encounter with Jesus; the second followed Jesus on the way to Jerusalem. The two together stand as symbols of the disciples' blundering attempts to follow Jesus." Hooker, *The Gospel according to Mark*, BNTC (Peabody, MA: Hendrickson, 1991), 200.

7. Luke fits the parable in his series of three parables on what is "lost" (a coin, a sheep, a son; Luke 15), while Matthew places the parable in the Community Discourse, which highlights care for those who are vulnerable and those who stray (Matt. 18); see Brown and Roberts, *Matthew*, 168.

(short) stories. Comprehending a Gospel in its entirety—with its overarching messages, with its subtle and not-so-subtle themes—is not a simple interpretive endeavor. It might seem achievable to fully analyze a Gospel pericope. But twenty-one chapters of John will leave one more breathless than certain. It is my hope that a narrative engagement with the Gospels will leave us all with something of a sense of mystery as we hear their profound invitations to ourselves and our communities.

Recommended Resources

Part 1: Introduction

Brown, Jeannine K. "Narrative Criticism." In *Dictionary of Jesus and the Gospels*, 2nd ed., edited by Joel B. Green, Jeannine K. Brown, and Nicholas Perrin, 619–24. Downers Grove, IL: InterVarsity, 2013.

Malbon, Elizabeth Struthers. "Narrative Criticism: How Does the Story Mean?" In *Mark and Method: New Approaches in Biblical Studies*, 2nd ed., edited by Janice C. Anderson and Stephen D. Moore, 23–49. Minneapolis: Fortress, 2008.

Merenlahti, Petri. *Poetics for the Gospels? Rethinking Narrative Criticism*. New York: T&T Clark, 2002.

Powell, Mark A. *What Is Narrative Criticism?* Guides to Biblical Scholarship. Minneapolis: Fortress, 1990.

Resseguie, James. *Narrative Criticism in the New Testament: An Introduction*. Grand Rapids: Baker Academic, 2005.

Rhoads, David, Joanna Dewey, and Donald Michie. *Mark as Story: An Introduction to the Narrative of a Gospel*. 2nd ed. Minneapolis: Fortress, 1999.

Part 2: Plot and Plotting

Bauer, David. *The Structure of Matthew's Gospel: A Study in Literary Design*. Bible and Literature Series 15. Sheffield: Sheffield Academic, 1988.

Brooks, Peter. *Reading for the Plot: Design and Intention in Narrative*. New York: Knopf, 1984.

Burridge, Richard. "Gospels: Genre." In *Dictionary of Jesus and the Gospels*, 2nd ed., edited by Joel B. Green, Jeannine K. Brown, and Nicholas Perrin, 335–42. Downers Grove, IL: InterVarsity, 2013.

Culpepper, R. Alan. *Anatomy of the Fourth Gospel: A Study in Literary Design.* Philadelphia: Fortress, 1983.

Genette, Gérard. *Narrative Discourse: An Essay in Method.* Translated by Jane E. Lewin. Ithaca, NY: Cornell University Press, 1980.

Tannehill, Robert C. *The Narrative Unity of Luke-Acts: A Literary Interpretation.* Vol. 1, *The Gospel according to Luke.* Philadelphia: Fortress, 1986.

Part 3: Character and Characterization

Bauer, David. "The Major Characters of Matthew's Story: Their Function and Significance." *Interpretation* 46 (1992): 357–67.

Bennema, Cornelis. *A Theory of Character in New Testament Narrative.* Minneapolis: Fortress, 2014.

Brown, Jeannine K. *The Disciples in Narrative Perspective: The Portrayal and Function of the Matthean Disciples.* Society of Biblical Literature Academia Biblica 9. Atlanta: Society of Biblical Literature, 2002.

Hunt, Steven A., D. Francois Tolmie, and Ruben Zimmerman, eds. *Character Studies in the Fourth Gospel: Narrative Approaches to Seventy Figures in John.* Grand Rapids: Eerdmans, 2016.

Kingsbury, Jack Dean. *Matthew as Story.* 2nd ed. Philadelphia: Fortress, 1988.

Malbon, Elizabeth Struthers. *Characterization as Narrative Christology.* Waco: Baylor University Press, 2009.

Rhoads, David, and Kari Syreeni, eds. *Characterization in the Gospels: Reconceiving Narrative Criticism.* Journal for the Study of the New Testament Supplement Series 184. Sheffield: Sheffield Academic, 1999.

Skinner, Christopher W. *Characters and Characterization in the Gospel of John.* Library of New Testament Studies 461. London: Bloomsbury T&T Clark, 2013.

Part 4: Intertextuality

Brown, Jeannine K. "Creation's Renewal in the Gospel of John." *Catholic Biblical Quarterly* 72 (2010): 275–90.

———. "Matthew's Christology and Isaiah's Servant: A Fresh Look at a Perennial Issue." In *Treasures New and Old: Essays in Honor of Donald Hagner*, edited by Carl S. Sweatman and Clifford B. Kvidahl, 93–106. Wilmore, KY: GlossaHouse, 2017.

Hays, Richard B. *Echoes of Scripture in the Gospels.* Waco: Baylor University Press, 2016.

————. *Echoes of Scripture in the Letters of Paul*. New Haven: Yale University Press, 1989.

Jobes, Karen H., and Moisés Silva. *Invitation to the Septuagint*. 2nd ed. Grand Rapids: Baker Academic, 2015.

Oropeza, B. J., and Steve Moyise, eds. *Exploring Intertextuality: Diverse Strategies for New Testament Interpretation of Texts*. Eugene, OR: Cascade Books, 2016.

Part 5: Narrative Theology

Brown, Jeannine K. "Is the Future of Biblical Theology Story-Shaped?" *Horizons in Biblical Theology* 37 (2015): 13–31.

Brown, Jeannine K., and Kyle Roberts. *Matthew*. Two Horizons New Testament Commentary. Grand Rapids: Eerdmans, 2018.

Gaventa, Beverly Roberts. "Toward a Theology of Acts: Reading and Rereading." *Interpretation* 42 (1988): 146–57.

Gaventa, Beverly Roberts, and Patrick D. Miller, eds. *The Ending of Mark and the Ends of God: Essays in Memory of Donald Harrisville Juel*. Louisville: Westminster John Knox, 2005.

Goldingay, John. "Biblical Narrative and Systematic Theology." In *Between Two Horizons: Spanning New Testament Studies and Systematic Theology*, edited by Joel B. Green and Max Turner, 123–42. Grand Rapids: Eerdmans, 2000.

Koester, Craig R. *Symbolism in the Fourth Gospel: Meaning, Mystery, Community*. 2nd ed. Minneapolis: Fortress, 2003.

Sweat, Laura C. *The Theological Role of Paradox in the Gospel of Mark*. New York: Bloomsbury, 2013.

Glossary

allegorizing. The mining of an individual narrative **pericope** for its storied details, which are then heard to speak within the reader's own context apart from what the author was communicating. The interpretive practice of allegorizing is distinct from a biblical author's intentional use of allegory.

allusion. A New Testament reference to an Old Testament text consisting of just a few words (e.g., two to four words), often including a thematic connection that assists in its recognition.

amalgamating (or harmonizing). The combining of accounts from the four Gospels into a single, harmonized text.

analepsis (or flashback). A narrative technique in which the author introduces an event out of sequence, after the point where it would fit chronologically within the story line.

atomizing. An interpretive focus on a Gospel's individual episodes or accounts (called **pericopes**) as if they were fairly autonomous, rather than on a Gospel in its entirety.

backstories. The various kinds of stories assumed by the Gospel writers that inform their stories of Jesus. Backstories include the Old Testament and other Jewish writings that the evangelists assume and use, as well as the sociohistorical settings that form another set of backstories to the Gospels.

causality. A key feature of plot in which subsequent events arise from and are the result of preceding events.

characterization. The techniques an author uses to construct and develop the persons in the story.

chiasm. A sequencing pattern using repetition, with its second half in reverse order from the first half (e.g., ABCDCBA). A chiasm may provide structural clues to a narrative.

christological figure. A literary (textual) figure drawn from the Old Testament or other Jewish writings that the **evangelists** use to illuminate the identity of Jesus as Messiah.

Christology. An area of theology that explores the question of the person, nature, and role of Jesus as the Messiah (Christ). It aims to answer the question, Who is Jesus?

citation. A New Testament reference to an Old Testament text involving significant verbal repetition, often including one or more Old Testament verses and sometimes preceded by an introductory formula (e.g., "as it is written . . .").

climax. The point in a story where the plot reaches the height of its tension, just prior to the final resolution. It is one of the four elements or movements of a plot (**exposition, rising action, climax,** and **resolution**).

composition criticism. A method for studying the Gospels that examines how the various units of the text (**pericopes**) are arranged and the purpose for that arrangement. It shares similarities with **redaction criticism**, building on the analysis of how a Gospel writer uses his sources.

conflict. A clash of, or a struggle between, two or more forces in a story. The presence of conflict is crucial for building tension in the plot.

direct agency. When a character acts in a narrative apart from intermediary means or figures.

discourse level. One of the two levels of a narrative identified by Seymour Chatman (the other being the **story level**). It consists of the author's use of literary devices within the narrative—such as **point of view**, irony, sequencing, and **pacing**—to orient the reader to the author's purposes.

divine passive. A passive verb whose action can be attributed to God even though God is not explicitly mentioned as the subject of the action (e.g., "The curtain of the temple was torn in two," Mark 15:38).

echo. A New Testament reference to an Old Testament text (or to something referenced in an Old Testament text) made by implicit evocation more than through verbal linkages. These connections are usually quite subtle and are often recognized only as related echoes accumulate across a New Testament book.

evangelist. One of the four Gospel writers: (as attributed to) Matthew, Mark, Luke, or John.

exposition. Descriptions of central characters and events usually found toward the beginning of a narrative that prepare the reader for the story ahead. It is one of the four elements or movements of a plot (**exposition, rising action, climax,** and **resolution**).

filial. Relationship of a child to a parent.

flat (character). A character that functions as a simple type, usually demonstrating a single trait (E. M. Forster's term).

form criticism. A method for understanding the Gospels that focuses on the oral forms involved in a Gospel's production. Form critics study individual Gospel units (**pericopes**)—their specific genres and how they functioned for the early church before being written down.

implied author. A textually derived construct for understanding the author, which is distinct from the empirical (flesh-and-blood) author. The implied author is the writing persona presupposed in the narrative itself.

implied reader. A textually based construct referring to either (1) the reader presupposed in the narrative itself, who fulfills the **implied author**'s intentions, or (2) the reader emerging from a combination of textual cues and the ways in which real readers respond to those cues.

inclusio. A literary, structural feature that bookends a section of narrative, with a repeated word, phrase, or theme occurring at the beginning and the conclusion of a passage or story segment.

intercalation. A narrative pattern in which one episode is embedded within another, producing a storied ABA pattern (a "sandwich"). A hermeneutical feature of intercalation is that the two stories are intended to be mutually interpreting.

interchange. A sequencing pattern of alternating scenes or other narrative units (e.g., ABABABA), with the goal of illuminating a comparison between the A and B items (e.g., John and Jesus in Luke 1–2).

intertext. A precursor text (e.g., Old Testament text) incorporated into a later text (e.g., a Gospel).

intertextuality. The various ways the Gospel writers engage the Old Testament, and the subdiscipline of New Testament studies that explores these connections.

metalepsis. A concept in literary theory that suggests that reference to an earlier text (whether in **citation, allusion,** or **echo**) can evoke the wider context beyond the part of the precursor text used.

narrative criticism. A method for understanding the Gospels that focuses on their literary and storied qualities by moving beyond understanding their smaller units (**pericopes**) to interpreting the entire story at the book level.

Narrative criticism interprets a Gospel in its final form rather than in relation to issues of the text's production (e.g., **source** or **form criticism**).

narrative development. The emerging and changing quality of a narrative that can be seen in its characters (character development) and its plotting (plot development), as well as on the **discourse level**, in its thematic development.

narrative theologizing. An **evangelist**'s intentional, theological reflection on the life and ministry of Jesus communicated in and across a Gospel's story line.

narrative theology. The theology of a Gospel that arises from the narrative itself and is impacted by its storied features, such as **plotting, characterization**, and **intertextuality**.

narratology. A narrative methodology arising within literary criticism for the study of literature. It was used in the development of **narrative criticism** within Gospels studies.

narrator. The voice of the implied author in the telling of the story. Although the narrator can be distinguished from the implied author (e.g., when the implied author uses a first-person narrator), in reference to the Gospels, "narrator" and (implied) "author" are often used interchangeably (as in this book).

oblique agency. When a character acts in a narrative through intermediary means or figures—for example, through other character(s).

pacing. The shifting rhythm and speed of a narrative as it varies across the story line and in the reader's experience.

pericopes. Individual story units in a Gospel, whether individual sayings or shorter narrative accounts.

plotting. The intentional sequencing of events in a narrative and the manner in which the story is structured and told.

point of view. The perspective of an actor in a narrative, whether characters or the narrator. In narrative analysis the evaluative point of view of any particular character is assessed in comparison with the reliable point of view of the Gospel's narrator.

primacy effect. The significant impact that material occurring early in the plot has for setting expectations for the rest of the story.

prolepsis. A narrative technique in which an event is introduced before its expected location in the sequence of the story line. Thus this "flash-forward" occurs out of chronological sequence.

redaction criticism. A method for understanding the Gospels that compares a Gospel with its sources (e.g., Luke's use of Mark) to determine the particular audiences and purposes of the **evangelist** (e.g., Luke).

resolution. The final turn of a narrative, coming on the heels of the climax of the story. It involves the narrative solutions to the story's key conflicts. It is one of the four elements or movements of a plot (**exposition, rising action, climax,** and **resolution**).

rising action. The early stages of narrative activity that signal the direction of the plot and build tension by introducing the central **conflict**(s) of the story. It is one of the four elements or movements of a plot (**exposition, rising action, climax,** and **resolution**).

round (character). A character that is complexly portrayed with numerous traits, often showing signs of character development (E. M. Forster's language).

scenes. Segments within a narrative with significant amounts of action, often playing a decisive role in the story's plot. Scenes have the effect of slowing down the pace of the story (cf. **summaries**).

Septuagint (or LXX). The Greek translation of the Old Testament that was the (language) version of the Old Testament used in the early church (and so most often used by New Testament writers).

sequencing. A Gospel writer's intentional arrangement of plot elements—particular episodes, dialogue, and sayings—that contributes to the "narrative logic."

source criticism. A method for understanding the Gospels that focuses on the question of the literary (compositional) relationship among the **Synoptic Gospels**—Matthew, Mark, and Luke. The goal of source criticism is to determine which Gospel was written first and was used by the others, with the general consensus being that Mark was a key source for Matthew and Luke.

source text (or text form). The version of an Old Testament text (Hebrew or Greek **Septuagint**) that a New Testament author seems to be using in any particular **citation** or **allusion**.

story level. One of the two levels of a narrative identified by Seymour Chatman (the other being the **discourse level**). It consists of the storied elements of settings, plot (action), and characters.

summaries. Segments within a narrative providing an overview of prior or subsequent action, usually involving minimal dialogue, often covering a long stretch of "story time" (days, months, or years). Summaries have the effect of speeding up the pace of the story (cf. **scenes**).

Synoptic (Gospels). The first three Gospels: Matthew, Mark, and Luke, which share numerous similarities (with John being more distinctive). The likelihood of a literary (compositional) relationship among the Synoptics has led scholars to compare their similarities to determine the nature of their literary dependence (using **source criticism**).

theology proper. Theological reflection on God—on the divine character and action. In the Gospels, theology proper can be distinguished (at least in part) from **Christology** (theological reflection on Christ) and pneumatology (theological reflection on the Holy Spirit).

travel narrative. Luke's lengthy middle section (9:51–19:27) that depicts Jesus resolutely heading to Jerusalem (from Galilee) to embrace his fate there. Much of Luke's unique material is found in the travel narrative.

Scripture Index

Subject Index